Myths and Folk Tales
Around the World

MYTHS AND FOLK TALES AROUND THE WORLD

Robert R. Potter, Ed. D.
LECTURER IN ENGLISH
UNIVERSITY OF CONNECTICUT

H. Alan Robinson
HOFSTRA UNIVERSITY
CONSULTING EDITOR

GLOBE BOOK COMPANY, INC.
Englewood Cliffs, New Jersey

ROBERT R. POTTER received his B.S. from the Columbia University School of General Studies and his M.A. and Ed.D. from Teachers College, Columbia University.

Dr. Potter has been a teacher of English in the New York City School System, a research associate for Project English at Hunter College, and a teacher of English at the Litchfield (Conn.) High School. He has held a professorship at the State University of New York and now teaches at the University of Connecticut's Torrington branch.

Dr. Potter is author of Globe's *Stories of Surprise and Wonder, Beyond Time and Space, Tales of Mystery and the Unknown, English Everywhere, Making Sense, Writing Sense, Writing a Research Paper, Language Workshop* and the consulting editor of *American Folklore and Legends* and the *Pathways to the World of English* series.

Third Edition 1987

ISBN: 0-87065-174-9

PRINTED IN THE UNITED STATES OF AMERICA
11   12   13   14

CONTENTS

INTRODUCTION

This is a book of stories compiled primarily for classroom use in the teaching of reading. Its purpose is to supplement instruction in the various reading skills with the essential *experience* of reading—the consuming involvement of the individual with the archetypal ideas and emotions by which he relates himself to other people, and to the peoples of the world. Myths, legends, and folk tales have established themselves in our culture mainly because of their inherent worth as good stories. Their themes are universal; they speak of the desires and the dreams, the frailties and the flaws basic to the human condition. Here is an attempt to select some of the best tales from the rich and varied storehouse of folk literature, and to present them in a fashion that will stimulate interest for the modern reader.

The book grows out of the observation of two prevalent attitudes: enthusiasm on the part of students for the old, time-honored stories; and dissatisfaction on the part of teachers with many of the books containing these tales. The excellence of many anthologies is lost to the student because they are too difficult. Other collections suitable for free reading prove unsatisfactory for guided classroom use. Let us consider some of the points of dissatisfaction mentioned by teachers and supervisors about the books and procedures they are now using:

What can be done with stories too long for one reading period?

Time schedules, or equally inflexible interest spans, too often put an end to reading before THE END is reached. The stories in *Myths and Folk Tales Around the World* are not only short enough for classroom reading, but are of approximately equal length, permitting the establishment of regular procedures in situations where reading periods are of a standard length. As the reading sequence progresses, the stories become slightly more difficult, but it is expected that the student's progress and increasing familiarity with the book will enable him to read all units in about the same length of time.

What can the faster and often better readers do while waiting for the others to finish?

The next story is usually too long to start reading, and is earmarked for another day. This problem has been met by providing a short section of ancillary reading at the end of each unit. Inspection will reveal that in most cases it is a little more difficult than the main selection, to provide some challenge for the more advanced.

How can vocabulary be built and story interest maintained at the same time?

Vocabulary development and story comprehension are, unfortunately, too often viewed as separate entities which war with each other for classroom time. Every teacher is familiar with the student's urge to "get on with the story," and with his anti-climactic attitude toward vocabulary exercises that immediately follow an engrossing tale. In truth, vocabulary development can often be made to proceed from story interest. Whenever possible, new words should be presented in meaningful contexts and reviewed through the medium of the material the student has read. Words *qua* words interest few people; words *qua* tools that afford the individual the delights of discovery and discussion are of interest to all.

Accordingly, *Myths and Folk Tales Around the World* has been written with attention to the context of the more difficult words. A preview of "Words We Need to Know" is provided for each unit. Learning of these words is indirectly reinforced by their reappearance in the comprehension questions on each story.

Why do even the best stories fail to hold the attention of many readers?

The chief aim of *Myths and Folk Tales Around the World* is to arouse, hold, and satisfy the interest of the modern reader. To this end, certain minor alterations have been made in a few of the stories. For the most part, these changes consist of the omission of essentially irrelevant material. It is not necessary, for instance, to go into Theseus' escape from the labyrinth of King Minos in order to tell the self-contained story of Daedalus and Icarus; nor is it advisable to dampen the reader's concern for Ceres by relating the extraneous middle sections of her story as it is usually told. Also, dialogue has been modernized and simplified without being vulgarized. To facilitate comprehension still further, deities in Greek myths have occasionally been given their equivalent Roman names. *Venus* and *Cupid*, for example, might already mean something to the reader, while *Aphrodite* and *Eros* almost certainly would not.

Comprehension, interpretation, and extension questions are located in the back of the book. It is not the author's intention to foster endless page-turning, nor to relegate this useful material to an inferior position. This division has been made merely to separate the vitality and spirit of the tales from the necessary but unavoidably artificial appendages of the schoolroom. Students must learn that there are values in reading a story other than those of simply being able to answer questions that immediately follow. The teacher is urged to use only as much of this material as will be helpful to the student. Some of the "Thought and Discussion" questions call on the student's ability to make inferences and use what he has read in new situations. Teachers may want to select questions to meet individual needs and abilities.

Following the questions will be found a tabulation of the number of words in each main story and a reading-rate chart, enabling the student to find his reading speed and to graph or otherwise record his progress. Again, the teacher is urged to use this device only when it will benefit the student. The primary purpose of this book is not to put the student on a chart, but to put him, in the words of Keats, "asleep in the lap of legends old."

OLD, OLD STORIES

. . . in which we learn just how old an old story can be.

Words We Need to Know:

ancestors [*AN ses ters*]—one's grandparents, great-grand-parents, great-great-grandparents, etc.
Ann told the class that some of her *ancestors* were on the *Mayflower*.

ancient [*AYN shent*]—very old; on the earth long ago
Ted's father owned some *ancient* coins.

characters [*KAR ik ters*]—people in stories
"Who are the important *characters* in this story?" the teacher asked.

plot [*PLAHT*]—the things that happen in a story
Most boys like stories with exciting *plots*.

printing press [*PRINT ing PRES*]—a machine that prints books, magazines, newspapers, etc.
Before the *printing press* was invented, books had to be copied by hand.

publisher [*PUB lish er*]—a man or a company that prepares and sells books
The *publisher* of this book is Globe Book Company.

translate [*trans LATE*]—to change things written or spoken in one language into another
At the United Nations, speeches are *translated* into many languages.

wisdom [*WIZ dum*]—knowledge and good sense
Our country must have leaders with *wisdom*.

The word *old*, like many other words, changes its meaning almost every time we use it. One month's calendar is *old* the minute the next month comes. *Old* chewing gum has been chewed a few hours. Newspapers become *old* in a few days. *Old* potatoes have been in the kitchen a few weeks. *Old* magazines have been in the living room a few months. When we talk about *old* clothes, we mean those a few years *old*, but countries do not grow *old* for a few hundred years. Just how *old* is an old story? Let's read to find out.

OLD, OLD STORIES . . . is our title, but first let's talk about a new story—one that hasn't even been written yet!

Let's suppose that right now our class were writing a story. We have already talked about the people in the story. By now our made-up characters seem almost real. We have also talked about the plot, so we know exactly what the characters do. Many exciting things happen before the story reaches its end.

But the class is no longer talking. It has split up into small groups, to write different parts of the story. When we finish, a good reader will read the whole tale. Then we'll know how good our story really is.

What will happen if no one likes what we've done? Maybe we'll be able to change the story into a better one. On the other hand, maybe we'll decide that it's just too poor to bother with. We can throw the story away, and write another, more interesting one tomorrow.

If the story is too poor to be changed, no one will trouble himself to take it out of the wastepaper basket. After school

3

some of us might tell the story to our friends. But, if it's not a good story, no one will remember it. In a few days the wastepaper will have been burned. The story will have been forgotten.

However, as long as we're supposing, let's suppose that the story is very good. Let's pretend that it's one of the best stories ever written! Our class has written another "Rip Van Winkle," or another "Pinocchio." What might happen to such a wonderful tale?

After school the teacher would type the story. Tomorrow every teacher would have a copy. Soon the whole school would have heard our tale. Then someone would send it to a magazine. It would be printed right away.

A book publisher would read our story in the magazine. He would write us a letter, wanting to know if he could put it in a book he was publishing. After the story was in the book, other publishers would see it. They would want it in their books. In a few years, millions of people would have read the story. It would have been translated into Spanish, French, German, and other languages. Years from now our own children would read it in their schoolbooks. Our great-grandchildren would read it a hundred years from now.

And why would all this happen?

Remember, we called our story *one of the best stories ever written!* A really good story grows old, but it never dies. It is read even after the author's name is forgotten. It is told long after the author's language is no longer spoken. A good story lives not hundreds of years, but thousands.

The first stories in this book are thousands of years old. They were made up by the ancestors of the modern Greeks. For thousands of years, the Greek people have lived in

Greece, a country in the southern part of Europe. The people in Greece have always been called *Greeks*, just as we have always been called *Americans*. But remember that when we use the word *Greeks* in this book, we are talking about the people who lived in Greece long ago, not the people who live there today.

Why should the stories of these ancient Greeks still be read three thousand years later? We already know why: a good story never dies. People all over the world like to read these old tales. We're going to like them, too. And we'll like them even better if we first learn something about the interesting people who wrote them.

Today we know a lot about the ancient Greeks. We have an idea what they looked like. Luckily for us, the Greeks left us many statues of themselves. If we can believe these statues, the Greeks were large, handsome people, with deep-set eyes, wavy hair, and straight noses. They dressed in long robes, graceful even when cut out of stone.

Can you guess what kind of life these people led three thousand years ago? We all know, of course, that they had no television sets, no cars, and no frozen foods. But how many of us know that the Greeks had no printing presses? Their few books had to be slowly copied by hand. For this reason their stories were usually told instead of read. Storytellers went from town to town telling their tales. Instead of going to libraries, the people of Greece went to listen to storytellers.

The Greeks were unlike us in other ways, also. For instance, they thought of themselves as citizens of cities. There was no government for all of Greece. Instead, every Greek city, with the land around it, was an independent country. These Greek cities were almost as different from each other as the countries of the world are today. Some of them were ruled by kings, some by dictators, and some by the people. And, like the countries of the modern world, they didn't always get along well with each other.

For a minute, try to think what the United States would be like if each city were a separate country, with its own laws and its own army. What would happen if an army left New York to fight Boston? Or if the people in San Francisco decided that Los Angeles should be wiped off the map? Or if New Orleans refused to let boats sail up the Mississippi River to St. Louis and Chicago? The answer is easy. The cities would wear themselves out fighting each other, and the United States would be beaten by another country. (This is just what finally happened to the Greek cities, but that is another story.)

Also, the Greeks had slaves. Their slaves were not people of another race. They were Greeks who had been captured in war by Greeks from another city.

Another way in which the Greeks were unlike us is that they didn't believe in one God. Instead, they had many gods. They even had lady gods, called goddesses. All this seems strange to us, but to the Greeks it was not strange at all. Remember that they lived many, many years ago.

The Greeks didn't have modern science to help them understand the things they saw around them. A Greek student couldn't have opened a book and learned that the world is round, or that the sun is many times larger than the earth. Even if the early Greeks had had printing presses and books, no student could have read these facts. No child could have learned these things because no adult knew them.

We have all heard that people laughed at Columbus when he said that the world was round. The world *looked* flat, so people believed it *was* flat. This is just what the Greeks thought. Some Greeks asked why the oceans didn't run off the edges of a flat world. The smarter Greeks thought and thought. Finally they said that the world must be shaped like a saucer, with a brim to hold the oceans in their places!

And what about the sun? It *looked* like a ball of fire, so the Greeks believed it *was* a ball of fire. It *looked* smaller than the earth, so the Greeks thought it really *was* smaller. The one thing the Greeks had trouble explaining was why the sun rose in the east every morning, moved across the sky all day, and set in the west when evening came.

When the Greeks couldn't explain something by looking at it, they made up a story. Here is how they made up a story to explain the movement of the sun:

It does not make sense, the Greeks told themselves, for this ball of fire to move across the sky by itself. Someone, or something, must pull it across the heavens. But who? Or what? The Greeks didn't know. They knew it couldn't be a man. No man could walk across the sky, and surely a human being would burn up if he were so close to the sun. The best guess the Greeks could make was that a god guided the sun across the sky. And what did the god use to pull the sun? God-like horses, of course! It was all very simple, although the sun was so bright that humans couldn't see exactly what was happening.

Today we have a special name for these stories. We call them *myths*. A myth is an ancient story made up to explain things that people couldn't understand. How did the ball of fire move across the sky every day? A myth said that a god of the sun pulled it across with horses. Why did storms sink boats on the oceans? Another myth said that a god of the sea was shaking the waters. What caused thunder and lightning? Still another myth said that an angry god was throwing lightning at people on earth.

We know very little about the authors of the Greek myths. Today we think that most myths were made up by the storytellers who traveled around ancient Greece. Just as we have popular authors today, so the Greeks had popular storytellers. The men who made up the best myths were the best storytellers. To make their myths more interesting and easier to remember, the storytellers often turned them into long poems.

It didn't take long for the Greeks to invent a large family of gods and goddesses. Among them were a god of music and a god of war, a goddess of wisdom and a goddess of beauty. The gods and goddesses never grew old. If they wanted to, they could live with people on the earth. Sometimes they even married human beings. But they soon grew tired of the earth and returned to Mount Olympus [o LIM pus], the home of the gods.

The top of Mount Olympus was high in the sky. It was separated from the earth by a gate of clouds. Above these clouds lived the gods. On the top of Mount Olympus no one ever grew old, and no one ever died. Gods and goddesses couldn't get sick, and hardly ever were they hurt. They spent much of their time talking about what was happening down on earth. At their meals they ate a special food called ambrosia [am BRO zha]. They drank only nectar [NEK ter], the sweet juice of flowers. It was truly a life "fit for the gods."

The Greeks had kings in their cities, so they thought the gods must have a king on Mount Olympus. This king the Greeks called Zeus [ZOOCE]. He was supposed to keep order among the gods and goddesses. Since the gods grew jealous and quarreled just like humans, Zeus's job was not

8

an easy one. The proud gods and goddesses did pretty much as they wanted. Zeus had no real control over them. But Zeus could do something no other god could do. He could throw thunderbolts, or flashes of lightning. When the Greeks saw big, black clouds rolling up in the sky, it meant only one thing: Zeus was angry, very angry, and people down on earth had better watch out!

The first few stories in this book are Greek myths. The characters have ancient Greek names. Take the time to learn how to pronounce them. Remember, our names would have sounded just as strange to the Greeks.

In the beginning:

THE WAY THE WORLD BEGAN   The people of long ago lived in a world full of strange sights, smells, and sounds. They walked upon an earth about which they knew very little. They looked about them in fear and wonder. What made the oceans roar with anger, or the sky darken with clouds?

But before any other question, these people must have asked themselves how the world started in the first place. Just what *was* this earth that fed them, clothed them, and gave them shelter? How had the world first come into being?

The Greek poet Orpheus [*OR fee us*], about whom we shall read later, had one answer. Orpheus said that in the beginning there had been nothing except Time. (This "Time" must be spelled with a capital "T" because it was thought of as something like a god, but without a body.)

After millions of years, Time brought forth Chaos [*KAY*

9

os], or confusion. Chaos was a huge dark space filled with rain. Then Time told Chaos to spin around, and for more millions of years the dark space was a spinning, swirling rainstorm. "Spin faster! Faster! Faster!" Time ordered. As the rain spun faster, it changed into an enormous egg. Suddenly the shell of the egg cracked. The egg broke in two. One of the halves became the earth, and the other became the heavens. The yolk of the egg turned into love, connecting the earth and the heavens.

Other ancient peoples had different stories about the beginning of the earth. In Egypt, for instance, the most important god for many years was Ra [*RAH*], the god of the sun. He was thought to be the one ancestor of the other gods, of man, and of heaven and earth. Of course, in order for Ra to have had children he must first have had a wife. But where could this first god have found someone to marry? For the people of Egypt this was easy: Ra had married his own shadow!

To Ra and his shadow were born a god of the dry air and a goddess of the waters. These two, in turn, gave birth to a goddess of the heavens and a god of the earth. In a short time the heavens were filled with gods, and the earth was crowded with humans.

The people who lived in the icy lands of Northern Europe had another strange myth about the way the world began. Like the Greeks, they thought that at one time there had been only a dark empty space filled with rain. The rain fell and formed twelve rivers, and the rivers flowed downward until they formed a huge block of ice.

Then a great fire came from the south. The flames melted some of the ice, and changed the water into a cloud. Out of the cloud came the first giant, and out of the ice came the

10

first god. As we might suppose, the giant and the god didn't get along together. A fight started. The giant was killed, and out of his body the god made the earth. The giant's blood became the sea, his bones the mountains, and his hair the trees.

Today people are likely to laugh when they hear these old stories. But do we really know how the earth and the heavens were made? Our scientists are not sure. The things they tell us sound almost as strange as the ancient myths. They talk about bursting suns, and about enormous clouds spinning around in space.

But people living today have other things on their minds. Many of us are too busy to look upward at the star-spangled heavens and wonder how it all began. Maybe ancient people had something that modern men have lost—the ability to wonder.

FROM
Greece and Rome

*T*his was the world of the ancient Greeks. It included Greece, in the center, and the nearby lands that could be reached in small boats. For us, this ancient Greek world can become an exciting new world of reading pleasure.

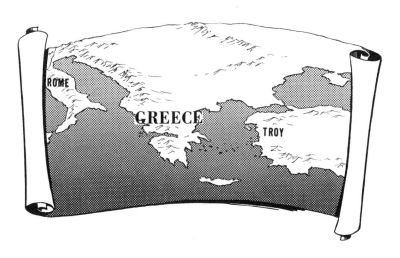

THE MYTH
OF PHAETON

. . . in which a boy disobeys his father's
wishes, and the sun stands still.

Words We Need to Know:

attendants   [*a TEN dents*]—servants, people who wait on others
The king's *attendants* stood in a row by the throne.
chariot   [*CHAIR i ut*]—a two-wheeled battle cart pulled by horses
The Greeks used *chariots* in wars, races, and parades.
fiery   [*FIRE ee*]—on fire, or colored like fire
In the evening we often see *fiery* red clouds.
reins   [*RAYNZ*]—leather straps used to drive horses
The rider pulled on the *reins* and made the horse stop.
shock   [*SHAHK*]—to surprise and frighten
The bad news in the telegram *shocked* the whole family.

What does having a father really mean to a boy? The average boy doesn't even think about it—unless he has no father. Phaeton [*FAY a ton*] was such a boy. He thought he had no father, until one day when he learned differently. And soon Phaeton was to learn some other things as well.

The story of Phaeton has been a favorite for thousands of years. Maybe this is because the most important character is not a god but a boy—a very human boy. This is the myth that explained to the Greeks how the sun moves across the sky, and why it once stood still. The myth explained more than this, however, as we shall soon find out.

THE MYTH OF PHAETON   Once, longer than long ago, there lived in Greece a boy named Phaeton [*FAY a ton*].

Phaeton was tall for his age. He had curly black hair, a straight Greek nose, and a smile that could light up a room. He was smart and did well in school. In fact, Phaeton had all that it takes to make a boy happy except one thing. He had no father. Ever since he could remember, he had lived alone with his mother.

When Phaeton was almost full grown, his mother told him about his father. What she said made Phaeton understand why his father didn't live at home. "You are almost a man now, Phaeton," she said one evening. "It is time you knew the truth. Your father is Helios [*HEE li os*], the god of the sun."

His own father a god! Was it possible? Yet the news had come from his own mother's lips.

Phaeton was too excited to sleep that night. The next day he couldn't keep his mind on his school work. He wanted to stand up at his desk and shout the news to the whole room. On the way home from school, he could keep his secret no longer. He decided to tell his friends about his father.

"My father is Helios, god of the sun!" Phaeton said suddenly.

His friends laughed. They had never heard anything so silly. "If your father is Helios," one of them joked, "then my father is the mighty Zeus. He can beat up your father."

"Take that back!" shouted Phaeton. But this only made his friends laugh louder.

That afternoon Phaeton arrived home with a black eye and a bad cut on his chin. He felt angry. He was beginning to wonder if his mother had told him the truth, or even if she knew the truth herself.

"How can I be sure that my father really *is* the god of the sun?" Phaeton asked his mother as she wiped the dirt from his face.

She looked at him a long moment. For the first time Phaeton noticed the tiny lines around his mother's eyes, like the tracks of a very small bird. Finally she said slowly, "My son, your father is a good god. Without him we would live in darkness. No food would grow, and the earth would become cold. If you go to Helios yourself, I think he will tell you the truth."

Phaeton was shocked. "What! Go to him myself? I may be his son, but I can't walk up in the sky."

"Helios rests on the earth every night," his mother said. "I'll go and pack some food and clothing. Tomorrow morning you can start for your father's palace."

The next morning Phaeton's mother awakened him before sunrise. They ate breakfast together by the light of a candle. When the red sun peeked over the purple hills in the east,

Phaeton's mother led him out into the yard. She pointed toward the sun.

"Walk toward the place where the sun rises," she said. "If you walk far enough, you will come to the palace of Helios."

With tears in his eyes, Phaeton kissed his mother good-by. Then he started the long journey to the edge of the earth. He walked, and walked, and walked. Every morning he would watch the sun rise, but it didn't seem to come any closer. Phaeton walked across Greece, across Persia, and across India. Late one day he came to some high mountains.

"This must be the edge of the earth," Phaeton told himself. "But it's getting dark. And how will I know the palace when I come to it? After all, I don't even know what it looks like."

Then Phaeton noticed a red glow in the sky ahead of him. He ran up and over a hill. There it was—a palace of light! The walls were made of gleaming gold. The towers shone like diamonds. The twelve heavy doors were made of silver. Suddenly Phaeton knew that his trip had come to an end. This was the palace of Helios!

Phaeton ran up the steps three at a time and entered the palace. Then he stopped short. The inside was so bright that it blinded him. He threw his hands up in front of his face. Tears flowed down his cheeks.

But as his eyes grew used to the light, Phaeton opened them wider and wider in wonder. Never could he have believed what he now saw. He found himself standing in a large room. At one end was a huge glittering throne. It was so bright that Phaeton couldn't tell of what it was made. Upon this throne, dressed in a purple robe, sat a powerful man with a wide forehead and eyes that seemed to see right through Phaeton. No, Phaeton thought, this wasn't any *man*.

This was a *god!* This was his father, Helios, god of the sun!

Around Helios stood his attendants. On his right were the Day, the Month, and the Year. On his left stood the Hours, each the same size as the others. In front of Helios were the four Seasons. Smiling Spring had her hair covered with flowers. Summer carried a bundle of ripe wheat. Autumn wore brightly colored robes. Frowning Winter's hair was white with frost. All were looking at Phaeton.

Helios spoke first. "Who comes here?" he asked in a deep voice. "And what does he want?"

Phaeton opened his mouth, but no sound came out. He swallowed and tried again. "My name is Phaeton," he finally said. "I am the son of an earth woman of Greece. My mother says that you, mighty Helios, are my father."

Helios said nothing. His forehead seemed to glow brighter.

"Please," asked Phaeton, "if I am your son, prove it to me, so that I can be sure."

Helios shook the rays of light from his broad shoulders. Then he stood up and put his hands on Phaeton's arms.

"My boy," said Helios, "only the son of a god could have come here alone, as you have done. Yes, you are my son. And I shall prove it to you. Ask anything you wish, and it will be yours."

Phaeton knew right away what he wanted. "All my life," he cried out, "I've dreamed of driving the chariot of the sun. Even for just one day!"

Helios smiled sadly. "Remember, Phaeton," he said, "you are an earth boy. Don't ask to do something only a god can do. Why, not even Zeus himself can drive my fiery horses across the sky. Surely, you wouldn't want to try it."

"But I do!" said Phaeton.

"Then you don't understand," explained Helios. "The first

part of the trip is steep and dangerous. The horses are almost wild. Do you want to try it if it means your death?"

"I do!" Phaeton repeated without thinking.

Without listening to Phaeton, Helios went on with his warning. "The middle part of the journey is high in the heavens. If I look down, I grow dizzy. Surely, no human thinks himself brave enough for that sight!"

"I do!" Phaeton cried. "I'm not scared of——'"

Helios raised his right arm. "He who is too brave is foolish," he told Phaeton. "Do you really think you could drive a god's wild horses among the stars?"

Then, without waiting for Phaeton's reply, Helios dropped to his knees in front of his son. "Look at me!" he cried. "Look at me now. A god on his knees!" He stretched his arms slowly toward the heavens. "If you were not my very own son, why should I be so worried about you?"

But Phaeton had his heart set on just one thing. He was going to drive the chariot of the sun across the sky. Helios talked for hours, but his words did no good. After a long time, one of the Hours told Helios that it was almost morning. "A god cannot break his word," Helios sighed. "And the sun must rise."

With a heavy heart, Helios led Phaeton to the room where the horses and chariot were kept. The horses were the largest Phaeton had ever seen. They were half asleep, but even so, fire shot out of their noses when they breathed. Behind them the chariot shone with the brightness of a hundred suns.

Phaeton jumped up on the chariot and took hold of the reins. Helios told Dawn to open the purple gates of morning. The horses started to move.

"Hold it!" shouted Helios. It was all Phaeton could do to stop the horses. Helios reached up and took his son's hand.

"Remember," he told Phaeton, "your job is to keep the reins tight. The horses will find the way if they don't get excited. Don't use the whip. Try to take the middle path. If you go too high, you'll burn the houses of heaven. And if you go too low——"

Phaeton never heard the rest of his father's sentence. The horses, now wide awake, had started moving. Out the gates of morning they ran, and up into the sky. The wind whistled past Phaeton's ears. He pulled with all his strength on the reins, but the horses went faster, and still faster. Up, up, up went Phaeton.

Soon the morning star zoomed past the chariot. Phaeton remembered what his father had said about going too high. But *how* high was *too* high? He turned and looked over the side. There lay the earth, spread out below him like a huge map. Phaeton started to feel faint. His head grew dizzy. He fell forward on the front of the chariot. The whip dropped onto the horses' heads. Down they turned. Down. Down. Down.

Back on earth, the people thought that the end of the world had come. Instead of rising slowly, the sun had seemed to shoot up out of the earth. Instead of moving across the sky, it kept on going up! Soon it was no larger than the head of a pin. The temperature fell to zero, and kept on falling. The blackest darkness ever seen covered the earth. People built huge fires for light and heat. They cried their prayers to the gods as they watched the sun grow fainter than the faintest star.

Then, just as everyone thought that the sun would disappear, it began to grow bigger. Before long it was back to its old size. People smiled—but not for long. The sun seemed to be standing still! But no! Now it was growing larger, and even larger. Soon it covered a quarter of the sky, then half the sky. People ran for cellars and caves. All the fish swam to the bottom of the sea.

Phaeton blinked his eyes, raised his head, and took a frightened look in front of him. He pulled madly on one rein, then on the other. The earth was rushing toward him. He shouted at the horses. "We'll crash! We'll crash into the earth!" Shutting his eyes tight, he waited . . .

But before long Phaeton felt the chariot moving up again. He opened his eyes and looked behind him. All the mountain tops were on fire. Large parts of the earth had been burned. Only hot, dry sand was left.

From their home on Mount Olympus, the gods watched Phaeton's wild ride. At first they laughed at the boy who tried to do a god's work. Then they became worried. It looked as if the boy might burn up everything, including Mount Olympus.

"A thunderbolt!" cried Zeus, the king of the gods. Then he grabbed the largest bolt of lightning he could find. He pushed a few clouds out of the way and took careful aim. Zoom! The thunderbolt flashed toward Phaeton with the speed of light.

In a way, Phaeton was lucky. He never knew what hit him. Wrapped in a ball of lightning, he fell like a shooting star into the sea. The tired horses no longer felt Phaeton pulling on the reins. They were excited no longer and soon found the path they took every day.

The sun set that night as it always has—and, we can hope, as it always will. For from that day to this, Helios has never let anyone else drive the chariot of the sun.

DAEDALUS AND ICARUS   The Greeks had another story about a trip through the sky. Here is the sad tale of Daedalus [*DED a lus*] and Icarus [*IK a rus*].

Daedalus was a famous Greek inventor. The Greeks were smart people, and Daedalus was one of the smartest. Maybe he was too smart. At any rate, a certain king once grew worried about Daedalus. The king didn't like anyone who was smarter than he was himself. One day he sent soldiers to arrest the inventor. But Daedalus wasn't put in an ordinary jail. Instead, he was made a prisoner on an island in the sea near Greece.

Daedalus was allowed to have his son, Icarus, with him. But even so, as the months passed he grew more and more homesick. The island was a prison without bars or walls. The king had ordered that every boat be searched before it left the island. There seemed to be no escape.

Then one day, as Daedalus sat looking out over the ocean, watching the sea gulls fly low over the water, he called his son to him. "Icarus," he said, "we cannot escape by land or sea. Only the air is left. Gather as many feathers as you can find. I will get string and wax to fasten them together. We shall make wings and fly back to Greece."

Icarus couldn't believe his ears. "Wings?" he cried. "You mean *fly* through the *air*? Like the birds? I thought only the gods could do that."

"There are times," replied his father, "when men must try to do what the gods can do without trying." He pointed at a flock of gulls winging in slow, lazy circles above the sea.

24

"Look there. See how easily the birds do it? Don't you want to go back to Greece?"

Icarus nodded his head.

"Then do as I say," ordered Daedalus. "Be off now, and bring me every feather on this island."

Soon Icarus had collected a huge pile of feathers—all shapes, all sizes, and all colors. Daedalus fastened them together with wax and string. When his own wings were finished, he made a smaller pair for his son.

Together, father and son climbed to the top of a high tower. They helped each other tie the wings to their arms and shoulders. A warm breeze blew in from the water. Worried sea gulls flew back and forth overhead, screeching at the strange birds with the ugly wings.

Icarus spread his wings and jumped up and down. He wanted to fly. It was all he could do to stand still. He had heard his father's plan a dozen times, and now he had to listen to it again. Daedalus was to jump off the tower first. If the wings worked, Icarus was to follow.

Moving slowly and carefully, Daedalus climbed up on the wall at the edge of the tower. He looked down at the hard ground. Then he looked out to sea, across the water, toward Greece. Oh, how Icarus wished to be off and away. But no —his father had still more things to say.

"When we get to the water," Daedalus warned, "you'll have to be careful. Fly only the middle path. If you fly too low, the water might wet the feathers. And if you fly too high, the heat of the sun might melt the wax that holds them together."

At last Daedalus was ready. He spread his large wings and jumped out into the air. Icarus was already testing his wings. When he saw that his father's wings worked, he held his arms close to his body and took a running jump off the tower. Suddenly he spread his arms. It was as if he had reached out and caught hold of the air! He was flying!

With a cry of joy, Icarus flapped his wings rapidly to catch up with his father. They were escaping! How wonderful it was to be free! To fly through the air! To feel the wind drying up the happy tears that ran down his cheeks!

Icarus forgot everything his father had said. Higher and higher he flew, until the hot rays of the sun started to melt the wax in the wings. One by one, the feathers began to come loose and flutter down toward the sea.

Little by little, Icarus began to fall. When he saw what was happening, he flapped his arms wildly. But this only made the feathers fly faster. In a frightened voice he called to his father.

But it was too late. Daedalus turned around to see his son falling down through the feathers. The boy's naked arms were still beating the air when he splashed into the sea.

That's the end of this sad story. Returning to Greece did not make Daedalus happy after all, for he had lost his son. In the years that followed, he often walked down to the water's edge. There he would stand for hours, looking out over the bright blue sea. No, Icarus was never seen again. But to this day, some people say, you can still see his rainbow of colored feathers flashing on the surface of the sunny sea.

CERES AND PERSEPHONE

. . . in which a girl disappears, a goddess is angered, and the human race almost comes to an end.

Words We Need to Know:

earthquake
: [*ERTH kwake*]—a shaking of the earth
The Pilgrims thanked God for the good *harvest*.
Not a house was left standing after the *earthquake*.

echo
: [*EK o*]—a sound heard again after bouncing off something
After the gun was fired, an *echo* came back from the hillside.

harvest
: [*HAR vest*]—food grown by farmers when it is gathered or picked
The Pilgrims thanked God for the good *harvest*.

pomegranate
: [*POM gran it*]—a dark red fruit with a thick skin
Most Americans have never eaten a *pomegranate*.

quiver
: [*KWIV er*]—a leather case made to hold arrows
The hunter took an arrow from his *quiver*.

sped
: [*SPED*]—went fast; the past form of *speed*
The racing cars *sped* around the track.

28

Winter was hated by the ancient Greeks. Without canned or frozen foods, their stomachs were often empty. Without rubber, their feet were often wet. Without stoves or furnaces, their bodies were often cold.

But, as they sat around their open fires, the Greeks would dream of an age long before when it had always been summer. The Golden Age, they called it. It had been an age without cold weather, without sickness, and without hunger. Ceres [SEE reez], the goddess of the harvest, had kept plants growing 365 days a year.

The Greeks loved Ceres. It was she who made the flowers bloom and the wheat fields wave with golden grain. All over Greece, people thanked Ceres for the food and clothing she gave them. They told each other the myth about Ceres and her daughter, Persephone [per SEF o nee]. It was a beautiful story, and it explained why summer no longer stayed all year long.

CERES AND PERSEPHONE   The Greeks believed that long, long before they lived it had been summer all year long. They thought that January had once been as warm as July, and March as sunny as May. Plants had stayed green twelve months a year. This was because Ceres [SEE reez], the goddess of the harvest, had loved the earth more in those days. The earth had been so dear to Ceres that she left Mount Olympus to live among the flowers and fields over which she ruled.

On earth, Ceres' life was like that of any other middle-aged housewife. She even looked like a middle-aged housewife. True, there was something strange about her eyes and forehead. But no one would have taken her for a goddess.

Her hair was almost gray, and the apron she wore almost always needed washing.

Ceres lived in the Valley of Enna, where it was always summer. Her cottage was deep in the woods near the shore of a blue lake. Here Ceres lived with Persephone [*per SEF o nee*], her daughter.

People said that Persephone was a pretty girl. And how right they were! The sun kept a healthy tan on her face the year around. Her fine, blond hair hung in soft bangs over eyes that were as blue and as calm as the lake.

But Persephone was more than *pretty*. She was *beautiful*, which means pretty from the inside out. Only really happy people can be beautiful, and happiness was Persephone's habit. She sang from dawn till dark, and she smiled even while sleeping. Although she was almost grown up, she still passed her days picking flowers and playing with her friends.

Ceres liked her daughter to pick flowers. Ceres always said that the two best sights in the world were the flowers Persephone picked, and Persephone herself. Once in a while Persephone thought of doing something else. But her mother *did* love flowers so! And, Persephone wondered, just how was the daughter of a goddess supposed to spend her time?

So Persephone kept on picking flowers. Every morning she skipped away from the cottage to join her friends. All day long she picked flowers, played games, and sang songs. And every evening, when she came home, her apron was filled with hundreds and hundreds of lovely flowers.

Then one night Persephone didn't come home. Ceres waited for her at the door of the cottage. Persephone's supper grew cold on the table. The sun went down behind the trees, and darkness started to move in over the blue lake.

Ceres stood waiting in the doorway. "Persephone!" she

called. "Persephone!" But the only answer was the echo of her own voice. "Persephone. . . . Persephone," came the faint echo from across the lake.

When it was dark, Ceres went back into the cottage. She sat down at the table and looked at Persephone's cold supper. The candle beside Persephone's plate grew shorter and shorter. The sound of the wind in the trees came through the open windows. But Ceres didn't hear it. She couldn't. She could think only of her daughter. There was nothing to do but sit and wait. For the first time in her life, Ceres wished she were human. A goddess cannot cry, and Ceres felt like crying.

Ceres didn't shut her eyes all night long. When morning came, she went outside to search for her daughter. She was sure of one thing. Persephone hadn't run away. The girl had been too happy to run away from the Valley of Enna.

First Ceres went to look for Persephone's friends. She found them playing in a nearby field where Persephone met them every morning.

"Where is Persephone?" the friends shouted when they saw Ceres. "It's getting late, and we don't want to start without her."

"That's just what *I've* come to ask *you!*" Ceres said. "Where *is* Persephone? She never came home yesterday."

Persephone's friends were surprised at the news. "We were picking flowers yesterday afternoon," they told Ceres. "Persephone went off a short way by herself. She was looking for a certain kind of flower. When she didn't come back, we thought she'd filled her apron and started home."

"Quick!" Ceres ordered. "Where did you see her last? Take me there."

Together they sped to the place where Persephone had

last been seen. Ceres couldn't run fast enough. What could have happened to Persephone? Had she fallen down? Twisted her ankle?

Alas, Ceres was to learn nothing of her daughter. They looked everywhere, but no Persephone did they find. What they *did* find was a pile of flowers—the same flowers Persephone had carried in her apron!

That afternoon Ceres walked all the way around the lake. "Have you seen my daughter, Persephone?" she asked everyone she met. "She is a pretty girl, and always seems to be smiling."

But no one had seen Persephone.

The next day Ceres left the Valley of Enna. She told herself that she would find Persephone, even if she had to go to the ends of the earth. Someone, she thought, must have carried Persephone away. But who? And where?

Ceres searched for many days. Since it was always summer, there were no winter storms to stop her. She went to every continent, and to every country.

"Have you seen my daughter, Persephone? She is a pretty girl, and always seems to be smiling." Ceres asked her question thousands of times, and thousands of times people shook their heads sadly and turned away. More time passed. Ceres began to wonder if Persephone could still be smiling. Ceres could not imagine her daughter without a smile, even though she herself had not smiled since the day Persephone had disappeared.

At last Ceres had traveled all over the world. Now she was almost back to the Valley of Enna. But the sight of her homeland only brought tears to her eyes. Persephone seemed to have disappeared from the earth.

When she came to a river not far from her home, Ceres felt that she could walk no farther. She had often come to this same spot with Persephone, years before the girl had disappeared. Ceres thought she was really going to cry, even though no goddess had ever cried before. She sat down on the grassy bank of the river and buried her face in her hands.

For a long time, Ceres sat without moving. Then she heard, or felt, someone drawing near her. But she didn't look up. She couldn't bring herself to open her eyes again on the cruel world. She hardly heard her voice as it said, "Have you seen my daughter, Persephone? She is a pretty girl, and always seems to be smiling."

In answer there came not a voice but a little noise. Suddenly Ceres felt as if she were again alone. She opened her eyes a crack and peered between her fingers.

There on the ground lay a wide red belt—Persephone's belt!

Ceres leaped to her feet. She looked around. Nothing. No one. But where had the belt come from? Had someone tricked her? She picked up the belt and twisted it in her hands. Yes, it was Persephone's belt. But Persephone was not on earth. Ceres knew that. She had looked everywhere.

"The worst has happened," Ceres told herself. "Persephone has been swallowed up by the earth!"

Sudden anger now filled the heart of Ceres. She kicked the ground hard. "Wicked Earth!" she cried. "All these years I've been good to you. I've kept you green twelve months a year. I've covered you with flowers and rich harvests of grain. And now you have taken my Persephone!"

With hate in her eyes, Ceres went on with her angry words. "No longer shall I let the seeds grow. No longer shall the trees give shade, or the flowers give beauty. From now on, cruel, wicked Earth, you shall be brown and dry. Forever!"

Ceres could stay not a moment longer on the earth. She left right away for Mount Olympus, the home of the gods. The flowers were sad to see her go. They hung their heads and waited for death.

Ceres had not been to Mount Olympus for many years. Zeus saw her coming. He met her at the gate of clouds. With him were most of the gods and goddesses. They whispered to each other behind their hands.

"Welcome, dear Ceres," Zeus said. "We've been waiting for you a long time—ever since the day Cupid [KEW pid] shot that gold-tipped arrow."

"What?" Ceres asked. She did not understand. Cupid, she remembered, was a playful little boy-god with curly hair. She remembered that he always carried a bow and a quiver of arrows.

Ceres looked around for Cupid. Soon she saw his wings sticking out from behind the skirts of his mother, Venus [VEE nus], the goddess of beauty. Venus looked embarrassed, or as embarrassed as Venus could look.

Zeus went on talking. "You should have remembered, Ceres. Here on Mount Olympus, the gods know everything. I will tell you what happened to Persephone."

Slowly the whole story became clear. It began with an earthquake. Pluto [PLOO toe], god of the underworld and king of the dead, had come up to see if any cracks had opened in the earth. He had been hit by one of Cupid's gold-tipped arrows. This meant that he would fall in love with the next person he saw.

Persephone, out picking flowers, had been that person!

34

She had tried to escape, but she could not run as fast as the coal-black horses of Pluto. He had gathered her up in his chariot, whipped his horses, and sped back to the land of the dead.

"And now," Zeus finished his story, "Persephone is married to Pluto. She is queen of the dead."

It took a moment for Ceres really to understand what Zeus had said. Her own daughter was the underworld queen! Ceres jumped toward Cupid, but Venus stopped her.

"Ceres, listen!" Venus cried. "Put the blame on me! It wasn't my Cupid's fault!"

Ceres looked down at Cupid. "You awful, awful little boy!" she cried. "Because of what you did, the earth will never again grow grain or flowers. And all the earth people will die!"

The gods disliked what Ceres had done to the earth. Already the trees were turning brown. Cows and horses could find no green grass to eat. Before long, the gods knew, the people would start to die. This would be terrible. Men and women were so very strange and interesting.

"I have an idea!" Zeus said suddenly. "I shall send Spring down to see Pluto. Who knows, maybe he will let Persephone return to earth!"

"But can anyone return from the underworld?" Ceres asked.

"It depends," Zeus told her. "Persephone can return if she has eaten nothing. But if she has eaten the food of the underworld, there will be no returning."

Ceres felt her heart grow heavy again. Was it possible that Persephone could have eaten nothing at all?

"Don't look so sad, Ceres," Zeus said. "Remember, the dead don't *have* to eat, you know."

35

Zeus gave directions, and Spring sped down to the palace of Pluto. When she arrived, she hardly knew Persephone. The person she saw was no longer a girl. Persephone looked every inch a queen, and Spring was a little afraid of her.

Had Persephone eaten anything?

Yes, said Pluto. She had sucked the juice from six pomegranate seeds.

No, said Spring. Sucking the juice from seeds could hardly be called "eating."

Spring and Pluto talked and talked. Persephone didn't know what to think. She had grown to like being a queen, even queen of the dead. But she had often dreamed of the flowers and trees back in the Valley of Enna. And most of all, she missed the good taste of the food of the earth.

It was Persephone who finally decided where she was to live. She would spend half of each year with her mother, and the other six months with her husband. Spring knew that Ceres wouldn't like this plan, but it was the only thing to do.

And ever since, Persephone has lived on earth half of each year. During the warm months, when Persephone is on earth, Ceres is happy. She lets flowers bloom and makes pumpkins grow heavy. Then Persephone returns to the underworld. Leaves turn brown and fall from the trees. Seeds lie on the ground until Persephone returns in the spring.

Another underworld adventure:

ORPHEUS AND EURYDICE   Some people have thought it strange that Persephone couldn't make up her mind about leaving the underworld. It's hard for us to know what to think. We can see why she might have wanted to

return to earth. But we must also realize tł
had a very interesting time being queen of thꞔ
One day, not long after her marriage to Plutꞔ
learned that a young man named Orpheus [OR
on his way down from earth. Now, thousands oł
young and old, made the trip to the underworld \   ᵤ.ₐy.
But Orpheus was different. He was famous—and he was still
alive!

Orpheus was probably the sweetest singer the world has
ever known. His name was famous from the bottom of the
underworld to the top of Mount Olympus. He played the
lyre, a musical instrument something like our guitar. It is
said that when Orpheus sang, the whole world stood still to
listen. Not only men and women, but animals, birds, and
even rocks and trees were charmed by his soft, sweet tones.

Orpheus at length appeared before Persephone and Pluto.
The hard journey had left its marks on his tired body and
hollow cheeks. But, Persephone thought, no journey, however hard, could have made his eyes look so sad. It would
take a deeper wound to do that.

Without speaking, Orpheus started to play his lyre. Then
he began to sing. The sad story he sang made Pluto himself
unhappy. Orpheus and a girl named Eurydice [yew RID i see]
had both been hit by Cupid's arrows. Their first look was
soon followed by an engagement to be married. The goddess
of love and the god of music attended their wedding two
weeks later. Never had two young people been so happy.

But joy changed to sorrow right after the marriage. Eurydice was bitten on the foot by a poisonous snake. In a few
hours her heart had beat its last weak beat. Now she was a
citizen of Pluto's kingdom of the dead.

"Please," Orpheus asked Persephone and Pluto, "let me

my Eurydice back to earth. Let us walk once more through sunny fields of flowers."

Persephone was surprised when Pluto said Eurydice could leave the underworld. However, there was to be one condition. Orpheus and Eurydice must walk straight out of the underworld, without once looking back. If either of them looked back, Eurydice was to return.

The two lovers were brought together again, and hand in hand they started the long trip up to earth. Eurydice's foot still hurt her, so Orpheus led the way. The climb was long and hard. Finally, just as Eurydice said that she couldn't walk much farther, Orpheus saw a glow ahead of them. He dropped Eurydice's hand and raced ahead. Yes! It was just as he thought!

"The sun!" Orpheus cried. He turned to smile back at his bride—and saw a look of horror come over Eurydice's face. She started to slide backward. She fell to her knees. One hand went out to Orpheus.

Orpheus ran toward her, his arms stretched out before him. But his hands felt only the empty air. It was too late. Orpheus had looked back before he reached the upper world.

"I'll wait for you," came Eurydice's voice as she passed out of sight. "I'll wait for you." Then she disappeared into the underworld, forever.

Eurydice didn't have to wait long. Orpheus died shortly after his return to earth. Soon he once again joined his beloved Eurydice. And ever since, it is said, they have been walking hand in hand, though not through sunny fields of flowers.

PROMETHEUS
AND PANDORA

. . . in which Zeus and some helpers make
the earth an interesting place.

Words We Need to Know:

creatures [*KREE cherz*]—living things; animals, insects, and birds
Horses, butterflies, and robins are all *creatures*.

slyness [*SLY nes*]—being tricky and sneaky
The fox is known for its *slyness*.

stubbornness [*STUB ern nes*]—having one's mind made up for good; being hard to deal with
The mule is known for its *stubbornness*.

timidity [*ti MID i tee*]—being afraid of things and easily frightened
The little girl's *timidity* made her afraid of the dark.

torch [*TORCH*]—a flaming light used before flashlights were invented
The Statue of Liberty holds a *torch* in her right hand.

Would you like to have lived with the gods on Mount Olympus?

Today, probably, most of us would just as soon stay right here on earth. Science has given us a world with more magic in it than the Greeks ever dreamed of. But the Greeks would have jumped at the chance to live on Mount Olympus. The life they made up for the gods was life as they would like to have lived it.

Most of the time the gods lived a life of ease. They often gathered happily in Zeus's palace. Here they feasted on ambrosia and nectar, while the god of music played heavenly tunes. Life was one big party without an end.

Life on Mount Olympus was not only comfortable, but it was also exciting and interesting. We know that the gods and goddesses sometimes did not obey Zeus. If they were caught, they were punished. Zeus's punishments could be hard and cruel. Once he threw Vulcan [*VUL kan*], the blacksmith of the gods, off Mount Olympus. Poor Vulcan tumbled through the air for six days. He fell faster and faster. When he finally landed on the earth, he broke the bones in his right foot, and ever afterward he limped.

But Vulcan's punishment was nothing when we think of what Zeus did to Prometheus [*pro MEE thee us*], the god who brought fire to man. Here is that story.

PROMETHEUS AND PANDORA   Long, long ago, in the days when the earth stayed green all year, human beings were not as they are today. In those times men lived much like animals. Of course, men were smarter than animals. But, since life was so easy, men never had to use their brains. Ceres saw that humans had more than enough to eat. The weather was always sunny and warm. People were not selfish, for they already had everything they wanted. Zeus had even taken all sickness off the earth. People died only of old age.

Men were unwise and happy, but the gods were wise and bored. They looked down from Mount Olympus and saw nothing interesting on the earth. Humans wandered about happily, eating fruits, berries, and nuts when they were hungry, and sleeping in the cool shade of trees when they were tired.

This kind of life pleased men and women, but it didn't please the gods. One day Zeus decided to make some changes. "It might be a good idea," he told himself, "if the creatures on earth were different. After all, why should a man spend his days like a monkey? Or a monkey like a man?"

Not long afterward, Zeus sent for Epimetheus [*ep i MEE thee us*], a young god who was not busy at the time. Zeus gave Epimetheus two boxes, a large one and a small one.

"I want you to take these boxes down to earth," Zeus ordered. "The big box is full of differences."

"Differences?" Epimetheus repeated.

"Yes," Zeus said, "differences—things to make the creatures of the earth different from each other. I want you to pass them out to the creatures on earth."

Epimetheus scratched his head. "What differences do I give to what creatures?" he asked.

"It doesn't matter," Zeus replied. "Just so you make things interesting."

"Is the little box full of differences, too?" asked Epimetheus.

"Ah!" the king of the gods answered. "That is Zeus's secret. All you need to remember is not to open the little box, unless you hear from me." Then Zeus slapped Epimetheus on the back. "On your way, now. The longer you stand around Mount Olympus, the longer I am bored."

Epimetheus wanted to ask Zeus more questions, but he

didn't dare. One didn't question Zeus's orders. One just obeyed them. The young god put one box on each shoulder and sped off through the gate of clouds.

Soon Epimetheus was on earth, walking along the dirt road that led from Mount Olympus. The boxes seemed to grow heavier and heavier. The god's arms and shoulders ached, for on earth he was no stronger than a man. Finally Epimetheus put the boxes down by the roadside. He sat down on the big box to rest.

A dusty, tired mouse came walking down the center of the road. The little animal didn't seem to notice Epimetheus. It had no enemies to watch for, and the young god looked much like a man.

Epimetheus stood up. "Stop a minute, mouse," he said. "I have a gift for you from the all-knowing Zeus." He opened the big box. The first difference he took out was strength.

"I can't give strength to such a tiny animal," Epimetheus thought. He put strength back in the box and looked for something more mouse-like. Timidity was hiding in a corner. Epimetheus gave timidity to the mouse. Suddenly frightened, the mouse took one look at the god and ran off into the bushes, as fast as its little legs would carry it.

The news spread quickly. Creatures big and little came running and flying to Epimetheus. They made a huge circle around the young god with the boxes. One by one, Epimetheus handed out the differences. He gave strength to the bear, loyalty to the dog, and cleanliness to the cat. Courage went to the lion, wisdom to the owl, and laziness to the pig. The bee got busyness, the fox got slyness, and the mule got stubbornness. Epimetheus went on passing out differences. Finally the box was empty. The animals went away, talking loudly about whose difference was the best.

Epimetheus was left alone by the side of the road. His

job was done, and he was now very tired. The sun was setting, so he decided to spend the night on earth. He could just as well return to Mount Olympus the next day. He found a bed of soft grass. The little box was just the right size for a pillow.

Epimetheus had had a hard day. He lay down and closed his eyes. But just as he was going to sleep, he heard a voice:

"What difference did you save for me?"

Epimetheus opened his eyes. He had made a terrible mistake. Man had been given no difference. And man was Zeus's favorite creature!

Epimetheus sat up and looked at the man. Then he looked at the raised lid of the empty box. "I have nothing left," he groaned. "The box is empty."

"What's in the little box?" the man asked.

"Only Zeus knows," answered Epimetheus. He felt very sad. He wanted to open the little box and give the man whatever was inside, but he remembered Zeus's warning. At any moment one of Zeus's bolts of lightning might flash down out of the sky.

Epimetheus knew he had to act quickly. First he called an eagle. Then he wrote a message to his brother Prometheus [*pro MEE thee us*]: SEND SOMETHING FOR MAN BEFORE ZEUS DISCOVERS MY MISTAKE. Finally he tied the note around the eagle's leg, and sent the bird flying off toward Mount Olympus.

When Prometheus received his brother's message, he knew right away what he would send—*fire*. For many years Prometheus had looked down at humans and felt sorry for them. He had often thought what man could do with the help of fire. But now Prometheus wasted no time thinking. He hurried to the palace of the sun-god to get a flaming torch.

44

Zeus noticed Prometheus as he was leaving the sun-god's palace with a large torch in his hands. "What can Prometheus be up to now?" Zeus asked himself. "We have no need for fire here on Mount Olympus."

When Prometheus reached the gate of clouds, he found Zeus waiting for him. The king of the gods stood quietly with his arms folded. He had an angry look on his face.

"Just what do you think you're doing with that torch?" Zeus asked.

Prometheus told the truth. He knew better than to lie to the all-knowing Zeus.

"You must not take fire to man!" Zeus thundered. "Not now, and not ever. Is that understood?"

Prometheus nodded. For a moment he stared at the tops of his shoes. Then he looked Zeus straight in the eye. "I think the mighty Zeus is selfish and thinks only of his own glory," he said slowly.

No one talked to Zeus like that. Prometheus expected Zeus to punish him, but the king of the gods made a long speech instead.

"Have you thought what would happen if men had fire?" Zeus asked. "They would be able to cook meat. Soon they would be killing other animals. They would melt gold and silver into coins, and start selling things for money. They would be able to get iron from rocks. With iron they could make guns and start killing each other. Wars would start. They might even learn how to make machines that could fly through the air, right over Mount Olympus." With one hand Zeus imitated an airplane in the sky above his head. "Oh," he groaned, "it's all too terrible to think about." And then, shaking his head sadly, he returned to his palace.

Prometheus stood by the gate of clouds, still holding the burning torch in his hands. What *would* humans do with

45

fire? He thought about what Zeus had said. It was true, of course, that men might use fire to kill each other. But it was also true that fire could make their lives more comfortable. There were thousands of interesting things men could do, if only they had fire.

Prometheus had spent many years watching men. He thought he knew them pretty well. He thought they could be trusted. Suddenly he opened the gate of clouds. Holding the lighted torch high above his head, he ran down to earth.

Prometheus knew he would be punished. But he had never dreamed of a punishment like the one he was to receive. When Zeus heard what Prometheus had done, he sent for Vulcan [*VUL kan*], the blacksmith of Mount Olympus. Vulcan was ordered to make a set of strong iron chains. Prometheus was chained to a huge rock high on a mountain. Here the hot sun burned into his skin. Rain whipped his helpless body. Ugly birds pecked at him when he tried to sleep. Many years were to pass before he would be rescued by a strong man named Hercules [*HUR kew leez*].

As for Epimetheus, he was not brave enough to return to Mount Olympus. He stayed on earth, hoping Zeus would forget, and maybe forgive.

But Zeus did not forget. Every day he looked down at the earth and saw humans busy with their new fires. The gods and goddesses tried to cheer Zeus up, but he refused to smile.

When Zeus finally did smile, it was a sly smile. "Epimetheus must be lonesome down on earth," he told the gods and goddesses. "Come, let's make a wife to keep him company. We shall make as perfect a woman as we can."

Every god and every goddess gave something to help make the new woman. Her beauty was that of Venus herself. When the woman was finished, Zeus breathed life into her. She opened her eyes and smiled.

"Your name is Pandora [*pan DOR a*]," Zeus told her. "You were made on Mount Olympus to be a wife for Epimetheus."

A short time later, Pandora walked into the house that Epimetheus had built for himself on earth. "My name is Pandora," she said. "I was made on Mount Olympus to be a wife for Epimetheus."

Epimetheus blinked his eyes. He had expected Zeus to send a thunderbolt, not a beautiful wife. Could there be some trick?

"In fact," Pandora added, "we are married already, I think."

Then Epimetheus took a closer look at Pandora. He couldn't take his eyes off her. Suddenly she smiled, and his doubts were gone for good.

Epimetheus had never been so happy as he was with Pandora. They passed their days much like humans. Epimetheus searched for food while Pandora looked after the house. Sometimes they took long walks together. They watched men doing things with fire. Pandora learned the names of the plants and animals of the earth. Epimetheus taught her everything she wanted to know—except one thing. He would not tell her what was in the little box that he kept on the top shelf of the bedroom closet.

"Please," Pandora teased him. "Just one little peek?"

"No!" said her husband. "Zeus said never to open it, and that's that!"

One day Pandora was cleaning the closet shelves. She lifted the box down and set it on the bed. Surely one little look wouldn't hurt. "After all," she told herself, "it isn't as if I were going to *steal* anything."

Pandora reached down and opened the latch on the box. The lid shot open with a bang. Out of the box flew greed, hunger, and fear.

It was a box full of troubles!

Pandora tried to close the lid, but the escaping troubles were too much for her. Measles, mumps, and chicken pox went out through the window. Pandora threw herself down on the bed. Soon the pillow was soaked with tears.

When Epimetheus arrived home, the last of the troubles were flying out the window and into the world. He raced into the house. Pandora lay crying on the bed. The open box was beside her.

"What have you done?" Epimetheus cried.

Pandora could not look at her husband. "Yes, I opened it," she said into the pillow. "The box was full of troubles, and I opened it."

Epimetheus stepped over to look inside the box. Something moved. The box was *not* empty!

Epimetheus took a closer look. There in the bottom, almost crushed by the escaping troubles, lay hope!

A shout of joy filled the room. "Get up!" Epimetheus yelled. "Look! Look in the box!"

Slowly Pandora rose to her feet. She peered into the box. Then she looked up at Epimetheus and smiled.

"The world may be full of troubles," Epimetheus told her, "but things won't be too bad, so long as we still have hope."

And Epimetheus was right. For from that day to this, hope has been man's best friend in a world full of troubles.

48

PYGMALION   Pandora, as we have read, was made by the gods on Mount Olympus. Here is a story about a woman who was put together right here on earth.

Pygmalion [*pig MAY li on*] was a famous maker of statues. He could turn a block of stone into a statue that looked more real than life itself. It is said that when a person first saw one of his statues, it appeared for an instant to be moving. Hunters used to shoot arrows at his stone animals, and people were forever saying things to his statues of men and women.

No one becomes perfect without practice, and Pygmalion had practiced twelve hours a day for many years. His practice had started when he was fifteen years of age. He had been jilted by a girl he loved dearly. From that day on, Pygmalion hated women and girls. He thought them stupid, dishonest, and more trouble than they were worth. If he had since made the greatest statues on earth, he had also made himself the world's loneliest man. He never spoke to women. This was too bad, for he was still young, strong, and handsome.

One day Pygmalion had an idea. "If the perfect woman cannot be found," he told himself, "I shall make her myself out of stone!"

The longer Pygmalion thought about his idea, the better he liked it. He searched all over Greece until he found a perfect piece of white stone. Then he set to work. Never had he taken more care. A creature of breath-taking beauty slowly took shape under his hammer.

49

Finally the day came when the statue was finished. Pygmalion stepped back to look at his work.

In front of him, carved out of white stone, was beauty itself! Pygmalion sighed. He could feel himself falling in love with the piece of stone. Try as he would, he could not help dashing forward to kiss the statue.

But the stone lips were hard and cold against his.

Pygmalion cried out to the heavens. If there was anything worse than falling in love with a girl, it was falling in love with a statue! He fell to the floor and beat his fists against his head. There was nothing he could do. All his skill could not put one drop of blood into the stone body.

It happened that soon there came the holiday in honor of Venus. This was the biggest celebration of the year. People danced in the streets and sang songs before the altar of the goddess of beauty. Pygmalion, when he had done his part, went forward and stood before the altar. "O Venus," he said, "who can do all things, give me a wife as beautiful as my stone statue."

But deep in his heart, Pygmalion knew that this was impossible. How could Venus grant his prayer? There *was* no woman as beautiful as his statue. As he walked home his sadness increased. Tears flowed down his cheeks when he opened the door and saw the statue he had come to love.

Suddenly Pygmalion blinked. He rubbed his eyes and looked again at the statue. Was it possible? Was the stone beginning to change color?

As Pygmalion watched, the stone cheeks of the statue started to turn pink. The lips moved and grew red. The eyes turned blue. Blood ran through the body.

"My love!" cried Pygmalion, rushing forward with joy.

And the statue?

She blushed.

BAUCIS AND PHILEMON

... in which the mighty Zeus visits the earth and decides to make some changes.

Words We Need to Know:

disguise   [*dis GIZE*]—to make yourself look like some-body else
Mary pinned up her hair and *disguised* herself as a boy.

magnificent   [*mag NIF i sent*]—wonderful; very good or large
There are many *magnificent* buildings in New York City.

messenger   [*MES en jer*]—someone whose job it is to carry messages or small packages
Bill worked as a *messenger* during his summer vacation.

paving stones   [*PAY ving STONZ*]—blocks of stone used to make streets or roads
Years ago many streets were made of *paving stones.*

temple   [TEM pel]—a large building used for religious services
Some *temples* in Greece are over two thousand years old.

vehicles   [*VEE i kelz*]—cars, trucks, buses, wagons, carts, etc.
Long ago *vehicles* were pulled by horses.

In the last story, we read that the gods' favorite creature was man. The gods were supposed to have found men interesting. Really, though, it was the other way around. It was the *Greeks* who found the *gods* interesting. For in truth, the gods lived only in the minds of the Greeks.

At first, the Greeks really believed in the gods. Then they learned more about science. They no longer needed the gods to explain things they couldn't understand. But the Greeks kept on making up stories about the wonderful gods they had invented. These new tales didn't explain anything. They were just good stories.

Our next story is just such a tale. It tells of a pitcher that never grew empty, and of a love that never grew old.

BAUCIS AND PHILEMON

Zeus was very worried. From his palace high on Mount Olympus, the great king of the gods looked down at the earth. Far below him, people hurried about like tiny ants. Men seemed to be very busy with their new fire and newer troubles. Humans had begun to build towns and cities. Roads, once little more than crooked paths through the woods, were now wide and straight. Someone had invented the wheel, and wagons, carts, and chariots moved in long lines along the new roads.

"It looks as if man can now do anything he wants," Zeus said to himself. "The trouble is, how can I know what he will want to do next."

Zeus sent for Hermes [*HUR meez*], his messenger. Hermes was the fastest of the gods. His shoes had little wings on them. He could almost fly through the air.

"I want you to go down to earth," Zeus told Hermes when he arrived. "I want to know what men are talking about.

53

I want to know if men still remember the gods. See if they think well of us, or if they are planning war."

Zeus watched Hermes step off into the air. Then he sat down to a meal of ambrosia and nectar. As Zeus ate, he thought about man. Everything—all Zeus's plans for the future of the human race—seemed to have gone wrong. Part of the trouble had been the work of Prometheus and his fire. But the rest had been Zeus's own fault. He should never have put Pandora in the same house as the box full of troubles. Zeus had planned to use the troubles to punish men if they ever forgot the gods.

Hermes had good news when he returned. "Everywhere I went," he told Zeus, "the people cheered me and held big parades. The leaders all made long speeches welcoming me to their fair cities. Here, look at these." From his pockets Hermes took enough keys to open a hundred gates. "The keys to the cities of earth," he told Zeus.

Zeus took the keys, but he didn't seem interested in them. "Yes," he said, laying the keys to one side. "Now tell me, do humans still remember the gods?"

"The name of Zeus is always on their lips," Hermes answered. "Before almost every sentence they say your name."

Zeus smiled. "Tell me about the temples they have built to worship me," he ordered. "Are they made of gold, or just plain silver?"

Hermes pulled on his ear. "I didn't happen to notice any temples."

"What!" cried Zeus. "You didn't notice any *temples?* Why, a temple should be the biggest building in a city." Zeus pointed down toward the earth. "Then tell me, what *are* those big buildings down there?"

"They call them stadiums," Hermes said. "Teams of men

play games in them, and thousands of people sit and watch."

Zeus shook his head sadly. "I fear, dear Hermes, that the earth people do not love us as much as you think. They saw you coming, and they put on a big show. But now I know that they have no temples. How can the gods be worshiped without temples?"

Hermes thought for a moment. As always, Zeus was right. "Yes," Hermes agreed, "I was fooled."

A frown appeared on Zeus's face. Fire and troubles had made men very wicked indeed. It was bad enough for men to do an evil thing, like forgetting the gods. It was much worse for them to pretend they were doing the right thing. Who could tell just how wicked humans had become?

"You will have to go to earth again," Zeus told Hermes. "This time I want you to travel in disguise. Take the wings off your shoes and dress like an old beggar. Have Venus paint lines on your face, so you'll look like an old, old man. She can also color your hair gray."

Hermes smiled at the idea. "This is going to be fun," he said.

"It *will* be fun," Zeus agreed. "In fact, I shall go with you! Together we shall see just what man has made of himself."

A few hours later, two old beggars passed through the gate of clouds. Slowly they made their way down Mount Olympus. They made a strange sight as they bent forward over their walking sticks and dragged their rag-covered bodies along the road.

The road grew wider when it reached the earth. It was covered with paving stones. Vehicles pulled by horses filled the road, so Zeus and Hermes had to walk in the ditch. The first town was still miles ahead of them.

Hermes was not used to the little steps of a man. His legs

55

grew tired. "Let's get a ride in the first empty wagon," he said.

The two gods leaned on their walking sticks until a wagon came along. Zeus held up his right hand and smiled at the driver. The horses stopped. "Would you be so kind as to give two old men a ride?" Zeus asked.

"Have you got any money?" the driver wanted to know.

"We are poor travelers," Zeus said. "We have no money."

"No money, no ride," replied the driver. His whip cracked over the horses' ears. The wagon rumbled on down the road.

"It is worse than I thought," Zeus told Hermes. "Men have become selfish. They do favors only for money."

As the sun was setting, the two gods walked into a small town. The village lay in a valley at the foot of a mountain. Zeus and Hermes stopped at the first house they came to. Hermes knocked at the front door.

The door opened—and just as quickly slammed shut in their faces. Before either of the gods could speak, they heard the click of a back door opening. Around the corner of the house came a barking dog. Zeus and Hermes had to run for their lives.

When the gods were safely in the middle of town, they turned in at another house. "This time you try to hold the door open," Zeus told Hermes.

A tired-looking woman with a baby in one arm opened the door. The baby looked at the two beggars and started to cry. Hermes held the door open with his foot. "Would you give two old men something to eat?" Zeus asked.

The woman just stood there.

"Please, let two old beggars look through your garbage," the king of the gods asked. "In the name of Zeus."

56

"Don't talk about Zeus to me!" cried the woman. "The only thing your great Zeus ever did was to fill the world with troubles."

Zeus looked angry. Then he looked as though his heart would break. He did not know what to say.

"Zeus is a mighty god," spoke up Hermes. "He might do you favors if you worshiped him properly."

"Go worship him yourself," replied the woman. She looked the strangers over from head to foot. "Look there at those rags you're wearing. You seem to need his favors more than I do!"

Zeus shook his head. "Take care," he warned. "Zeus might punish you someday."

The woman laughed and closed the door.

Tired, hungry, and sad of heart, the two gods turned away from the door and walked out of the yard. Boys threw stones at them as they walked down the main street of the town. Soon they had left the village behind. The road ahead went almost straight up the side of the mountain. Neither Zeus nor Hermes spoke as they started to climb.

A small cottage soon appeared ahead of them. Its walls were gray with age. There was no glass in the windows. In a garden beside the cottage, an old man bent over a hoe. A big white goose in the yard saw the gods coming and made a loud hissing noise.

The old man looked up when the goose hissed. "Welcome, strangers," he called. "What brings you this way? Only an errand for the mighty Zeus could send *me* along this road with night falling."

The two gods stopped and stood looking at each other. They were too surprised to speak. Here was a man who remembered Zeus!

"Why not stop here for the night?" said the old man. "You can go on in the morning."

Gratefully, Zeus and Hermes said there was nothing they would rather do. The old man, whose name was Philemon [*fi LEE mon*], called his wife, Baucis [*BAW sis*], from the house.

Baucis smiled at the travelers. "What we have is not much," she said, "but you are welcome to it." Then Baucis took a quick look at the goose. She nodded to her husband. Philemon jumped toward the goose with his arms stretched out before him. The big bird hissed and ran around a corner of the cottage. Philemon followed it, as fast as his old legs would carry him. Hissing and honking, the goose led Philemon around and around the cottage.

"Stop!" cried Zeus, when he saw what the old man was going to do. "Don't kill your goose. We are used to hunger, and can eat but little."

Philemon stopped running. His face was red, and he was too short of breath to speak. Baucis asked the two gods into the cottage.

The inside of the cottage looked even older than the outside. Summer rains had leaked through the roof and left dark, cloud-shaped stains on the walls and ceiling. The feet of Baucis and Philemon had worn paths in the dirt floor. Baucis put two old chairs in front of a cold fireplace. She asked her guests to make themselves comfortable while she set the table.

In a few minutes Philemon brought a tiny cabbage in from the garden. Then he reached up in the chimney and took out a little piece of bacon. A small pitcher half full of wine was put on the table, and the four old people sat down to eat.

The food was not enough for two people, let alone four.

58

The wine glasses were less than half full. The two gods tried to act as if they didn't notice how small the servings were. But their hosts could not be fooled. Baucis and Philemon wore faces of shame. When Hermes picked up the pitcher to refill his glass, Baucis was so ashamed that she shut her eyes. She knew that she had just poured the last of the wine herself.

Then Baucis heard a strange sigh escape Philemon's lips. She opened her eyes. Hermes was filling the fourth glass with wine! Baucis watched with her mouth open as Hermes set the pitcher down on the table.

The pitcher was full to the brim, as if nothing could have been poured out!

"Look!" Philemon pointed a shaking finger at the pitcher. "It was empty, and now it's——"

Philemon never finished his sentence. His eyes met his wife's. At once they knew that their guests were not beggars, but gods.

"Forgive us," Baucis and Philemon asked together, falling to their knees beside the table. "Forgive us for insulting the gods with such poor food."

Zeus stood up. He put his right hand on Philemon's shoulder, and his left on the white head of the old woman. Then he started to speak, in his god's voice for the first time. "You gave all you had," he said. "No one can give more. Come, stand up now. I want you to step outside and look at the town."

Zeus and Hermes led their shocked hosts out into the yard. In the valley where the town had been, a huge lake now lay peacefully in the light of a rising moon. The whole town was under water!

The eyes of the old people grew wide with wonder. It

was Zeus who finally broke the silence. "Now, Baucis and Philemon, turn around and look at your house."

Behind them, their old cottage stood no longer. In its place was a magnificent temple, covered with silver that gleamed in the moonlight. On the very top of the temple stood a golden statue of Zeus.

"A temple of Zeus!" Philemon cried.

"Yes," Zeus said. "I have placed it here so that people will never again forget the gods. And you good people, who never did forget us, you will watch over this temple as long as you live."

Baucis and Philemon lived out their lives looking after the temple of Zeus. When they died, Zeus saw that they were buried beside the temple, in the same ground that had once been Philemon's garden.

If you go to Greece today, people will show you this temple that Zeus is supposed to have built. They will also show you the two old trees that now mark the graves of the gentle Baucis and the good Philemon. Some say that if you listen carefully, you can still hear the two trees talking together, whispering their prayers to the all-knowing Zeus.

A short myth:

ECHO AND NARCISSUS   "Baucis and Philemon" is a story about love. It tells of two old people who loved the mighty Zeus. It explains very clearly what might happen to people who do not love the gods.

But "Baucis and Philemon" tells us little about people loving one another. For this, the Greeks had another story.

We remember reading that people fell in love when they

were hit by Cupid's gold-tipped arrows. The Greeks believed that if you were hit by one of these arrows, you fell in love with the person you were looking at, or with the next person you saw. (Some books will tell us that Cupid also carried blunt arrows tipped with lead. These are supposed to have brought hate instead of love. But this seems hard to believe.)

It was Cupid who started all the famous Greek love stories. But not all the love matches he started had happy endings. Cupid was careless. Once, for instance, he shot an arrow at a girl named Echo as she walked through the woods on a warm summer day.

Echo didn't feel Cupid's arrow, though for an instant she had a slight pain in her heart. Soon she came to a bubbling stream. As she stood on the bank wondering how to get across, she saw, on the other side, a young hunter named Narcissus [*nar SIS us*]. She could not take her eyes off him. She thought he was the most handsome youth she had ever seen. Without thinking, she jumped into the stream and started to wade through the water.

Their eyes met as she crossed the stream. Those of Echo were filled with love, and those of Narcissus—well, the less said, the better. Cupid had gone off to start new romances. He hadn't bothered to shoot Narcissus. The youth did not return Echo's love, even though she refused to leave his side.

"Go away!" stormed Narcissus, as Echo followed him through the woods. "Why should I love you?"

"I love you," Echo repeated. "I love you."

"I'd rather die than let you marry me!" shouted Narcissus.

"Marry me," came the echo. "Marry me."

Narcissus became more and more angry. Whatever he said to this girl, she always had to have the last word.

61

Finally Echo saw that her love would never be returned. She went off to cry by herself. Looking ahead of her through the tears in her eyes, she found a cave in the woods. Here she could be alone with her sadness. Every day her sorrow increased. Having nothing to live for, she became thinner and weaker, thinner and weaker, thinner and weaker, until only her voice was left. The voice of Echo still lives on, replying to those who call, and always having the last word.

As for Narcissus, well, he too was finally hit by one of Cupid's arrows. It happened just as he was leaning over to drink from a pool of still water. Narcissus saw his own face in the quiet pool. It was love at first sight. He reached down, but his fingers rippled the still surface of the water. The face he loved disappeared whenever he touched it.

Poor Narcissus! He loved himself so much that he couldn't leave the water's edge. For days he neither ate nor slept; and soon he, like Echo, had died for love.

A short time after the death of Narcissus, a new kind of plant came up out of the soil on which he had rested. The plant grew, budded, and blossomed. The body of Narcissus had been changed into the flower that today bears his name.

KING MIDAS and the GOLDEN TOUCH

...in which a famous but foolish king learns a lesson that most of us should already know.

Words We Need to Know:

embroider [*em BROY der*]—to decorate with a needle and colored thread
Janet wanted to *embroider* a handkerchief for Mother's Day.

solid [*SOL id*]—made of only one thing; forming the whole
Sally had a *solid* gold ring.

sunbeam [*SUN beem*]—a ray of sunlight
Not a *sunbeam* came through the thick leaves of the tree.

vault [*VAWLT*]—a locked box or room in which valuable things are kept
Banks have *vaults* where they keep large amounts of money.

Does anyone you know have a "one-track mind"? By a "one-track mind" we mean a mind that can think about only one thing. For instance, most of us know a boy who can think only about cars. This boy thinks about cars during lessons at school. He talks about cars during his lunch period. He draws pictures of cars in his notebook during study periods. After school he puts on old clothes and works on cars. In the evening he reads about cars in magazines. Then he goes to bed and dreams about cars.

Some girls can think about nothing but records. Such a girl doesn't just like records; she loves them. She will carry a record around with her all day, even to places where there is no record player. She does this because the record reminds her of a song, or the person who sings it. Other girls have a "one-track mind" when it comes to clothes. Still other girls can think of nothing but make-up and movie stars. Then there are girls who can think only of boys, and boys who can think only of girls.

Maybe you know people who can think only about money. These people often carry all their money around with them. They like to take it out and look at it. Usually they are not generous, for they want more money, not less. They don't like the things money can buy. They like money for its own sake.

The ancient King Midas [*MY dus*] was such a person. In his day money meant gold, so his story will be about a man who could think of nothing but gold.

KING MIDAS AND THE GOLDEN TOUCH   In the days of long ago, when this world of ours was both a younger and a stranger place, there lived a very rich king named Midas [*MY dus*].

King Midas loved gold more than anything else in the world. He loved his kingdom only because of the gold in its hills, and he loved his crown only because it was made of solid gold. He saw gold in the morning sunlight, gold in the daytime flowers, and gold in the hair of the beautiful daughter he kissed on the head every night.

This little girl, Iris by name, was the only family that the rich King Midas had. Indeed, it would be hard to say which Midas loved more, his gold or his daughter. But one thing was sure. The more Midas loved his daughter, the more he wished to become the richest man on earth. "My darling," he often told his daughter, "when I die, I want you.to have more gold than any man, woman, or child on the face of the earth."

Iris, however, had grown tired of gold, gold, and more gold. She had been named for the goddess of the rainbow, and she liked the blue of the sky, the green of the trees, or the red of the sunset fully as much as the yellow of gold. And while she loved her father dearly, she *did* get tired of looking at the long rows of buttercups, yellow roses, and sunflowers that grew in the palace garden. Iris could remember when the flowers had been of every color in the rainbow. But that had been before her father became so interested in gold. It had been back in the days when the palace rang with singing and music.

Alas, the only music that pleased Midas now was the sound of one gold coin striking against another. The only flowers that pleased him were yellow flowers. He liked to think how much his garden would be worth if each of the many flowers were made of gold. In fact, Midas had so fallen in love with gold that he could hardly touch anything that was not made of the yellow metal.

Every morning after breakfast, Midas went down to a dark vault in the basement of his palace. It was here that he

66

kept his gold. First he would carefully lock the door. Then he would take a box of gold coins, or a pail of gold dust, and bring it from a dark corner of the room into the one small sunbeam that fell from the one small window. Then he would count the coins in the box, or let the gold dust flow through his fingers into the pail. "O Midas," the rich king would say to himself, "what a happy man you are!"

Midas called himself a happy man, yet deep in his heart he knew that he was not quite so happy as he might be. The vault was small. Midas would never be really happy until the whole world had become a vault filled with gold which he could call his own.

One day, as Midas sat counting his money, a shadow suddenly fell across the single sunbeam in his vault. He looked up into a face that was young, handsome, and smiling. Midas couldn't help thinking that the stranger's smile had a kind of golden glow about it. Indeed, the whole room seemed to glow with the stranger's smile.

The king knew that he had carefully turned the key in the lock. No man but Midas himself had ever entered the underground vault. Who could the stranger be? And how had he got through the door? Again Midas looked at the stranger with the sunny smile.

Of course—this was a god! Midas was sure of it.

But what god could he be? What god could be as pleasant as the smiling stranger? And what god would have a reason to visit the rich King Midas?

"Bacchus [*BAK us*]!" Midas said suddenly. "The god of happiness!"

The stranger nodded his head. "Friend Midas, you are a smart man," he said. "And a rich one. I have never seen so much gold in one place as you have piled up in this room."

"Yes, I have done pretty well," Midas agreed. "But when I think of all the gold in the world——"

"What!" cried Bacchus. "With all this gold, you are not the happiest man alive?"

Midas shook his head.

Bacchus sat down on a box of gold coins. "I find this strange, friend Midas," he said. "Tell me, just what *would* make you really happy?"

Midas thought for a minute. He had felt from the beginning that the stranger meant no harm, but instead had come to do him a favor. This was an important moment. Midas must not say the wrong thing. In his mind he piled golden mountain upon golden mountain, but even mountains were too small. At last he had a bright idea. It seemed fully as bright as the yellow metal he loved so much.

"I wish," said King Midas, "that everything I touch might be changed to gold."

"*The golden touch!*" Bacchus cried. "I said before that you were a smart man, King Midas." The god's smile grew very wide. It seemed to fill the room, like a bursting of the sun. "But are you quite sure that this will make you more happy than you are now?"

"Why not?" said Midas.

Bacchus smiled again. "And you will never be sorry you wanted it?"

"How could I?" asked the king. "I want nothing else to make me as happy as a man can be."

"Then it is as you wish," replied Bacchus. "At sunrise tomorrow, the golden touch will be yours."

Once more Bacchus smiled. This time his smile was so bright that Midas had to close his eyes. When he opened them, the god had disappeared. Only the one small sunbeam remained to light the room.

That night Midas found it hard to fall asleep. His mind raced with thoughts of the golden touch that would be his in the morning. It was after midnight when he finally stopped tossing and turning.

The sun was high in the sky when Midas opened his eyes. The first thing he saw was a blanket woven of the brightest gold. He shook the sleep out of his head and looked again. This time he noticed his hand resting on the blanket, with the tips of his fingers touching the golden cloth.

The golden touch was his!

Midas jumped up with a shout of joy. He ran about the room, touching everything that happened to be in his way. He touched the foot of the bed, and a bed of gold gleamed before his eyes. He touched the dresser, and it too turned to gold. He touched the table—gold! The curtains—gold! The walls—bright gold! "O Midas," the king cried, "what a happy man you are! What a very happy man you are!"

As quickly as possible, Midas dressed himself in a robe of golden cloth. He was pleased to find that the cloth stayed as soft as it had ever been. From a pocket he took a handkerchief that Iris had embroidered for his last birthday. The handkerchief, too, was gold, with the girl's many-colored stitches now changed to bright yellow.

Somehow or other, this last change did not quite please King Midas. For an instant he wished that he held the same handkerchief that little Iris had given him.

But it wasn't important. Singing to himself, Midas opened a golden door and walked down a flight of golden stairs to breakfast. He wanted to surprise his daughter, so he was careful not to touch anything. Midas really loved the child, and he loved her so much the more now that such good luck had come his way.

By good fortune, the small bell Midas rang for his meals had long been made of gold. Iris would notice nothing strange except the golden robe, for Midas was careful not to place his hands on the table in front of him, or on the chair in which he sat. At length an attendant appeared with a golden tray. On the tray was the king's usual breakfast: a fresh orange, two pieces of buttered toast, and a large cup of steaming coffee. The servant told Midas that Iris had eaten hours before, and was now playing in the garden. Midas ordered that she be called.

Then the king turned to his meal. It was by now the middle of the morning, and the sight of the food made him hungry. But when he picked up the orange—of course!

"What!" said Midas, as he looked at the golden orange in his hand. "Now, this *is* a problem."

Very carefully, Midas reached out and touched one of the pieces of toast. At once it turned to gold. Only the butter still looked real. The coffee cup, too, and the coffee in it, became gold at the king's touch.

"I don't quite see," Midas thought, "how I am to get any breakfast."

Breakfast! Why, he would never be able to eat again! Already he was very hungry. By dinner time he would be starving. The poorest man in the kingdom, who sat down to the poorest supper, would be better off than he.

Moving quickly, Midas picked up the good piece of toast, rushed it to his mouth, and tried to swallow it in a hurry. But the golden touch was too quick for him. The hot metal burned his lips and tongue. Midas cried out in pain and jumped up from the table.

At this moment, Iris entered from the garden. She found

her father, dressed in a strange robe of golden cloth, dancing around the room like a wild man. Suddenly he stopped and looked at her. Iris watched two big teardrops work their way down her father's face. For a moment she tried to find out what was the matter with him. Then, with her heart full of love, she ran forward and threw her arms around her father's waist.

"My darling, darling daughter!" cried Midas.

But the girl made no answer.

Alas, what had the golden touch done now! It took Midas a moment to free himself of the metal arms around his body. He could not make himself look at the golden statue of what had once been his very own daughter. With a loud roar, he left the room and sped down to the only place he could be alone—his underground vault. He sat down on a box of gold and covered his face with his hands.

How long he sat there not even Midas could have said. With his eyes shut, he thought of all the times he had told Iris that she was worth her weight in gold. But now, now he felt differently. He wished that he were the poorest man in the whole wide world, if only the loss of his riches might bring the rosy color back to his daughter's cheeks.

A sudden change in the light made Midas open his eyes. There in front of him stood Bacchus. The god still had a sunny smile on his face.

"Well, friend Midas," said Bacchus, "how do you like the golden touch?"

Midas shook his head. "I am the most unhappy of men."

Bacchus laughed. "Let us see, then. Which of these two things do you really think is worth the most—the gift of the golden touch, or your own daughter Iris, as warm and loving as she was yesterday?"

"My daughter!" cried Midas. "My daughter! I would not

have given the smallest dimple in her chin for the power to change this whole earth into a solid lump of gold!"

For the first time, the smile left the god's face. "Yesterday," said Bacchus, "I said you were *smart*. But today I say you are *wise*. Now I will tell you how you can lose the golden touch. Wash yourself in the river that runs next to the palace garden. Wait!" The god poured a pail of gold dust out onto the floor. "Take this pail. Bring back some water, and sprinkle it over anything which your greed has changed to gold."

Midas lost no time. He raced to the river and jumped in. Then he sped back to the palace, in such a hurry that he didn't notice that he no longer wore a golden robe. He poured the whole pail of water over the golden statue of his daughter.

"Father!" cried Iris. "Look! See how my dress is all wet!"

The girl could remember nothing that had happened since she had thrown her arms around her father's waist.

And Midas was wise enough not to tell her. For he knew now that there was something better than all the gold in the world. This was the beating of one small and tender heart that truly loved him.

More about Midas:

KING MIDAS AND APOLLO   It would be nice to think, as many people do, that the troubles of King Midas came to an end with his daughter's return to life. But the truth is hard to hide. In a moment we shall see why.

Midas had learned his lesson only too well. For now he hated gold fully as much as he had once loved it. The very sight of the yellow metal would make him cover his eyes and cry as if in pain. He had the stairway leading to his vault filled with sand. He had all things made of gold thrown into the river. He had the yellow flowers in his garden picked before they bloomed.

But still the king was unhappy. He wanted to be the poorest man alive, but he found it impossible to be a poor king. Even though he dressed in rags and slept behind the stove in the palace kitchen, he was still the owner of the stove, of the kitchen, and of the whole palace. He could get rid of his gold, but not of his palace or of his kingdom. It would be years before Iris would be old enough to marry the next king, and she would not hear of the palace being destroyed.

The only happy hours left to Midas were those he spent walking through woods and pastures far from his home. As time passed, he began to leave the palace for days and weeks at a time. A few roots and berries were a dainty meal to set before this king, and a bed of grass pleased him more than a bed of gold. He became a follower of Pan, the god of the forests and the fields. Pan was a small god with the legs and feet of a goat. It was he who played the pipes that Midas loved to hear echoing across the valleys.

One afternoon, as Midas sat in the woods eating a handful of gooseberries, he heard the sound of voices raised in argument.

"I am!" came one voice.

"No, *I* am!" came another.

Then the first voice said, "But who is to decide?"

Midas stood up and made his way toward the voices. Soon he came upon Pan. The goat-footed god was jumping up and down before a taller god dressed in a purple robe. The big god held a stringed instrument called a lyre in his right hand. Midas knew that this could be only Apollo [*a POL o*], the god of music. Standing beside the excited Pan, Apollo looked as calm as a cloud.

Midas was joyous. "O Midas," he told himself, "what a happy man you are! What a happy man you are!"

"Ah!" Pan cried when he saw the king. "Here is a man who can be our judge. Be seated, friend, and tell us who plays the better music."

Then, before Midas had a chance to sit down, Pan started to play merry music on his pipes. Midas found his foot tapping to the gay country tune. His body began to rock from one side to the other. Soon the old king was dancing a wild jig. He danced so hard that Pan finally took pity on him and stopped playing.

Now it was Apollo's turn. Without a word, the god of music pulled up the sleeves of his purple gown. At the first heavenly note from his lyre, the birds in the trees became silent. At the second note, the wind stopped to listen. For the five minutes that Apollo played, the only other sound was the noise of the old king's breathing.

Midas spoke up while Apollo's last note still hung in the air. "There is no question," he said. "The better music is played by Pan."

Apollo was no longer quiet. "You dirty little goat-god!" he shouted. Then he turned to Midas. "And as for you, sir, your ears are deaf to music. You have the ears of a donkey!"

Midas heard a strange buzzing sound. He cupped his hands over his ears. Why, his ears were growing longer! They became pointed. Soon they were covered with hairs. He felt them move at the roots. He *did* have the ears of a donkey!

74

Alas, Midas had received another unwanted gift! Embarrassed and ashamed, he covered his head with leaves and returned to his palace. For the rest of his days he wore a turban, a long piece of cloth wound around his head.

This story, it is said, comes from his barber.

ULYSSES
AND CIRCE

. . . in which men become pigs, and a beautiful witch becomes almost human.

Words We Need to Know:

conquer [*KON ker*]—to win something in a war
        Hitler thought he could *conquer* all of Europe.
enchantress [*en CHAN tris*]—a beautiful witch
        The *enchantress* could change men into trees.
oars [*ORZ*]—pieces of wood made for rowing boats
        You use *oars* to row a rowboat, and paddles to
        paddle a canoe.
overboard [*O ver bord*]—over the side of a boat
        Knowing how to swim might save your life if you
        should fall *overboard*.

Could the gods die?

No, said the Greeks. One reason the gods were gods was that they lived forever.

But the gods did die. They died just as soon as the Greeks stopped believing in them. And with the death of the gods came the birth of the heroes.

When the Greeks stopped believing in their gods, the gods in their stories became less important. Human heroes became more important. Finally the Greeks were telling tales in which the gods hardly mattered at all. These old stories about famous people are called *legends*. The characters in many legends really lived, but the plots are almost always made up.

Some of the best Greek legends are about a clever king named Ulysses [*yew LIS eez*]. In real life, Ulysses was king of the island of Ithaca [*ITH a ka*], one of the many small countries that made up the land we know as Greece. His life was full of battles, adventures, and narrow escapes. Hundreds of years after Ulysses died, the Greeks were still telling legends about him. Today no one knows which stories really happened. After you read this legend, you can decide for yourself if it is true or false.

ULYSSES AND CIRCE   The city of Troy was the most magnificent in the ancient world. It was built high on a hill. It looked out over a sea that protected it from its enemy, Greece. Above its strong walls, towers of white stone gleamed in the sunlight. The palace of the king of Troy was as well known as the Empire State Building is today. Everyone in the ancient world dreamed of seeing Troy before he died.

The Greeks not only dreamed of seeing Troy, they dreamed of conquering it. In the days of the brave Ulysses [*yew LIS eez*], the small Greek kingdoms joined together

79

to form a large army. The soldiers sailed across the sea to Troy. It was a terrible war. Many men lost their lives.

After ten years of fighting, the Greeks won. They made slaves of the Trojans, as the people of Troy were called. The Greeks filled their stomachs with Trojan food, and their pockets with Trojan gold. They loaded everything they could carry into their boats to take home. Then they destroyed the things they couldn't carry. Finally they set sail for Greece.

As the wind filled their sails, the Greek soldiers sang songs of joy. They had beaten the Trojans. Slaves and riches made their small boats float low in the water. They were returning as heroes. The cities of Greece would soon be greeting them with parades, games, and dancing in the streets.

Or so they thought. Little did they know of the adventures that lay waiting on the way home. Little did they know that many of them would never live to see Greece again.

Their first stop was the harbor of an unfriendly city. Six soldiers from every Greek boat were killed. Then, when they were again on the sea, a dark cloud suddenly cut off the rays of the sun. More black clouds rolled up in the sky. In a few minutes it was almost as dark as midnight. Soon it started to rain. Water poured down into the open boats. The wind broke the masts and blew the sails into the sea. The waves rose higher and higher. The little boats were tossed up and down like toy boats in a bathtub.

The Greeks thought that Neptune, the god of the sea, was angry with them. They knew that the sea-god had been a favorite of the Trojans. To please Neptune, they started throwing overboard all they had stolen. Food, statues, silver, gold, and even slaves went into the angry waters.

This made the boats lighter. They floated higher. Not as

much water came in over the sides. "Old Neptune will forgive us!" the soldiers cried. Above the screaming winds and the roaring waves, they shouted their prayers to the god of the sea.

But Neptune must have been very angry. In a few minutes the wind screamed louder than ever. The waves again towered above the boats. Most of the Greeks stopped praying and waited silently for death.

There was one Greek, however, who would never give up hope. This was a short man, with a face like a stone, deep-set gray eyes, and black hair that broke in waves over his forehead. He was the ruler of the small Greek country called Ithaca [*ITH a ka*], and his name was Ulysses.

"Row toward the shore, my brave men of Ithaca," Ulysses cried. "Our only safety is on land."

Luck, as usual, was with Ulysses. His boat reached the shore safely. For two days and two nights, the Greeks lay on the beach, tired, cold, hungry, and wet. But on the morning of the third day, the storm was over. Rays of golden sunlight swept the clouds from the sky. The blue waters again whispered quietly beneath the sun.

The storm had ended, but Ulysses' troubles had hardly begun. The Greeks' next stop was the land of the Lotus-Eaters. These people ate the fruit of a strange plant that made them forget the past and brought sweet dreams of the future. Then the men from Ithaca landed in a country ruled by a race of cruel giants. Finally they sailed to within sight of their homeland, only to have a storm come up and blow them far out to sea.

Now the Greeks were surely lost. Around the boat the sea stretched out for miles, until it faded into the blue of the sky. No land was in sight. The soldiers rowed and rowed,

81

but the boat seemed to stand still. They rowed until the sun sank into the western sea. On through the night they rowed. Ulysses steered the boat by the stars.

When the first light of dawn showed in the east, the men laid down their oars. Everyone looked for land. Land would mean food, fresh water, and a chance to rest. As the sky became lighter, they could see farther across the water.

"Look!" one of the men shouted. "An island!"

Far in front of the boat, a small island lay on the edge of darkness. The men grabbed their oars and rowed as they never had before. The boat almost flew through the water.

Soon the Greeks were stepping out of the boat onto dry land. They fell to their knees and kissed the ground. Ulysses stood to one side, smiling. A long time passed before he gave orders.

"My friends," Ulysses began, "we know nothing about this island. We don't even know where it is. But someone must live here. A while ago, I saw some smoke rising above the trees."

The soldiers froze with fear. They remembered their narrow escape from the cruel giants. What new dangers lay waiting here? None of the soldiers wanted to explore the island. But what else could they do? Sail without food into an unknown sea?

Ulysses divided the men into two groups. One group he told to explore the island. The other group stayed behind with Ulysses. While they waited on the beach, Ulysses made the men forget their troubles by telling them stories. He told them the tale of Prometheus, and about Pandora's box, and about hope being man's best friend in a world full of troubles.

82

Hours later, a loud, crashing noise came from the woods. Something was coming! Ulysses and his soldiers reached for their swords. They waited. The noise grew louder.

A single man ran out of the woods. His clothing was red with blood, and his body had been scratched by branches and thorns. He ran down the beach and fell to the ground at Ulysses' feet. Only then was Ulysses sure that this was one of his own men.

"What is it?" asked Ulysses. "Is a monster chasing you?"

"A monster?" the man repeated. He stopped for breath. "It's worse than a monster. It's an enchantress!

"We went into the woods to look around," the man went on. "At first we found nothing. But in the center of the island we found a clear place in the woods. In the center of this clearing was a palace. A woman's voice—or we *thought* it was a woman's voice—came from the windows. It was singing the sweetest song anyone ever heard."

"Go on," ordered Ulysses. "Go on."

The man slowly sat up on the sand. "Then, as we watched," he said, "a woman came out of the palace. She was a walking dream, too beautiful to be real. She came toward us. We couldn't take our eyes from her face. When she understood we were hungry, she smiled and invited us inside. It seemed too good to be true."

A shiver passed down the man's back as he thought about what had happened next. "The others went into the palace," he told Ulysses. "But I stayed outside. Something seemed wrong. I walked around the palace, looking for the windows of the dining hall. Finally I found them. And then! There our men sat, each eating a whole pie. On the table in front of them lay what little was left of a huge meal. The men were so full, they sat at the table like stuffed animals, unable to move. Not one of them saw the woman take out her magic wand."

"Go on!" cried the soldiers. "What happened? What did she do?"

The man picked up a handful of dry sand. He watched it fall from between his fingers. When his hand was empty, he spoke again. "The enchantress touched each man on the head," he said slowly. "And they were changed into pigs—big, fat pigs!"

The soldiers looked at the woods above the beach with fear in their eyes. For a moment even Ulysses' eyes grew cloudy. What could he and his men do now? He put his hands against his eyes and tried to think.

When Ulysses lowered his hands, his eyes were once again clear. He picked up his sword. "Show me the way to this island palace," he said. "I think I'll be able to handle the enchantress."

"No! Don't go!" cried the man. He jumped up and grabbed Ulysses' arm. "I haven't told you the worst of it. As I was leaving, I passed the pen where the enchantress keeps her pigs. There our friends were, all of them. They looked up at me. There was a strange look in their eyes. Suddenly I knew what was wrong. One part of them hadn't been changed—their *minds!* They still had the minds of men. Don't ask me how, but I know it!"

The eyes of the soldiers grew wide. The same plan raced through every mind—to jump into the boat and get away from the island right away.

But this Ulysses refused to do. "Wait here, then," he said. "I'll go to the palace alone."

Without another word, Ulysses marched off into the dark

forest. He fought his way through the thick bushes until he was within sight of the palace. Just then the god Hermes, in the disguise of a young boy, appeared before him.

"Foolish man," said the boy. "Just where do you think you're going? Do you think you can change the pigs back into men? No, even the clever Ulysses cannot do that. You'll end up as a pig, too. But here—I know a way to help you."

The boy pulled a small medicine bottle from his pocket. "Drink this," he told Ulysses. "It will protect you from the enchantress."

Ulysses lost no time in drinking the drug. Then he thanked the boy and walked on toward the palace. Suddenly he heard a woman's voice singing a simple, sad song. It echoed through the woods with a strange beauty. As Ulysses stopped to listen, a door in the palace opened slowly. The enchantress stepped out into the sunshine.

Never had Ulysses seen a being so beautiful—or so enchanting. Waves of blond hair flowed down over a robe of deep-sea blue. She moved forward with the gracious steps of a princess. Her sudden smile was as warm as the sun.

"Come in," the enchantress said. "A meal is waiting for you."

"Who are you? What is your name?" Ulysses said.

"My name is Circe [*SUR see*]," she replied. "Come, you look hungry."

Ulysses allowed Circe to lead him into the dining hall. While his meal was being put on the table, she gave him something strange to drink. Ulysses had never tasted anything like it before. But he drank it at once, knowing the drug would protect him.

All the time, Ulysses kept watching Circe out of the corner of his eye. Soon he saw her take a wand from the folds of

85

her blue gown. Then she passed behind his chair. He felt the wand touch him lightly on the head.

"Now, be off to the pigpen," Circe said. "Go and lie in the mud with your friends."

"Aaaaaaaaaaah - Eeeeeeeeee - Oooooooooow!" Ulysses roared. It was a cry that made the blood run cold. He jumped to his feet. Out came his sword. Circe screamed and dropped her wand. Ulysses chased her into a corner.

"Know ye that I am the mighty Ulysses, King of Ithaca and conqueror of Troy!" Ulysses shouted. "Promise that you will never try that again, or else you shall feel the cold steel of my sword."

Circe nodded without speaking. Ulysses watched two teardrops form slowly in the corners of her eyes. In another minute she had become a crying girl. She was very lonely on the island, she said. It made her so angry!—angry enough to turn men into pigs. But she had to do something. She would give anything, if only Ulysses would stay and keep her company. And she would start by preparing the best meal Ulysses had ever eaten!

"Circe," said Ulysses, "no man whose friends have been changed into pigs could really enjoy a meal. If you want me to eat, set my soldiers free. Make them men again, and let me see them."

Once more Circe did as she was told. She took her wand and went to the pigpen. In an instant the pigs were soldiers again, crawling around in the mud. They looked surprised and ashamed at first. Then they got to their feet and cheered Ulysses. They looked younger and stronger than ever.

Before long, all the Greeks were feasting at Circe's big table. Now they found it hard to leave Circe's island. The days turned into weeks, and the weeks turned into months.

86

For a whole year, the Greeks lay in the sun of Circe's island and ate five meals a day. But they couldn't forget the island of Ithaca. At last the day came when they were too homesick to stay another day. It was with tears in their eyes that they finally waved good-by to the sad Circe and pointed their boat once again toward Ithaca.

A close escape:

ULYSSES AND THE SIRENS   Not long after leaving the sad-eyed Circe, the Greeks saw another island ahead of them. Circe had told them to watch for this island. From the way it sparkled like a diamond set in the blue sea, Ulysses knew that this was the island of the Sirens.

Circe had warned Ulysses about the Sirens. "Not far from here," were her words, "you will pass an island where live the most beautiful creatures on earth. They will smile and wave at you from flower-covered fields. But be careful, Ulysses. These are the Sirens. They are charmers. Their voices will make you forget your wife back in Ithaca. If you hear their singing, you will jump into the water and try to swim to the island."

Ulysses smiled at Circe. "And what happens when I get there?"

"No one knows," she sighed. "No man has ever reached the island. All who have tried have been killed by the waves and sharp rocks. The sea around the island is filled with the bones of men."

Ulysses stood looking at Circe. Was she sending him to his death? If the Greeks could not safely pass the Sirens' island, how were they ever to get home?

"But there is a way to sail past the island," Circe went on. "Stuff your ears with wax. It will make them deaf to the Sirens' songs."

Now, as Ulysses sighted the island of the Sirens, he prepared to follow Circe's instructions. He heated some wax in the sun. But he didn't fill his own ears with wax. He wanted too much to hear the Sirens. Instead, he had his men tie him to the mast. Strong ropes ran around his ankles, legs, wrists, and arms. The ropes were tied with double knots. In this way, Ulysses would be able to hear the singing without throwing himself overboard.

The tiny boat sailed onward toward the island of the Sirens. Soon the creatures could be seen. They were dressed in flowers. Beautiful blond goddesses they seemed, smiling as they sang and waving as though they had never before seen a man.

Soon the Sirens' voices began to drift into Ulysses' ears. "Untie me!" he shouted. "Untie me, do you hear!" He pulled at the ropes until his skin was rough and red.

"I am the king here!" Ulysses howled. "Cut me loose, you cowards!"

But Ulysses' cries could not be heard. His men had their ears stuffed with wax. They had orders to tie the ropes tighter if they saw Ulysses shouting. They were not to free Ulysses until the island was out of sight behind them.

Ulysses pulled at the ropes and shouted like a madman. He seemed not to notice the blood that ran down his arms and legs. He howled like a trapped tiger—until, finally, the boat passed out of hearing.

The distance between the boat and the island slowly became greater. When the dot of land had disappeared under the curve of the sea, the soldiers cut Ulysses from the mast. They laid him in the bottom of the boat and washed his sores with sea water. In a few hours Ulysses was himself again, the only man in history to have heard the Sirens sing —and lived to tell about it!

ULYSSES AND
THE CYCLOPS

. . . in which Ulysses meets the ugliest creature ever to walk the earth.

Words We Need to Know:

fleece   [*FLEECE*]—sheep's wool before it is made into yarn
       Every spring the farmer sold the *fleece* from his sheep.

herd   [*HERD*]—to watch over animals
       A shepherd's job is to *herd* sheep.

rage   [*RAJE*]—to move or shout with anger
       The lion *raged* when it saw the hunters.

shrug   [*SHRUG*]—to raise your shoulders to show you don't know about something
       Jane *shrugged* when her sister asked the date of the school play.

The Greek myths are so old that their authors have been long forgotten. The first author we know anything about is the man who wrote the legends about Ulysses. His name was Homer. (The Greeks used only first names. Last names were invented later.)

Except for his name, we know very little about Homer. We don't know where he was born, when he was born, or when he died. We think that he was born nearly three thousand years ago. Legends about Homer himself tell us that he was a blind storyteller. His friends are supposed to have led him from city to city.

Today some people believe that no "Homer" ever lived at all. These people think that he is as much of a legend as any of the characters he is supposed to have invented. Homer, they say, should be thought of along with the strange beings in his stories—Circe, the Sirens, and the Cyclopes [*sy KLO peez*].

We have already met the beautiful, sad Circe. Some of us have read about the dangerous Sirens. Now, let us hope, we are ready to meet the Cyclopes, the most ugly monsters that ever *never* lived. For as makers of monsters, the Greeks have never been beaten.

ULYSSES AND THE CYCLOPS   Day after day, the small boat holding Ulysses and his men sailed toward Ithaca. Around them, as far as the eye could see, there was nothing but blue water. Were they never to see their families again? Were they never to see the one place in the world they called *home*?

It seemed not. There was no escape from the hot sun and the restless waves. They ate the last of their food. Their water was almost gone too. Each man was given only enough to

93

wet the inside of his mouth twice a day. But still they sailed on, hoping to see land.

The worst thing was the lack of water. This was strange, for there was water all around them. But Ulysses knew that the sea water was too salty for his men to drink. It would make them more thirsty than they already were. And too much salt would make them ill.

As time passed, the burning sun did strange things to the men from Ithaca. Some of them went blind for hours at a time. Others began to see strange and wonderful sights. They thought they saw friendly green islands in front of the boat. They saw big meals floating in the air before their eyes. The food looked real—until they tried to eat it. Then it disappeared.

Finally the Greeks saw something that was very real. The water around the boat was changing from blue to green. "This means that the water is becoming shallow," Ulysses said. "Watch carefully from now on. We may be nearing land."

Ulysses was right. That night they came to an island. Working in the dark, they pulled their boat up onto the beach. They had no idea where they were. But it didn't matter. It was enough to sleep on dry land.

In the morning, when the men awakened, they cried for joy. They seemed to be on an island. Close to them a stream bubbled down out of the green hills. Wild goats dotted the hillsides. Joyful tears flowed down the faces of the men from Ithaca. They were saved!

But their tears soon became tears of sorrow. Not far from the island was a large body of land. One look told the Greeks that this was the land of the Cyclopes [sy KLO peez].

The Cyclopes were giant monsters. They looked something

94

like humans, except that they had only one eye. These horrible eyes were set right in the middle of the monsters' foreheads. The Cyclopes had no government and no laws. They lived alone. They never washed. Everyone in ancient Greece had heard about the Cyclopes. But few people had seen them—and no one had ever left their land alive.

Ulysses' soldiers looked across the water at the Cyclopes. They lost all hope. But not Ulysses. "There seem to be no Cyclopes here on this island," said the clever king. "They must not know how to make boats. Come, let's explore the island, feast on the goats, and forget about the Cyclopes."

The Greeks could explore the island and feast on the goats. But they couldn't forget about the Cyclopes. They could see the smoke from the monsters' fires. When the wind was right, they could hear the monsters shouting at one another.

Ulysses sat on the shore watching the Cyclopes. He became more and more curious. Finally he called his men together. "My friends," he said, "I'm going to visit the Cyclopes. I want to find out what they're really like. Are they as cruel as we have heard? Or, when they see that I bring no harm, will they treat me as a guest?"

The soldiers backed away from Ulysses. Had their king gone mad?

"Anyone who wishes may come with me," Ulysses went on. "The rest of you will stay here and wait."

A few of the braver soldiers joined Ulysses at once. Then more decided to stick with their king. Soon the soldiers had divided themselves into two groups. Ulysses took those who were going with him and got into the boat. Silently they rowed across the water to the land of the Cyclopes.

"I wish we had a gift for the Cyclopes," Ulysses whispered.

"We need something to show them that we come as friends." Suddenly a light came to his eyes. He reached into the bottom of the boat and came up with a jug of wine. He looked at the jug and smiled.

"I've been saving this," he told his men. "Had we not found land, it might have tasted good. But now, I think the Cyclopes should have our wine."

They reached the shore of the land of the Cyclopes. Ulysses told some of the men to stay with the boat. Then, with twelve of his best friends, he set out to meet the monsters. As yet the Greeks had not been seen.

"Be careful," Ulysses warned. "A Cyclops [SY klops] has only one eye, it is true. But his one eye can see more than our two."

Soon the Greeks passed around a huge rock and found themselves looking into the mouth of a cave. "A Cyclops' cave!" Ulysses said in a loud whisper. "The monster must be out herding his animals."

Ulysses stepped into the cave first. It was a large, damp room. Hundreds of spiders ran for cracks in the stone walls. The only light came from a fire in the center of the dirt floor. Baskets of cheese were scattered here and there. In the back of the cave was a pile of wood for the fire. On one side was the giant's bed. On the other side were pens full of hungry little lambs.

Ulysses held a piece of cheese to his nose. "It looks as if the Cyclopes can do one thing well," he said. "Here, taste the cheese."

The men did as they were told. The cheese was so good, they couldn't stop eating.

"Listen!" one of the soldiers cried suddenly. "Do you——"

96

"Shhh!" Ulysses put a finger to his lips. All was quiet for an instant. Then came the sound of the monster's steps.

The men ran to all parts of the cave. Some hid under the giant's bed. Others ran behind the pile of wood. Still others dived in among the lambs.

In a minute the Cyclops began to herd his sheep into the cave. He had a huge head, long arms covered with hair, and feet like a bear's. His ugly eye was at least four inches wide. The skins of three sheep were stitched together around his dirty body.

Thirteen pairs of eyes watched every move the Cyclops made. He had not seen or heard the Greeks, for he went about his work as though nothing had happened. First he threw wood on the fire. Then he put the sheep in their pens. When this was done, he reached outside and pulled the huge rock up against the mouth of the cave.

Suddenly someone sneezed. "Ker-*chew!*" The sound echoed from wall to wall.

"Ha!" cried the Cyclops. His one eye looked around the cave, now well lighted by the roaring fire. Then the eye came to rest. It was looking at a foot that stuck out from behind the pile of wood.

The Cyclops pulled the owner of the foot from his hiding place. "Ha! Ho! Ha!" he laughed, walking around the cave. He pulled men out from everywhere. Before long the Greeks were lined up in front of the sheep pens. The monster's huge eye moved slowly up and down the line.

"Who are you?" he asked in a deep voice. "Are you pirates? Robbers? Have you come to kill, or to be killed yourselves?"

Ulysses took a step forward. "We are Greeks, men from

Ithaca," he told the giant. "We come as friends. And we wish to leave as friends."

The Cyclops said nothing. Again his eye moved up and down the row of men.

"Come, Cyclops, let's not quarrel," said Ulysses. "True, you are bigger than we are. But the gods look down on us both."

The Cyclops seemed to burst with anger. "The gods!" he raged. "Do you think we Cyclopes fear the gods? No, we are *above* the gods! If I want to kill you, Zeus himself can do nothing to stop me."

The monster was now looking at the largest of Ulysses' men. Before the Greeks knew what was happening, he had grabbed the man and smashed his head against the wall. Then he killed another man. He cut the bodies in pieces and ate them quickly, bones and all. The Greeks cried like babies and prayed for the help of Zeus.

For a short time, at least, they were to be saved. The big meal soon made the monster sleepy. He yawned a few times and lay down on the bed. Before long he was asleep. When he started to snore, Ulysses walked toward him on tiptoe. The king pulled out his sword and placed its tip over the Cyclops' heart.

Suddenly Ulysses stopped. If he killed the giant, how could the Greeks get out of the cave? The rock that covered the doorway was too big to be moved by human hands.

Ulysses sat down sadly on the other side of the cave. There seemed to be no way out. They were trapped in a cave with a man-eating monster!

Things got no better. When the Cyclops woke up, he ate two more of the Greeks. Still Ulysses could think of no way to escape. Then he remembered—the monster had not yet discovered the wine! But six men had been eaten before the clever Ulysses was ready with his plan.

Ulysses went up to the Cyclops as soon as the sixth man had been swallowed. "Cyclops," he said, "after your meal, wouldn't you like a drink of this wine. You have treated us badly, but we still want you to have the wine."

"Wine?" said the Cyclops. "If you brought me wine, you are truly my friends."

The monster reached his hair-covered hand out for the jug. He jerked out the cork and poured a large drink down his throat. He licked his lips with a loud *smack*.

"This is very good wine," the giant said. "It makes me feel kindly toward my friends. What is your name, friend?"

"My name is No-man," Ulysses lied.

"Well, I like you, No-man," replied the Cyclops. "I will treat you as a friend. I will eat you last."

As soon as the giant was again asleep, Ulysses put his plan into action. "The monster is going to lose his one eye," he whispered. First the sharp end of a long pole was put in the fire. When the point was red-hot, Ulysses took it from the fire. He carried it toward the sleeping Cyclops.

Before long a loud cry came from the Cyclops' cave. "Ow! Oo! Oh!" cried the blinded monster. The noise could be heard all over the land. Other Cyclopes came on the run and gathered outside.

"What's the matter?" they shouted. "Is an enemy in there? Is anyone hurting you?"

"No-man is in here!" the monster called back. "No-man is hurting me."

The other Cyclopes looked at each other. "If no man is in there, our friend must be all right," they agreed. Then they shrugged and walked back to their own caves.

Inside the cave, the blind Cyclops ran around trying to catch the Greeks. His big feet were burned as he ran through the fire. He crashed into the sheep pens, then tripped over the sheep that ran about the floor. Finally he bumped into a wall and bounced back flat on the ground. He lay there a long time.

When the Cyclops sat up, he blinked his one blind eye and rubbed his head. Then he slowly got to his feet. He felt his way along the walls until he reached the mouth of the cave. With one hand, he pushed the huge rock out of the way.

"Look!" the men cried. "He's going to lock us in here!"

But the monster had no such idea. It was now morning, and the Cyclops wanted to let his animals out to eat. He sat down in the mouth of the cave and stretched out his arms.

Before long one of the sheep lifted its nose and smelled the grass outside. The animal tried to get past the Cyclops. When the monster was sure it was a sheep and not a man, he let it go by.

Ulysses watched with interest. Then, without a word, he caught the largest sheep in the cave. He led it almost to where the blind Cyclops was seated. As soon as the sheep had smelled the grass outside, Ulysses crawled under the animal. He grabbed the fleece on the sheep's neck and gripped its body between his knees. Very slowly, he raised himself off the ground.

The Greek soldiers held their breath as they watched their king. Ulysses held on tight. The sheep started to walk toward the Cyclops.

Soon the monster felt the sheep press against his leg. His huge, hairy hand passed over the animal's woolly back. Then the sheep passed outside. Ulysses was free!

One by one, the Greeks made their escape by hanging on

to the sheep. When all were safely out of the cave, they ran down to the boat. Soon they were once again on the blue sea.

Ulysses stood up in the back of the boat. He looked back at the land of the Cyclopes. "Blind Cyclops," he called across the water, "know now who has blinded you. I am the mighty Ulysses, King of Ithaca and conqueror of Troy."

The Cyclops was still seated in the mouth of the cave. He stood up and raged in a voice like thunder. Suddenly he picked up a great rock, as big as the top of a mountain. He threw it far out over the water.

But luck was still with Ulysses. The big rock just missed the Greek boat. Ulysses and his soldiers were soaked by the splash. The King of Ithaca and conqueror of Troy wisely decided to wait until they were farther away before he called again.

The end of the road:

ULYSSES RETURNS HOME   After many years of wandering, Ulysses finally reached Ithaca. He found his kingdom in bad order. Most people had come to believe that their king had drowned.

His wife, Queen Penelope [*pe NEL o pee*], had not yet remarried. But it was clear that she would soon choose a new king. More than a hundred men spent their time in Ulysses' palace. Each hoped Penelope would marry him. These suitors were eating Ulysses' food, drinking Ulysses' wine, and giving orders to Ulysses' old servants.

Worst of all, no one who saw Ulysses knew who he was. He had been a young man when he left for Troy. Now he returned, twenty years later, looking older than his years. His face was browned by the sun and lined by the sea. His clothes were those of a beggar.

Ulysses decided to tell no one who he really was. For a while, at least, he would be a spy in his own kingdom. With his own eyes and ears he would see just who had remained loyal. He started out on foot for the royal palace. The green fields and groves of olive trees were just as he remembered them. But most of all, he liked meeting the people. They told him what had happened in Ithaca since the mighty Ulysses had been swallowed up by the sea.

At last the beggar-king reached the royal palace. Music and laughter drifted through the open windows. But he didn't go in at once. He stood looking at a thin dog that lay in the dust by the gate. This was his old dog, its body now stiff with age and weak from lack of food.

The dog raised its eyes and looked at Ulysses. Very slowly, its tail started to wag. It tried to drag itself toward Ulysses. But it couldn't. The dog seemed to know that now, with its master home, it could die in peace. And in another minute the old dog lay dead.

Ulysses made his way into the palace. For the first time, he saw the men who wished to take his place. They were feasting and drinking in the great dining hall. Not one of them really looked like a king. Excitement was in the air, for Penelope had said that she would soon choose her new husband.

Ulysses went from man to man, begging for food. He wanted to see which of the suitors were good, kind men. Some of them took pity on him. Others did not. "What!" they cried. "A new beggar? Don't we have enough beggars in the country now?"

"Do you want something, old man?" laughed one of the suitors. He picked up a small stool. "Here, then. Take this!"

The stool sailed across the room toward Ulysses. It hit him on the shoulder. But the king didn't fall. Instead, he moved away without a word. He knew that his time would come.

Ulysses had not long to wait. Penelope's plan for choosing one of the suitors was an interesting one. She entered the room holding Ulysses' old bow and a quiver of arrows. "This bow," she explained to the suitors, "belonged to my beloved king, the lost Ulysses. It has not been used since he bent it with his own strong hands. I will let each of you shoot an arrow. The man who shoots the straightest arrow will be the new king."

Right away all the suitors wanted to try their skill with the bow. They couldn't agree on who would go first. But finally one of them stepped forward to shoot the first arrow. He took the old bow in his hands. "What!" he said to himself. Something was wrong. He couldn't even bend the bow! After trying three times, he handed it to the next man in line.

One by one, the suitors learned that the bow of a great king was too much for them. They tried to bend it until their hands were sore. When the old beggar asked for a chance to shoot an arrow, all they could do was laugh.

Ulysses not only bent the bow, he sent an arrow flying straight toward the target. He had won back his own kingdom and his own wife!

CUPID
AND PSYCHE

. . . in which a princess with the beauty of
a goddess finds she is too human to marry
a god.

Words We Need to Know:

exquisite [*EKS kwi zit*]—carefully made; very fine or beautiful
The queen kept her jewels in an *exquisite* silver box.

four-poster [*FOR POST er*]—a large bed with four tall bedposts and a high cloth cover
George Washington probably slept in a *four-poster*.

planet [*PLAN it*]—a heavenly body that travels around the sun: Mercury, Venus, Earth, Mars, etc.
Today there is a lot of talk about life on other *planets*.

suspicion [*suh SPISH un*]—doubt; lack of trust; a feeling that something is wrong
The woman had a foolish *suspicion* that everyone was trying to cheat her.

suspicious [*suh SPISH us*]—doubtful, mistrustful; likely to feel that something is wrong
A very *suspicious* person would probably trust no one but himself.

The tale of Cupid and Psyche [*SY kee*] is not so old as the stories we've read so far. People have been telling it for only about 1800 years! It comes not from Greece but from Rome, an ancient country known today as Italy.

The Romans lived after the Greeks. Some of their stories, like "Cupid and Psyche," they made up themselves. Most of their tales, however, they just borrowed from the Greeks. The Greek gods and goddesses were given Roman names. *Zeus*, for instance, was called *Jupiter* by the Romans. In this book we've used Roman names when they were better known than the Greek names. The Roman *Venus*, for example, is better known than the Greek *Aphrodite* [*af ro DY tee*].

In this story we meet Venus again. She is the same proud, beautiful goddess we read about in the Greek myths. But her son Cupid has changed. He has now grown up. The Romans thought of Cupid as a handsome young man, more as a god of love than as a playful little boy. Sooner or later, of course, some Roman was bound to make up a story in which this grown-up Cupid falls in love with a human. Here is that story.

CUPID AND PSYCHE   In days of old, there once lived a beautiful young princess with the beautiful name of Psyche [*SY kee*]. Her life was a comfortable one. She slept in a four-poster, between sheets of the richest red satin. At a snap of her fingers, the palace clown would come to make her laugh. She ate her meals from a silver plate, and she drank from a golden cup.

But all this did not make Psyche happy. For, like most princesses, Psyche was born with as many problems as anyone else—and maybe even a few more.

Psyche's problem was a strange one. She was very, very beautiful. She was so beautiful that most boys did not dare speak to her. And if she spoke to them, they turned red, stared at their shoes, and backed away with silly smiles. Her sisters, who were both very pretty, disliked her because she was so much better looking. Men and boys turned to stare at Psyche in the street. At first she hadn't minded. But it was getting annoying.

A crowd now stood outside the palace every day. They said they were waiting for the king, but Psyche knew differently. Many times she had put her ear to the window and heard them talking. "Why should we go to the temple of Venus to worship beauty?" they would ask each other. "Here is a creature even more beautiful than the goddess of beauty—and with real red blood in her, too!"

Was it true? Psyche often wondered. Did people no longer worship the goddess of beauty?

Alas, it was all too true. And no one knew it better than Venus herself. As more and more people stayed away from her temple, Venus became more and more worried. Finally the day came when not one person entered the temple of Venus.

The goddess was very angry. "Are people to forget me, just because this silly girl has a pretty face?" she asked herself. "No, this Psyche will not so easily take the place of the goddess of beauty. I will give her a reason to be sorry—very sorry!"

Then Venus called her son Cupid to her side. "This girl must be punished!" Venus said. "Somewhere on earth will be found the most wicked, mean, and ugly man alive. I want you to make Psyche fall in love with that man."

The handsome Cupid prepared to carry out his mother's wishes. He took from her a small jug of magic water. When sprinkled on Psyche's eyes, it would make her fall in love with a man who was wicked, mean, and ugly. Cupid tied the jug to the top of the quiver that held his arrows. Then he spread his white wings and flew down to earth.

Cupid found the girl asleep in her four-poster. She lay on her back under a satin sheet. Her left arm was thrown across her eyes, for a lamp burned low in the far end of the room. The god tiptoed silently across the smooth stone floor. He took an arrow from his quiver. With its golden point, he touched the white skin of Psyche's shoulder. Now he had to sprinkle the magic water over the girl's closed eyes. But first he would have to remove her arm from her face. Still holding the arrow in his right hand, he reached down with his left and slowly lifted Psyche's arm.

Such beauty! Cupid was not ready for such a lovely sight. He dropped Psyche's arm and stepped back. In his surprise he scratched himself with the arrow. But he didn't even know it, for his mind was on Psyche, not on himself.

Why, Cupid thought, even a goddess could not have such an exquisite face, much less a young girl. No wonder Venus had been angry . . .

. . .That same night Psyche had a strange and wonderful dream. She dreamed that she opened her eyes—was it a bump on the nose that awakened her?—and found herself looking into the eyes of a man who could be real only in a dream-world. Curls of light brown hair tumbled down over his wide forehead. His good-looking face seemed to glow with a light all its own. A kind smile tickled the corners of his mouth. His eyes were as blue as the sky. In them Psyche felt she could see not only the whole world, but the heavens as well.

Psyche had no idea how long she stared into these eyes. But finally, the dream-man started to move away. "Wait for me," he said in a soft voice, his eyes still upon her. Now he was fading away faster. "Wait for me," he said again. Psyche sat straight up in bed, suddenly wide awake.

But her dream-man had disappeared.

Psyche awakened the next morning a much happier girl. She no longer worried about boys. It was enough to wait for her dream-man. She refused to go outside where people could see her, except under cover of darkness. Slowly, the crowd around the palace gave up waiting for her to appear. The people went back to the temple of Venus.

Psyche stayed shut up in the palace. She spent most of her time reading. She read about the wonders of modern Rome, and about the strange ways of the ancient Greeks. This went on for months, and then for years. The king began to worry about her finding a husband. But Psyche just smiled to herself. She never told anyone about her secret dream.

One summer evening, Psyche climbed to the top of a hill near the palace. She liked to be alone in the night air, and to feel the breeze blowing through her hair. She looked up in wonder at the thousands of stars. The planet Venus was not in the sky. This made Psyche happy. She had come to hate Venus.

"Why do people worship Venus?" Psyche wondered. "If people knew what it's like to be so beautiful, they would hate the goddess of beauty, not love her! No, it isn't easy to be very beautiful. The trouble is that people see only the outside of you. Your beauty is like a shell, in which you, the *real* you, have to live."

As Psyche stood on top of the hill, with her mind full of questions and her eyes full of wonder, a strange thing happened. The friendly wind raised her slowly from the earth.

The wind's touch was so soft that she felt no fear. She was carried away easily, and was soon laid to rest upon a bed of soft grass. She could see nothing in the darkness. But still she was not afraid. The sweet smell of flowers, and the merry sound of a nearby brook, made her feel that she was not alone. She closed her eyes, and soon she was fast asleep.

When Psyche awakened, she found herself resting on the ground near a magnificent palace. It was built of a gleaming metal—not gold, not silver, but a blue metal that Psyche had never before seen. She knew at once that the building was not the work of human hands, but the happy home of some god.

Should she enter? Psyche didn't know. But soon she found that her feet were taking her toward the high doors. Then, as if by magic, the doors opened by themselves. Psyche entered a huge room. The walls were covered with pictures of every kind of animal, all painted with exquisite care. Statues of the gods stood here and there on the polished floor.

Going onward, Psyche came to a dining table set for a single person. On it were a pitcher of rich milk and an apple that looked too good to be real. She picked up the apple and bit into it carefully. It *was* real, and Psyche found that she was hungry.

Psyche spent the rest of the day going through the palace. She wandered through hundreds of fine apartments, and through room upon room filled with magnificent treasures of art. Everything she met filled her with joy. When the sun went down, she came to another dining table. Like the first table, it was set for only one person. But there was more food on the table than any one person could eat. There were three hot lamb chops, a huge white cloud of whipped potatoes, four kinds of rare vegetables, and a bowl of strawberries and cream. The food looked so good that Psyche sat right down to eat, even though she had seen only a small part of the palace. After all, there would be tomorrow, and the day after tomorrow, and the day after that. And when she had seen everything, she could start in at the beginning again.

As Psyche ate, she looked at the most beautiful sunset she had ever seen. The clouds in the western sky changed from red, to pink, to yellow. Then darkness came with a rush. It was like the quick coming of night in the North that she had read about in books. Soon it was too dark to see the little food that was left on the table.

Just as the last glow of light faded from the sky, Psyche felt a breath of air on the back of her neck. She turned her head, but in the dark room she could see only a black shape near her. Then, without warning, a soft voice seemed to come out of the air:

"Thank you, Psyche. Thank you for waiting."

As a strong hand took hers in the dark, Psyche knew that this was a voice she had heard only once in her life—long, long before in a dream.

For many minutes Psyche said nothing. She didn't want to break the spell by speaking. Finally she could hold her question no longer. "Who are you?" she whispered into the darkness. "Please, tell me your name!"

"My name you must never know," came the reply, low against her ear. "And my face you must never see."

"What!" cried Psyche. Was she never again to look upon the face of her dream-man!

"Is there anything you want that is not here in the blue palace?" the gentle voice asked.

Psyche thought for a moment. "No," she said softly.

"Do you doubt my love?"

"No."

"Is it that you don't trust me?"

"No!" Psyche cried. "Oh, no."

"Then please," said the voice, "never ask again to see me. That is all I wish. I want you to love me as an equal, not as your master."

This pleased Psyche for a time—but it was a short time. As the days passed, she wanted more and more to see her husband. He came only with the darkness, and he sped away before the light of dawn. Psyche's need to see her husband began to do strange things to her mind. During the long daylight hours, she would wonder if he were neither a god nor a man. Maybe he was an ugly monster! Why else would he hide from her eyes? But then, during the night, such thoughts seemed impossible. Psyche would lie awake and hate herself for thinking such things. This would make her want to see him all the more.

Finally Psyche could stand it no longer. One day she hid a candle under her bed. When she remembered it that night, she laughed at herself for having been so suspicious. But sleep refused to come. Her hopes and fears kept her awake. What harm could it do to light the candle? One look, and she would be sure for the rest of her life. Soon the first faint light of dawn began to show in the east. Unless she hurried, he would be gone. She reached for the candle. As her fingers closed around it, she knew what she was going to do.

Psyche rose from her bed. She felt around on the dresser for a match. Her hand shook as she lighted the candle. Then she walked toward the sound of the deep, even breathing on the other side of the room.

In the dim light of the candle, Psyche looked down at the brown curls and handsome face of her dream-man. And how strong he looked! Then she noticed something gleaming on the wall above his head. Why, it was gold. A quiver of gold-tipped arrows and a bow!

This was Cupid, the god of love! Not even in her wildest dreams had Psyche thought such a thing. Holding the candle nearer the god's face, she leaned over to have a closer look. Oh! A drop of hot wax fell on his arm.

In an instant Cupid's eyes were open, full upon her. Without a word, he jumped up on the other side of the bed. Then, taking his bow and quiver from the wall, he moved away. There was just enough light in the room for Psyche to see him disappear through the door .

"Wait!" Psyche cried. She dashed out of the room. She followed the sound of his footsteps down the long, long hall, and out of the palace. "Wait! Wait!"

Suddenly Cupid stopped in his tracks. He turned toward Psyche. She wanted to throw her arms around his strong shoulders. But the look on his face told her to stay where she was. "Good-by, Psyche," Cupid said. His voice was hard and cold, but Psyche thought there was a note of sadness in it, too. "After I left my mother, and made you my wife, is this the way you have trusted me? Love and suspicion cannot live in the same house, Psyche. So the god of love must go."

As Psyche watched, Cupid seemed to disappear into the morning air. Her eyes filled with tears. She ran a few steps after him. Then she fell forward into the soft grass.

When Psyche had cried herself out of tears, she raised her head and looked around. But the blue palace was nowhere to be seen. It seemed to have disappeared with the god of love. She found herself on the hilltop near her home, where she had stood when the gentle wind picked her off her feet. It was very early in the morning, and only the planet Venus was left to light the heavens.

Was it the tears in Psyche's eyes? Was it a trick of her mind? Or did the planet Venus really look down at her and wink?

An ending without an end:

THE TRIAL OF PSYCHE One who has lived with the gods can never again walk happily in the ways of men. Psyche's life was now without joy of any kind. The food of the earth had lost its taste, and not even the palace clown could bring a smile to Psyche's lips.

Alone and unhappy, Psyche could think only of her lost Cupid. She wondered by day and wandered by night. Many times she climbed to the top of the hill where the wind had carried her away to the blue palace. She would close her eyes and stand waiting for something to happen. But she would feel only the breeze, and hear only the sad singing of the birds of the night.

At last there was but one thing left for her to try. As much as Psyche disliked the mother of Cupid, she knew that she would have to go to the temple of Venus and ask the goddess for help.

Psyche entered the temple of Venus before the rising of the sun. She wanted no one to be there to stare at her beauty, or to make fun of her prayers. Behind the altar stood a huge statue of the goddess. Psyche dropped to her knees and shut her eyes.

"O Venus," Psyche began—but what should she say to the angry goddess? What *could* she say? Then, as Psyche searched for words, she heard the voice of the goddess talking to her from above:

"O girl of little faith, have you come here to worship Venus? Or have you come to find your husband? Cupid is still sick at heart because of the way you treated his love."

So Cupid had missed her!

Psyche looked up into the green eyes of Venus. The goddess's white body shone faintly through a robe of deep-sea green. "Why," Psyche thought, "her beauty is nothing at all like mine! Hers is the proud beauty of a goddess. But how can such lovely lips twist themselves into so cruel a smile?"

Venus stared down her straight nose at Psyche. "You are too thin," she said, "much too thin. In fact, you are not beautiful at all. No wonder my Cupid left such a weak little creature. Surely, the only way you could keep a man with you is by worry and a lot of hard work."

"I would do anything," Psyche said truthfully. It pleased her to be thought of as a busy housewife who was not at all beautiful.

Venus reached down and took Psyche by the hand. "Come with me, then," the goddess said. "I will give you a trial. If you do a good day's work, you can have your Cupid—no, *my* Cupid—back again."

Psyche was led down a flight of stairs to a dark and dusty storeroom. On the stone floor was a great pile of wheat, corn, oats, and barley. The seeds were mixed together as food for Venus's pigeons. "Separate all these seeds," the goddess told Psyche. "Make four piles, one in each corner of the room. I'll be back before dark to see how you've done." Then Venus left, locking the door behind her.

Psyche picked up a handful of the seeds. Why, it would take an hour to separate just this many! To sort through the whole pile would take weeks, maybe months. She let the seeds fall slowly through her fingers. For a while she stood looking at the impossible task Venus had given her.

"Why!" Psyche said aloud. "Look at that!" Seen through her tears, some of the seeds seemed to be moving. She blinked her eyes to clear them. Then she bent down and looked at the pile again. Some of the seeds still moved.

No! It was not seeds that moved, but ants! The pile was covered with thousands of tiny ants. Thousands more were crawling out of cracks in the floor. Soon Psyche saw that whole armies of ants were marching from the pile to the four corners of the room. And each ant was carrying a seed!

Seed by seed, the ants separated the large pile exactly as Venus had ordered. When they had finished, they disappeared as silently as they had come.

Psyche stood alone in the storeroom, looking at the four neat piles of seeds. She could hardly believe it. She had passed the trial Venus had given her. Cupid was now hers to keep!

Unknown to Psyche, it had been Cupid who sent the ants. He had missed her as much as she had missed him. Before long they were married again, and this time as equals. The beautiful Psyche was made a goddess—which is why we know so little about her from this time on.

FROM
Northern Europe

Northern Europe is a land of short, cool summers and long, dark winters. Here the ancient people told stories as different from those of the Greeks as North is from South. We now enter a land of cruel Frost Giants, brave knights in armor, and magic everywhere.

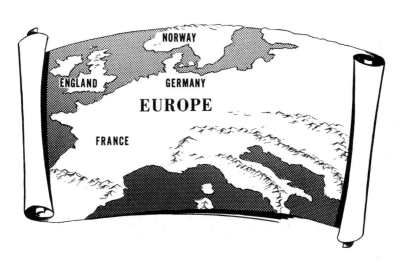

THE HAMMER
OF THOR

. . . in which Thor, the god of thunder, loses
his mighty hammer.

Words We Need to Know:

dwarf   [*DWORF*]—a very small person, something like a midget
A *dwarf* is the opposite of a giant.

raven   [*RAY ven*]—a black bird something like a large crow
Some people say a *raven* can talk if its tongue is split.

remodel [*ree MAHD el*]—to make into a new model; to decorate
Mrs. Marshall wanted to *remodel* her kitchen.

sledge [*SLEDJ*]—a heavy hammer with two flat ends, used for breaking rocks, etc.
The bent bumper of the car was straightened with a *sledge.*

tremble [*TREM bel*]—to shake with fear or excitement
Susan *trembled* when she heard someone breathing in the dark room.

veil   [*VALE*]—a piece of cloth worn in front of the face
Many women's hats have small *veils* on them.

The Greeks, as we have read, invented a large family of gods and goddesses. Then the Romans, who lived near the Greeks in Southern Europe, borrowed the gods the Greeks had invented. But what of the people in Northern Europe? They knew nothing about the Greek gods. If these people were to have gods, they would have to invent their own.

This is what they did. The names of some of their gods are still with us today. Look again at the title of this story and see if you can tell anything about our word *Thursday*. It comes, of course, from *Thor's Day*, named long ago for Thor, the god of thunder. Thor was also the god of marriage and family life. At one time the day named for Thor was a holiday, as Sunday is today.

In this myth we will meet more new gods. From Woden [*WO den*], the king of the gods, we get *Woden's Day*, or *Wednesday*. From Freya [*FRAY a*], the goddess of love and healing, we get *Freya's Day*, or *Friday*. But Loki [*LO kee*], the god of evil and wicked ways, is not remembered by any day of the week. This is a good thing, as we shall see by reading the tale of Thor and his famous hammer.

THE HAMMER OF THOR   It was a bad day in Asgard [*AHZ gard*], the home of the gods. Thor the Thunderer had lost his mighty hammer.

Lightning flashed from Thor's angry eyes down to the tops of the mountains on earth. Thunder rumbled across the heavens as Thor's goats pulled his chariot through the streets of Asgard. Big, black clouds rolled across the sky as Thor flopped them over to look beneath. But the hammer was not to be found.

When Thor had looked on earth, in Asgard, and under every cloud, he let out a cry of anger that made the other

123

gods come on the run. The big, red-bearded god was very proud of his short-handled sledge. A light tap would split a mountain in two. A heavy blow would make the whole world tremble. The hammer always hit what it was thrown at. And, more wonderful still, it returned by itself to the hand of its owner.

Soon the gods of Asgard stood in a circle around Thor's goat-chariot. "I have looked everywhere," thundered Thor. "Now I know for sure—somebody has stolen my hammer!"

Then, as Thor looked at the blank faces of the gods, he knew in a flash who might have stolen his hammer. Loki [LO kee], a small, sly god with a wicked mind, stood blinking his red eyes at Thor.

"You thief!" shouted Thor. He jumped from his chariot and grabbed Loki by the neck. "Where did you put my hammer?"

"I never touched your hammer," Loki squeaked.

"Then who did?" asked Thor. His fingers grew tighter on Loki's throat.

Loki was good at one thing, and this was talking. Now he spoke fast to save his neck. "Your hammer is not in Asgard?" he asked Thor.

"I have looked in Asgard," Thor said. "And my hammer is not here."

"Your hammer is not on earth?" asked Loki.

"I have looked on earth," Thor replied. "Nowhere did I see my hammer."

"Ah!" said red-eyed Loki. "Then I can tell you where to find your hammer. If it isn't in Asgard, and if it isn't on earth, then it must be in the icy land of the Frost Giants."

In reply Thor gave Loki a bang on the ear. Why, not

even the king of the Frost Giants would dare steal the hammer of Thor! With one hand, the Thunderer tossed Loki into the air. Loki's arms and legs turned like a windmill, until he folded up on the ground at Thor's feet. In a second Thor was beating the daylights out of him. It was lucky that Thor *didn't* have his hammer. His fists did Loki enough harm.

Thor might have killed Loki, had not a strong wind stopped him. He looked up and saw that the wind came from the wings of two huge ravens. The birds circled around the head of Woden [*WO den*], the king of the gods. The ravens, named Thought and Memory, were the two birds that Woden sent out every morning, to fly low over Asgard, the earth, and the land of the Frost Giants. Now they beat the air with their wings as they landed on Woden's wide shoulders. They stood whispering the news of the day into Woden's ears.

All the gods, even Loki, looked at Woden. Their king was a huge god with a long white beard. He wore a black patch over an eye he had once traded for his wisdom.

"Loki is right," said Woden, when the ravens had stopped rattling their split tongues. "The king of the Frost Giants stole Thor's hammer."

"Impossible!" cried Thor. "He couldn't——"

Woden made Thor keep quiet by looking at him with his one good eye. "The Frost Giant stole your hammer from under the cloud you used last night as a pillow," Woden said. "And what's more, he will return it only if we send Freya [*FRAY a*] to be his bride!"

"*Me?*" cried Freya the Fair. The goddess of love and healing stood a little apart from the group. She was fairest of all in Asgard. It was her smile that brought the bloom to flowers, and her tears that brought the dew. For a moment the gods were too surprised to speak.

All except Loki, that is. "Go pack your bag," Loki told the lovely Freya. "Mrs. Frost Giant you shall be."

"Marry that ugly monster?" whispered Freya to herself. Her nose wrinkled up like a dried apple as she thought about it. "Must I?"

"There are no flowers in his cold mountain cave," said Loki. "But home is where your husband is, I always say."

"No!" Freya cried. "I *will* not go." She fell to her knees in front of Woden. "I know Thor wants his hammer. But don't you want your little Freya to stay here in Asgard? Please, Father Woden, please. You will not make me go?"

"But my hammer!" cried Thor. "I must have my hammer back again!"

Red-eyed Loki added his voice to Thor's. "And how will we protect ourselves? Without the hammer of Thor, we will be attacked by the Frost Giants."

Now, Woden had not traded one of his eyes for nothing. His wisdom had saved Asgard from the Frost Giants before. The gods waited eagerly for their king to speak.

"The Frost Giant will have his bride," said Woden finally. "And Thor will have his hammer. We will do just what this Frost Giant wants, but we will do it our own way. Now listen closely." Woden waited for the gods to gather in front of him. "Freya, you are to make Thor look like a bride. Dress him in your best blue robe. We shall send him down to the Frost Giant to get his own hammer."

"Dress like a girl!" the Thunderer shouted. "Never! I will fight for my hammer, yes. But I will never cover this body with a woman's robe!" He looked toward Loki to agree with him.

But the slyness in Woden's plan had pleased Loki. The wicked little god couldn't wait to see the mighty Thor dressed in women's clothes. "Listen, Thor," said Loki, "with your hammer to help them, the Frost Giants are sure to conquer Asgard. The king will take our Freya anyway. He will make slaves of the rest of us. Come, do as Woden says. And let me go along as your maid."

Freya touched Thor's arm and looked up at his bearded face. "Please, Thor," she said, her eyes filling with tears. "Please, for my sake."

This was too much for Thor. "All right," he sighed. "I will go. I will go." Suddenly he jumped into his goat-chariot and drove away in anger.

Several days were needed to remodel the Thunderer. Freya's robe had to be made larger. New shoes were made for Thor's wide feet. Freya's purple veil hid his angry face and sparkling eyes. Long gloves of white leather covered the big hands that itched for just one thing—to hold the handle of the stolen hammer.

At last the costume was finished, and Thor stood before the gods dressed as a bride. Loki laughed so hard that he fell to the ground. And in truth, Thor *did* look very funny. Freya turned her head to smile. Even Woden could not keep from laughing.

"Ah, what a beautiful bride he is," said Loki between howls of laughter. But a flashing fist from under Thor's robe put a quick end to Loki's jokes.

"Come, let's get this over with," said Thor, his face blushing behind the veil. He took his maid by the elbow and turned his back on the laughing gods. Then he led Loki through Asgard and across the rainbow bridge to earth. It would have been pleasant to stay on earth a while, but the two gods had a job to do. They went straight down to the palace-cave of the Frost Giant king.

The king himself was seated on a barrel near the mouth of his cave. He was throwing live pigs to a dog the size of an elephant. When he saw, far away, the blue robe and purple veil of Freya the Fair, he let out a cry of joy that made the mountains shake.

"My crown! My crown!" the king shouted, dashing into his mountain palace. "Get out the jewels! Set the table! Prepare a feast! I am to be married!" Then he washed some of the dirt off his face and wiped some more off on a towel. His beard looked like a rats' nest, but there was no time to comb it now. He got back outside the palace just as Thor and Loki arrived.

"Fairest one," said the Frost Giant, taking Thor's gloved hand, "I have waited for this moment for many years."

Thor was so angry that his hand shook against the lips that kissed it. The Frost Giant dropped the hand in surprise.

Loki spoke up at once. "Your Freya is so, so happy," he said. "She trembles with joy."

"Of course," said the king softly. "And now, my bride to be, shall we see the palace?"

Thor nodded, but it was Loki who replied. "Little Freya has talked about you for days, and now her voice is gone."

"Of course," said the Frost Giant again. He gave Thor's shoulder a pat. "Well, we shall start with a look at the mines."

Thor wanted to see only his hammer. But first he had to follow the Frost Giant into the mountain palace, and down,

down, down the damp, dark tunnels that led to his mines. They passed through gold mines, silver mines, copper mines, tin mines, and iron mines. They went past rooms where ugly little dwarfs bent over benches and hammered away at pieces of metal with tiny sledges. Then, with the sound of the dwarfs' hammers still ringing in their ears, they traveled through still more tunnels. At last they found themselves in the great hall of the Frost Giant king.

Thor's eyes searched the room for the stolen sledge. The great hall was long and narrow. It was lighted by candles that hung from the high ceiling. The walls were covered with gleaming jewels. A long table reached from the king's throne to the other end of the room, nearly out of sight. On the table were huge oxen roasted whole and wedding cakes as big as haystacks. Thor's mouth watered at the sight of the food.

Hundreds of Frost Giants sat at the table. When their new queen entered, they cheered wildly and banged their forks against large copper plates. The king sat down at the end of the table, with his bride and her maid at his right. The Frost Giant served himself with half an ox from the platter in front of him. But to Thor he gave only a small steak.

"This is food enough for Freya," Thor whispered to Loki. "But not for Thor. I shall starve unless I eat as large a meal as I get at home." He reached out and helped himself from the platter.

The eyes of the Frost Giant grew wide with wonder as he looked at his bride. He saw a whole leg of beef disappear under her veil. "Why," he said, "I never thought my little Freya would be able to eat so much!"

"The truth is," explained Loki, "your little Freya has

eaten nothing for days, so eager was she for this wedding feast."

"Of course," said the king, his head nodding. This pleased him, and his heart swelled with love. He leaned forward to give Freya a kiss. Reaching out, he raised a corner of her veil—but his hand jumped back when he saw the flash of Thor's eyes. "My bride's eyes!" he cried. "They burn through me like lightning!"

Again the maid explained. "The poor girl has not slept for days. Her eyes are red with tears and bright with hope."

"Of course," said the Frost Giant with pride. The more Loki told him of Freya's love, the happier he became. Suddenly he shouted to his servants. "Bring the wedding present," he called. "Bring out the hammer of Thor, to be returned to Asgard."

Two attendants appeared. On a satin pillow between them rested the mighty hammer of Thor. Thor's heart beat with a wild joy. He held on to the arms of his chair to keep himself from leaping forward at once. Slowly, slowly, the hammer came toward him. Oh, to feel it in his hand once again! The attendants were about to lay the hammer at Thor's feet, when suddenly he reached out and grabbed the handle in his strong fingers.

The Frost Giant jumped up from his throne, for his bride was now shaking the hammer of Thor over her head. "Be careful!" the king warned. "Why, I never thought my bride would be so strong."

"This is *not* your bride," explained Loki, as Thor cried with anger. "This is Thor the Thunderer!"

The Frost Giant's eyes swelled to the size of saucers, then to the size of plates, then to the size of platters. He turned, started to run, turned back again, and stood as if

130

frozen. The dirt stood out on his white face. His mouth dropped open. *"Of course!"* was all he could say before the hammer of Thor cracked into his forehead.

Thor's second blow was aimed at the wall of the cave. The gleaming jewels tinkled to the floor. The candles fell from the ceiling. The whole mountain rumbled as the mines below caved in one by one. From far away came the cries of frightened dwarfs. Thor and Loki raced out of the great hall and sped toward the mouth of the cave. They reached it just as the mountain moved quickly to one side, shook for an instant, and disappeared into a cloud of dust.

Loki's sides split with laughter. "O Thor," he cried, "if you could only see yourself——"

"That's enough, you red-eyed rat!" Thor said. His women's shoes flew off into the dust of the mountain. He tore the long white gloves from his hands. Then he ripped off the purple veil and the blue robe. Loki smiled again. Under Freya's robe Thor had worn his own clothing!

"The joke is all over, Loki," Thor warned, shaking the hammer slowly over his head. "Never laugh at me again, and never, *never* speak of the time I wore Freya's clothes."

The two gods started the long walk back to Asgard. And Loki said not another word. For he was careful to note that the hammer of Thor never again left the hand of its owner.

The end of time:

THE TWILIGHT OF THE GODS   There had been a beginning of time, the gods believed, and they were wise enough to think that time would have an end. One day everything would be destroyed—the earth, the land of the

Frost Giants, Asgard, and the gods themselves. But the end would not come suddenly. First there would be a period of slowing down, a long sunset before the endless night, a twilight before the end of time. It would start when the Frost Giants attacked the earth with a triple winter. Snow and cold winds would cover the earth for three years. Then, when the body of the last man lay frozen in the snow, the Frost Giants would attack Asgard. There would be a long battle, but in the end everyone on both sides would be killed.

Small wonder that Thor was so eager to get his hammer back! The gods lived in fear of the Frost Giants. They took every chance they had to protect themselves. Woden had traded an eye for the gift of wisdom. His two ravens, Thought and Memory, told him all they saw and heard. Another god had a sword that by itself would attack a large army. And the watchman of Asgard had eyes that could see a hundred miles, and ears that could hear wool growing on the backs of sheep.

One day, as Woden sat thinking about the future of Asgard, he had an idea. "The soldiers who lose their lives down on earth are wasted," he told himself. "Why not bring them to Asgard to be our army?"

The longer Woden thought about his idea, the better he liked it.

Soon a magnificent hall, gleaming with gold, was built in Asgard for the dead soldiers. It was called Valhalla [*val HAL a*], the Hall of Heroes. The roof was made from the shields of fallen soldiers. The room was so huge that 800 men could march side by side through each of its 540 doors.

Here Woden met with his soldiers every morning. After he left, the soldiers went outside, to fight again the battles

132

they had fought on earth. They cut each other in pieces until the last man lay dead. Then Woden's magic brought them all back to perfect health. They marched once more into Valhalla, to spend the evening feasting, singing songs of war, and telling tales of battles fought long before.

Not all soldiers who died on earth received this reward. The job of choosing only the bravest of the fallen soldiers, and of bringing them to Valhalla, was given to the nine daughters of Woden. Dressed in shining white, with their horses well hidden in a cloud, the daughters of Woden spent each day watching a battle on earth. When night came, they sped down and picked up the bodies of the bravest soldiers. Then they rode back across the night sky to Valhalla. Their white clothing caught the light of the stars and the moon. Today we can still see these flashes of light in the sky. We call them the northern lights.

Maybe, wherever Woden is now, he can also see the northern lights. His nine daughters are bringing more brave soldiers to Valhalla. Woden knows that every man counts, for the Frost Giants must be held off for as long a time as possible. But that time is not forever. Sooner or later, Woden knows, will come the twilight of the gods. The stars will fall, the sun will grow dim, the earth will become cold, Asgard will disappear into night, and time will be no more.

SIR GAWAIN and the GREEN KNIGHT

. . . in which Sir Gawain of the Golden Tongue makes a strange bargain with a headless knight.

Words We Need to Know:

armor   [*AR mer*]—metal "clothes" worn by knights to protect themselves in battle
The knight's *armor* was so heavy that he had to be lifted onto his horse.

gallop   [*GAL up*]—to run fast, as a horse runs
Horses can walk, trot, and *gallop*.

helmet   [*HEL met*]—a metal head covering worn by knights and soldiers
The knight's *helmet* covered all of his head and neck.

shield   [*SHEELD*]—a flat piece of metal, leather, or wood carried by a knight to protect himself
A five-pointed star was painted on the knight's *shield*.

136

Old legends tell us that there lived in England, about the year 500, a king named Arthur. This King Arthur is supposed to have gathered about him a group of the bravest, most polite knights that the world has ever known. They were called the Knights of the Round Table.

The Round Table itself stood in the great hall of King Arthur's palace. It had neither "head" nor "foot." The knights were thought of as equals of each other, and of Arthur himself. Around the table were twelve chairs, one for each of the twelve apostles of Jesus Christ. One of these chairs was never used. This was said to be the chair of Judas, the man who pointed Christ out to the men who wanted to kill him. If a person sat in this chair, the earth was supposed to open and swallow him up. Other chairs were often empty, too. When a Knight of the Round Table died, his chair stayed empty until a better knight was found to take his place. Some chairs stayed empty for years.

Every year, during the Christmas season, the Knights of the Round Table came together in the palace of King Arthur. Here they feasted and told of their latest adventures. It was Arthur's habit, as he sat at the Round Table with his knights, never to eat until some exciting tale had been told. Here is a story about his knight Gawain, called Gawain of the Golden Tongue because of his voice and pleasant manner of speaking.

SIR GAWAIN AND THE GREEN KNIGHT   It was
New Year's Day. A howling snowstorm beat against the towers of King Arthur's palace at Camelot [KAM a lot]. But inside the walls, beneath the high ceiling, all was warm and happy. In the great hall of King Arthur, the Knights of the Round Table and their ladies feasted before a roaring fire.

Suddenly, a loud knock came at the door. And then, just as quickly, the heavy door swung open. The whistling wind blew snow against the hot, red faces of the knights. Everyone stopped laughing. All eyes turned toward the open door.

A knight on horseback appeared from out of the snow. The stranger wore green armor and carried a green shield. A heavy, green battle-ax hung from his waist. His green horse galloped to the center of the hall, turned around twice, and stood still.

"Who is King Arthur?" called the knight in green armor. "I want a word with him."

Arthur stood up behind the Round Table. "I am Arthur," he said. "Welcome to our palace, Sir Green Knight. Feast with us, and tell us your adventures."

"No," answered the stranger, his voice sounding hollow inside his helmet. "I want only to say this. I have heard that the bravest knights in the world come here for the holiday season. I want to know if one of you is brave enough to do what I ask."

Arthur looked at Sir Gawain of the Golden Tongue on his right. He looked at Sir Agravain of the Hard Hand on his left. "Any knight here is brave enough," he said. "What is it that you ask?"

The Green Knight got down off his horse. He was very tall, almost a giant. He took off his helmet. The ladies screamed. The hair that tumbled down onto his shoulders was bright green.

"Have no fear, good ladies," said the Green Knight. "I come only to give this battle-ax to the knight who will take it in his hands and strike me one blow." His eyes moved around the circle of knights as he held up the battle-ax. "Look, the handle is made of green wood. The blade is sharp enough to shave with. It is made of a green metal that never grows dull."

138

No one spoke. The knights could not believe their eyes —or their ears.

"What!" roared the Green Knight. "Are the Knights of the Round Table all cowards?"

Arthur, who was still on his feet, spoke up quickly. "Sir, what you ask for makes no sense. You ask for nothing but your own death. Be careful, Green Knight, or you shall have the blow you want so much."

The Green Knight laughed.

Sir Gawain of the Golden Tongue, the tallest of Arthur's knights, jumped forward. "No man laughs at the Knights of the Round Table," he warned. "Hand me that ax, and I will strike your laughing head from your body!"

Gawain took the battle-ax from the Green Knight. He swung it around his head so fast that the blade hummed as it sliced through the air.

The Green Knight made no move to protect himself. He stood quietly, looking at Gawain. Then he held up a green hand. "Just a minute," he said. "Let us be fair with each other. In return for the blow you are about to give me, I surely have the right to give you one."

"You have the *right*, yes," answered Gawain. He lowered the ax and stood feeling the sharp blade with his thumb. "But I warn you, no man has ever returned a blow given him by the arms of Gawain."

"We shall see," said the Green Knight, a strange smile on his green lips. "You must promise to come to my castle next New Year's Day. There *I* will hold the ax, and there *you* will receive the blow."

Gawain smiled at the foolish promise he was to make. "All right," he said. "It is as you wish. We will trade blow for blow."

139

The battle-ax started to move in a big circle over Gawain's head. Faster and faster it went, until one could no longer see the shining blade. It hummed and then whistled a note that went higher and higher. Suddenly Gawain took a step forward. In an instant the Green Knight's head was bouncing on the floor near his feet.

The headless stranger did not fall. His body stood quietly until the head stopped rolling. Then he reached down and picked up the head by its green hair. Soon the Green Knight was back on his horse. He held the head in both hands in front of him.

The eyes in the head moved slowly about the room. They went past the ladies who had fainted, past the white faces of the knights, and came to rest on Sir Gawain. At the same time the mouth started to move. The lips smiled a cruel smile as they began to speak. "Remember, my brave Gawain. One year from today at my Green Castle. It is in the North Country. Just ride north, and ask for the Green Castle."

Suddenly the green horse raised its front legs into the air, turned, and galloped out of the hall so fast that sparks flew from beneath its hoofs.

There was little laughter at Camelot for the rest of the holiday season. And the following year, when the knights and their ladies came together again, there was no laughter at all. Gawain's chair at the Round Table stayed empty. No one could forget that Gawain was keeping his promise to the Green Knight.

But the year after that, joy once again filled the great hall of King Arthur's palace. For Gawain was back! When the knights sat at the Round Table for the first time, it was Gawain's adventure that they wanted to hear. The room fell silent when Arthur called on the brave knight to tell his story.

The worst thing was the waiting (Gawain said). Spring came, summer passed, and the leaves fell from the trees. When the first snowflakes melted on the ground, I put the saddle on my horse and set out for the North Country. Everyone I met seemed to have heard of me, but no one could tell me anything about the Green Knight. November passed into December. I began to worry about finding the Green Castle before New Year's Day.

On Christmas, I was leading my horse through deep drifts of snow. I had not seen a house in two days, and all I had left to eat were a few raw potatoes. That evening my horse fell forward and lay in the snow, too weak to go on. I walked on through the night, and through the next night. I lost all track of time. Once I fell asleep on my feet and dreamed of life here at Camelot, only to wake up when I fell into the snow. I could make my body do what I wanted, but not my mind. I began to see lights that weren't there. Green castles in front of me disappeared as I ran toward them.

Finally I saw a light that became brighter as I neared it. This light was real! It came from a castle! I heard laughter and music. Cries of "Happy New Year!" came through an open window. I fell into the snow by the door and tried to make my knocking heard above the noise inside.

The door was opened by a very big man, the lord of the castle himself. He helped me to a chair by the warm fire. Then his lady, who seemed much younger than her husband, brought me a bowl of hot soup. But before I ate anything, I asked the lord about the Green Castle.

"The Green Castle!" he cried. A strange look came over his face. "I have never seen it, but it's not an hour's ride from here. A monster of some kind, some say a Green Knight, kills everyone who comes near."

I told the lord of my promise to be at the Green Castle on New Year's Day. For the rest of the evening, he treated me like a man who was soon to die. He asked what I wanted for supper, and saw that I was served with the best. Shortly after midnight, he led me to a large guest room. I was so tired that all I could see was a huge bed. In no time at all I was sound asleep.

I awakened with the first light of dawn. For a few minutes I lay there in the half-sleep of early morning. Then I heard a little noise at the door. I opened one eye a crack. It was the lady of the castle. She entered the room on tiptoe, shut the door carefully, and came toward the bed. I let her think I was still asleep. The lady's shoes squeaked softly as she came across the floor. Then I felt her sit down very slowly on the side of the bed. I could almost feel her eyes looking at my face.

There was but one thing to do. I opened my eyes, stretched my arms, and acted as if I were surprised. The lady seemed very lovely, with red on her cheeks and laughter on her lips.

"Good morning, Sir Gawain of the Golden Tongue," she said brightly. "Is this how you became a famous knight? Sleeping so soundly that a person can creep up on you?" She laughed and shook her finger at me. "If I were your enemy, what would your life be worth now?"

"Very little," I replied. This was my day to meet the Green Knight, and I didn't feel like playing games. But I was the lady's guest.

"Do you value your life?" she asked.

142

I replied as a knight should. "Only my honor do I hold dearer."

"Then I will give you one chance to live," she said. "But you must do what I ask."

"Your wish is my order," I said. "What must I do?"

The gay smile disappeared as the lady leaned toward me. "*You must escape, right now,*" she whispered. "I will get you a horse. You can ride far, far away from the Green Castle."

So *this* was her game! I said that her offer was a kind one, but that Gawain of the Golden Tongue had never been known to break a promise.

The lady stood up. "Don't you know the Green Knight will kill you?" she asked. "Escape now, quickly. I will swear that I saw you ride toward the Green Castle. No one will ever know the truth. My husband has gone out to hunt. He will not see you."

"I will always know the truth," I told her. "And I will not be called a coward, even by myself." Then I said, "Now, kind lady, I will thank you to leave the room."

She left the room without another word. Two hours later I was standing in front of the Green Castle.

The building seemed to have been made from one large block of green stone. It showed no signs of life. There was not even a footprint in the snow by the doorway. "Here stands Gawain of the Golden Tongue," I shouted at the blank wall of the castle. "I have come this New Year's Day to keep my promise to the Green Knight."

All was silent and still for a moment. Then the door began to open. Out stepped the Green Knight. He was still dressed in green armor. In his right hand he carried a new green battle-ax. He acted as if he expected to see me, saying not a word of greeting. When he took off his helmet, I looked closely at his neck. There was not even a scar!

"Are you ready?" asked the Green Knight.

The answer stuck in my throat, for he was already swinging the battle-ax. Around and around it hummed, closer and closer to my neck. Then, with a loud cry, he stepped forward. This was the end.

I blinked my eyes. I turned my head from one side to the other. I felt my neck. Yes, I was still alive! The battle-ax had stopped just as it cut the skin!

It was then that the Green Knight greeted me. I saw him smile as his battle-ax dropped to the ground. I do not want to boast, so I will repeat his words exactly as he spoke them:

"Gawain of the Golden Tongue, you have passed every test of a man who calls himself a knight. You fought for your honor. You were brave in the face of death. You kept your promise, even when my wife wanted you to run away.

"Now, take a closer look at me. Whom do you see? That's right, your host of last night, the lord of the castle. Ask not who I am, Sir Gawain. Ask not why my skin is now green. Know only that I am the Green Knight—sent to test that one knight who has no equal among men!"

Another tale of honor:

LADY GODIVA AND PEEPING TOM   Sir Gawain of the Golden Tongue became famous by keeping a strange promise made to an even stranger knight. But Gawain is not nearly so well known as the famous Lady Godiva [go DY va]. Like Gawain, Lady Godiva gained fame by keeping a strange promise. Here is a tale that will never be forgotten.

Lady Godiva was the wife of a proud, selfish lord named Leofric [*LEE o frik*]. Some nine hundred years ago, Leofric was the ruler of the English city of Coventry [*KUV en tree*]. He was proud of the great house—really a small castle—that he had built for himself with the people's money. He was even more proud of his gardens, in which all citizens had to work one day a week. But most of all, he was proud of his wife, the lovely young Lady Godiva with beautiful, long golden hair.

One day Lady Godiva was riding her white horse through the streets of Coventry. As usual, she had a smile on her face and a good word for everybody. But today she noticed that no one returned her friendly greeting. No one smiled. Even the children looked up at her with big sad eyes. A shoemaker who usually sang at his bench now sat silently in front of his shop.

"Good shoemaker," called out Lady Godiva, "why is there no joy today in Coventry?"

"Alas," sighed the shoemaker, "Leofric has doubled all taxes."

Doubled taxes! Why, she thought, Leofric could not spend all the gold he already had, even if he lived to be a hundred. Why should he raise taxes? The people barely had enough to eat now. Yes, she would go right home and give Leofric a piece of her mind.

But Leofric also had something on his mind. He stood waiting for Lady Godiva at the door of his small castle.

"Wife," Leofric said in an icy voice, "you have this day made me very angry. How many times do I have to tell you? You are not to ride through Coventry in those old clothes you have on."

Lady Godiva looked down at her plain white blouse and

long woolen skirt. They were not fancy clothes, she thought, but there was nothing really wrong with them. Must she *always* be dressed like a lady?

"So I made you angry, did I?" she said, her fair cheeks red with anger. "Well, *you* have made *me* angry, too. Why did you double the taxes these poor people must pay?"

"Taxes," Leofric told his wife, "are not the business of any woman."

"And my clothes," cried Lady Godiva, "are not the business of any man!"

"You are my wife," said Leofric coldly. "And I tell you this. You will dress as I say, and not worry your empty little head about things like taxes. If people have too much money, it makes them lazy and hard to rule."

"But people have to *eat!*" cried Lady Godiva. "If you don't lower your taxes, I will——"

"Just what will you do?" Leofric asked.

"Why," replied his excited wife, "I will—I will ride through Coventry without any clothes on at all!"

Leofric let out a laugh. "In broad daylight?" he asked.

"Yes," she cried. "In broad daylight!" Her foot stamped the ground. "At noon!"

A few hours later, Lady Godiva's attendant nailed a notice to the door of the town hall:

If my husband does not lower his taxes by noon on Saturday, I, Lady Godiva, promise to ride through the streets of Coventry without any clothes on at all.

When they read the notice, the people thought that Leofric would soon remove the new taxes. Surely their proud ruler would never let such a thing happen to his wife. They waited for another messenger to appear with the good news that Leofric had changed his mind.

But no news arrived. Saturday morning came, and still no news. The people gathered in front of the town hall, waiting for a notice from Leofric to be nailed to the door. The hours passed. Finally it was clear that the good Lady Godiva would have to carry out her promise.

No one in Coventry wanted this to happen. "But what can we do?" the people asked. "If Leofric can't stop her, how can we?"

There was one thing, however, that the people could do. As the clock in the town hall rang the hour of noon, they entered their houses and shops. They pulled the curtains and sat with their backs to the windows. All they knew of Lady Godiva's passing was the clackity-clack of her horse's hoofs on the stone street. Only one person, a tailor named Tom, lifted his curtains to see Lady Godiva seated on her huge white horse, dressed only in her long golden hair.

History does not tell us if Leofric lowered his taxes. But we do know that Tom, the tailor, soon lost his sight for some strange reason. He has been known ever since as Peeping Tom of Coventry.

THE PIED PIPER
OF HAMELIN

... in which a strange rat-catcher rids
Hamelin of more than its rats.

Words We Need to Know:

compartments   [*kom PART ments*]—sections, separate places or parts
The drawer in the kitchen table had *compartments* for knives, forks, and spoons.

patchwork quilt   [*PACH work KWILT*]—a quilt, or bed covering, made from pieces of cloth of many colors
Lisa's grandmother made a *patchwork quilt* for her bed.

peddler   [*PED ler*]—a traveling seller of small articles
The *peddler* went from town to town selling his knives.

pied   [*PIDE*]—dressed in many different colors
Pied birds have feathers of many colors.

Have you ever found yourself face to face with a rat—a real, live, ugly, long-tailed, four-legged rat? Some people have never seen a rat. They have the idea that a rat is some kind of over-grown mouse. But the rat and the mouse are two very different animals. The rat is not only larger, but it is also smarter and braver.

Many people of today live in concrete or brick buildings that make poor homes for rats. Rats can find little to eat if garbage is kept covered. But in the Middle Ages things were different. Most people lived in wooden houses. They threw their garbage into the streets. Modern rat traps and poisons were unknown.

The rats chewed holes in the wooden walls of the houses. They stole people's food, and left nothing in return except sickness. Sometimes whole armies of rats would enter a city, much faster than they could be killed. If the sickness they brought started to spread, the people moved to the country, leaving the city to the conquering rats.

In the year 1284, an old legend tells us, rats came to the small city of Hamelin [*HAM a lin*], Germany. One day a strange man walked into Hamelin and started to play music on a long pipe. He said he could get rid of the rats—for a price. Here is the story of what happened to the rats—and of the price that was paid the Piper.

THE PIED PIPER OF HAMELIN   The short, fat Mayor of Hamelin [*HAM a lin*] didn't look up from his desk when the dogs barked in the street outside. In fact, the mayor didn't even hear the dogs. He had something far more im-portant on his mind. He was thinking about rats.

Yes, rats! For rats were taking over the small city of Hame-lin. Even the mayor's house, the grandest in town, had become a rat hotel. There were rats in the cellar, rats in the kitchen, and rats in the attic. There were rats in the walls, rats in the closets, and rats in the pockets of the mayor's Sunday suit. His black Sunday hat held a whole family of rats. "There must be more rats here in Hamelin," said the mayor to himself, "than in the rest of Germany put together. Rats! Rats! *Rats! Rats!* RATS! RATS! RATS!"

If the mayor's head hadn't been so filled with rats, he might well have looked into the street when the dogs barked. And if he had, he would have set eyes on a most odd-looking man. The stranger who walked into town was at least six feet tall, probably seven. His face was small, round, and red. A long nose always seemed to be pointing. Long, pointed shoes made his feet seem huge. Fingers like carrots hung from the sleeves of his jacket. The right sleeve of this jacket was red. The left sleeve was yellow. The back of the jacket was a patchwork quilt of bright colors. And the pants beneath!—one couldn't tell what was patch and what was pants.

Yet even more strange than the man himself, or his odd clothing, was what he carried on his back. Strapped high on his shoulders was a very large cage. It was made out of fine wire, and was big enough to hold a family of eagles. But the cage held no birds of any kind. It was separated into two compartments, like a two-layer cake or a two-story house. On the first floor of the cage were ten fat rats. And on the second floor were about a hundred squeaking mice.

Walking with long, easy steps, the stranger made his way past the town hall where the mayor sat worrying about the rats. Then he walked out into the market-place square. At his heels were all the dogs in town, most of the children, and a few adults as well. The people of Hamelin had never seen anyone like the pied stranger. Some thought he was just another peddler, wearing odd clothes to draw a crowd. But, if he were a peddler, what was he trying to sell? Did he think that anyone in Hamelin would buy a mouse? Or especially a *rat?*"

The man stopped when he reached the center of the market-place square. He took the cage off his back. From its bottom he folded down four legs, like the legs of a card table. For a moment he stood still, looking at the crowd around him. His tiny blue-gray eyes gleamed like the heads of bright, new nails. Suddenly he cleared his throat and started to speak in a high voice.

"Ladies and gentlemen," he began—in spite of the fact that there was neither a gentleman nor a lady in the crowd. "Ladies and gentlemen, let me tell you who I am. I am called the Pied Piper. 'Pied' for my clothes, and 'Piper' for the pipe which I show you now."

From under his coat he took a shiny brass pipe. The horn was fully three feet long. Its finger holes were too far apart for any hands smaller than the Pied Piper's. "Step closer, friends," he said. "This is the only chance you will ever have to see a mouse march."

The crowd laughed at this. The adults shook their heads and turned away. But they stopped in their tracks at the first high note from the stranger's pipe. And they turned back when the children cried, "Look! Look in the cage!"

In the top of the cage, the mice were now lining up like soldiers. Soon ten rows of mice stood without moving a leg.

Still playing his pipe, the Pied Piper started to march around the cage. He made a funny sight, moving his head up and down in time with the music, and lifting his thin knees high in the air. But few people watched the Piper. All eyes were on the cage. For the mice, too, were marching to the Piper's happy tune. Around the inside of the cage they went—one, two, three times, all in perfect order.

Suddenly the Piper stopped playing. And just as suddenly the cage became as it had been before. The hundred mice again ran in a hundred different directions.

"Now watch the rats," said the Pied Piper. "But they march to a different tune." A second time he marched around the cage. This time he played slowly and softly, and the fat rats marched around like old soldiers in a parade.

"Hurrah! Hurrah!" A loud cheer went up when the Pied Piper stopped playing. Never had anyone seen animals so well trained.

The noise in the square was loud enough to make the mayor look up from his desk. When he saw the Pied Piper, he jumped to his feet, ran down the stairs, and made his way toward the crowd of people. "Make way for the mayor!" he ordered. "Make way for the mayor!" Soon he was staring into the little eyes of the Piper.

"You are the Mayor of Hamelin?" asked the Pied Piper.

"That is correct," replied the mayor, mopping his forehead with a big white handkerchief. "I am the mayor of the fair city of Hamelin, which lies between the Weser River and Kuppelberg Hill, having——"

"There is no time to waste," cut in the Pied Piper. "I am going to the palace of the King of France. I pass through Hamelin only because I have heard of your rats."

"Rats!" repeated the mayor, his eyes rolling in his fat face. "Have we got rats! Rats! Rats!——"

"For a price," went on the Piper, "I will march every one of your rats into the Weser River. Here, let me show you." Again he played the soft, slow tune on his pipe. And again the rats marched around the inside of the cage.

"But these are ten trained rats!" cried the mayor. "You have taught them to march."

154

"Oh, no," said the Piper. "I can make all creatures march to my pipe." He smiled for the first time. "For every creature I have a different tune."

"Well," asked the mayor, "what is your price, Piper?"

"A thousand pieces of silver," came the reply.

A thousand pieces of silver! Now, the mayor had spent much more than a thousand pieces of silver trying to get the rats out of Hamelin. But to pay this price to a crazy Piper with ten trained rats! It was enough to make a man laugh.

And laugh the mayor did. "Piper," he said with a smile, "if you can get the rats out of Hamelin, I'll pay you *fifty* thousand pieces of silver! *Fifty* thousand, do you hear? But only *after* the rats are gone."

As the mayor laughed, the Pied Piper lifted his pipe to his lips. He threw his head so far back that the pipe pointed straight up in the air. Then he started to play the rat tune, much louder and faster than before.

A little whisper of noise could be heard in Hamelin. The whisper grew to a rumble, and the rumble grew to a roar. Rats came crawling out of doors and tumbling out of windows—big rats, little rats, old rats, young rats, fat rats, thin rats, brown rats, black rats, and white rats. Fathers, mothers, babies, cousins, and second cousins—whole families of rats, great waves of rats—came running toward the Pied Piper.

Soon the market-place square was filled with rats. Then the Piper started to lead them through the streets of Hamelin. Up and down, back and forth, past every house marched the Piper. Deaf rats sleeping deep in cellars woke up and rushed to join the parade. When every rat in Hamelin was marching behind him, the Pied Piper pointed his nose toward the Weser River, on the edge of town.

The Piper didn't stop when he reached the river. He

marched straight into the water. He kept going until the water was up to his shoulders. Then he turned around to face the rats, still piping his tune. And the rats kept marching, marching, a hundred to a row, jumping into the river with a single splash.

Almost an hour passed before the body of the last rat had floated down the Weser River. Then the Pied Piper returned to the market-place square. He walked up to the mayor and asked for his thousand pieces of silver.

The mayor had never stopped laughing. "*One* thousand pieces of silver?" he asked the Pied Piper. "I thought I said *fifty.*"

The Piper finished putting his cage back on his shoulders. "My price," he told the mayor, "was, and still is, *one* thousand pieces of silver."

A strange look now came over the mayor's face. "I thought you were joking," he said to the Piper. "*I* was only joking, at any rate. But the job was well done, Piper. I still say fifty." The mayor's heavy, red cheeks shook with laughter. "And that's what you'll get, my friend—fifty pieces of silver!"

It was then that the Pied Piper smiled for the second time. "You'll pay my price, Mr. Mayor," he warned, "or I shall pipe a different tune."

"Go ahead!" laughed the mayor. "The rats are gone now. You can pipe till you burst open, for all I care."

And the Piper did play a different tune. Again a whisper was heard on the streets of Hamelin, and then a rumble, and then a roar. Was it rats? No, they were gone. Was it mice?

No! This time it was the children of Hamelin who came running to the Piper. They lined up, bright-eyed and laughing, and stood clapping their hands to the gay music. They seemed so happy that no one thought anything was wrong, not even when the children started marching toward the river. It was only as the Pied Piper neared the water's edge that the people knew what was happening.

"Look!" they cried. "He's going to drown the children! Just like the rats!"

Suddenly the Piper turned. Now he marched along the bank of the river. The people sighed, for the children were now marching toward Kuppelberg Hill. The children were safe.

But no! As the people watched, a hole opened in the side of the hill. It was like the opening of a very large mouth. Into this cave disappeared the Pied Piper. He still carried his cage on his back. He still moved his pipe up and down. He still threw his pointed shoes out in front of him as he marched. Row upon row of laughing children followed him into the cave.

The men of Hamelin rushed toward Kuppelberg Hill. But when they got there the hole had closed up. They found not even a crack in the earth.

There were no rats in Hamelin after that day. But there were many, many sad people. Saddest of all was a lame boy who had thrown down his crutches when he heard the Piper's tune. For the first time in years he had walked without help. But his bad leg had given out a few yards from the opening in Kuppelberg Hill. He had lain on the ground and looked into the huge hole. Ahead of him was a land where everything was strange and new. The air was clearer and the grass was greener. Everything was half its usual size. It was a wonderland for children.

The legend of the Pied Piper says that this happened in the year 1284. The city of Hamelin still lies on the banks of the sleepy Weser River. We can go there to see the pictures of the Pied Piper painted on the houses. People have never forgotten the Pied Piper of Hamelin. Nor have they forgotten the lesson he taught the world: *One must always pay the Piper*. For since 1284 the Pied Piper is not known to have carried off a single child.

A hero of all the world:

WILLIAM TELL   "The Pied Piper of Hamelin" is a strange story. The things that happen in it are strange. The Piper himself is a strange kind of character. Though the Pied Piper is famous, he can hardly be called the "hero" of the story.

But here is a hero the whole world loves. The story of William Tell comes from Switzerland, a small country south of Germany. About the time the rats were pouring into Hamelin, the Swiss were having their troubles, too. But it wasn't rats that troubled the Swiss. It was soldiers from Austria. The little country of Switzerland had been conquered by the Emperor of Austria.

The Swiss have always been a proud people. They gave the Emperor of Austria no peace. His army was always on the move, rushing all over Switzerland to put down small wars. Finally, the Austrian Emperor decided to show the Swiss exactly who ruled Switzerland. He sent a cruel man named Gessler to rule Switzerland with an iron hand.

Gessler was a hard ruler. When he passed through a town, all men had to salute him. Anyone who refused to salute was taken to a cold, damp prison. But even this was not enough for Gessler. He wanted people to salute him when he wasn't there. So he had one of his hats placed on a pole. His soldiers were to make sure that the hat was saluted.

A Swiss legend tells of a proud giant of a man named William Tell. One day Tell walked from his home in the hills to the market town of Altorf. He carried his bow, a quiver of arrows, and some rabbits he had shot in the woods. Beside him walked his young son. The boy kept a tight hold on his father's hand. It would have been easy to get lost in the crowd.

William Tell marched right past the pole that held Gessler's hat. He did not salute. He kept both hands at his sides. His body stayed as straight as a tall pine tree in the hills. In no time at all, Austrian soldiers had grabbed both his arms.

"Didn't you see Gessler's hat?" asked the soldiers.

"Yes, I saw it," said William Tell.

"Then why didn't you salute it?" the soldiers barked.

Tell looked at the hat above him on the pole. Then he looked at the soldiers. "I would not salute that hat," he said, "not even if it were sitting on top of Gessler's fat head!"

The soldiers decided to show Tell exactly who ruled Switzerland. They marched their prisoner and his son to Gessler's office in a nearby city. When the small group arrived, Gessler was just finishing an enormous dinner at a sidewalk restaurant. Again William Tell refused to salute.

"This man needs to be taught a lesson," Gessler said, standing up. His lips twisted into a cruel smile as he looked at Tell's bow and quiver of arrows. "You look like a man who's good with a bow and arrow," he said. "Am I correct?"

"It all depends on what I'm shooting at," answered William Tell.

Gessler laughed. "We shall see," he said. He picked up an

159

apple from a pile of fruit on the table. "I will have this apple placed on the head of your son. You are to walk a hundred steps up the street. Then you will hit the apple with one of your arrows."

With hate in his eyes, Tell stood looking at the savage Gessler. The Austrian sat down again to eat.

Gessler's soldiers dragged the boy to the center of the street. They placed the apple on his head. Then Tell walked a hundred steps away. The joke was too cruel for the Austrian soldiers. They had the boy stand looking away from his father.

"Turn around and look at me," Tell ordered.

The boy turned around very slowly, keeping the apple balanced on the top of his head.

William Tell planted his feet firmly on the ground. He placed an arrow in his bow. He tested the bow a few times. Then he raised it straight up and down in front of him. He took careful aim. Zoom!

Crack! The apple split into two halves. They fell to the ground on either side of the boy. A cheer went up from the crowd. Even the Austrian soldiers clapped their hands.

Only one person was not happy. "You did it, but you were never too sure of yourself," shouted Gessler. "What's that second arrow I see there under your coat?"

Tell looked down. A second arrow he had put under his belt had slipped into sight as he walked toward Gessler.

"This arrow," Tell said, "was to use in case I shot too low." Now he held the arrow in his right hand. "It was meant for you, Gessler."

"That's enough!" shouted Gessler. But no sooner had the words left his lips than Tell's second arrow hit his chest. In a minute the cruel Gessler lay dead with an arrow through his heart.

The crowd was too much for the few Austrian soldiers. By that evening the city was free. The next day messengers galloped all over Switzerland with the news. "Liberty will be ours!" they cried. "Fight for your freedom!" Soon the whole country was at war—and the Emperor of Austria was taught exactly who ruled Switzerland.

FROM
Eastern Europe

*T*he ancestors of millions of Americans came from Poland, Russia, Hungary, and the other countries of Eastern Europe. In the strange folk tales of Eastern Europe anything can happen— and almost always does!

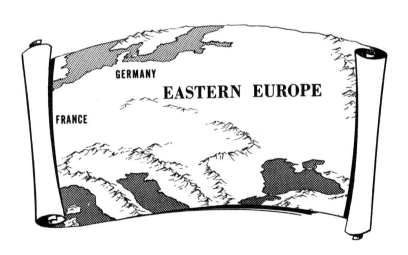

THE EVIL EYE

... in which we learn what happens to a man who has both an evil eye and a kind heart.

Words We Need to Know:

glance   [*GLANCE*]—a quick look
Charlotte took a *glance* at her homework, but didn't really read it.

pupil   [*PEW pil*]—the black circle in the center of a human eye
Our *pupils* become smaller when we look at bright lights.

ruin   [*ROO in*]—great damage; destruction
The army left a path of *ruin* behind it.

sleigh   [*SLAY*]—a sled pulled by horses
Long ago people rode in *sleighs* when there was snow on the ground.

Did you ever meet a witch? No, we don't mean someone dressed up like a witch on Halloween. Nor do we mean the kind of witch that is said to ride the handle of a broom. We mean a real, live witch. Ever meet one?

Probably not. Not many people today believe in witches. But a few hundred years ago, before the age of science, many people thought witches were real. There were things people couldn't understand, so they invented witches to explain them. When sickness or bad luck came to a person, he looked around for a witch to blame for his troubles.

Witches were supposed to do their work in many ways. Some witches made little dolls that looked like real people. Pins stuck in such a doll, it was thought, would bring pain to the person it looked like. Other witches had "evil eyes." These eyes were supposed to bring ruin, sickness, or death to all they looked at.

No one knows who first thought of the evil-eye story. The tale has been told in many different ways in different parts of the world. Here is the story as it was told in Poland. It is a strange tale, for the reader can feel nothing but sorrow for the character with the evil eye.

THE EVIL EYE   Through the beautiful country of Poland runs a great, winding river called the Vistula [*VIS choo la*]. On one bank of this river, many years ago, there stood an old stone house that was both very large and very strange. Dark green moss covered its tree-shaded walls. All the windows were on the side toward the river, where a field of brown grass ran down to the water's edge. On the other three sides the window holes had been filled with stones. Not a window looked out over the pleasant green fields. The lawn was full of weeds. Tall grass grew between the stones in the

167

front walk. But it was a walk that was never used. For in this house lived the man with the evil eye.

His name was Casimir *[KAS i mer]*. He had come to the old house from a village far away. Farmers in the neighborhood stayed out of sight of the big stone house. They walked miles out of their way in order not to look at it. Strange tales were told about the man who lived there.

Bad luck came to whatever Casimir looked at. Sometimes, if he were happy, his eyes would do no harm. But if he were in a bad mood, hardship or sickness would follow where his glances fell. The grass outside his windows refused to grow. For years boats had been running into trouble on that part of the river that could be seen from Casimir's house.

Casimir had been born with the evil eye. His eyes had brought bad luck to parents he loved dearly. At three years of age, Casimir had watched his father's barns burn to the ground. Both Casimir's parents had died before the boy was twenty. On his twenty-first birthday, Casimir sold his family's lands. Then he set out across Poland, to search for a lonely house where his eyes could do no harm.

With Casimir went an aged servant. The old man had always carried in his heart a strange, sad love for the unlucky boy. Casimir had never in his life looked at the servant with angry eyes. For this reason, the old man had always enjoyed perfect health. As they rode through Poland, the old man would tell Casimir when they came near an animal, a person, or a town. Casimir would then cover his eyes until the danger of doing harm was over. If Casimir had not done this, he would have left a path of ruin behind him. It made him angry when his glance did even a little bit of harm, and when he was angry his eyes carried death or fire. The more Casimir's heart wanted to do good, the more did his eyes do evil.

168

Finally, the big stone house was found. It seemed a perfect place for Casimir to live. The nearest town was miles away. Casimir's eyes could do little damage on the wide river. The windows that faced the fields could be closed up. Living quietly in this house, Casimir thought, he could do little damage. For Casimir had the kindest of hearts. There was, in fact, nothing evil about Casimir except his eyes. His face was both handsome and interesting. No one, at first, would have noticed his strange eyes. Only after a careful look would a person have seen that his eyes were hard and glassy, and that the size of the pupils never changed.

"For the thirty years of my life," Casimir said once to his servant, "I have lived like a criminal in hiding. I have done nothing but bring hardship, sickness, and death to others. Yet I know my heart is filled with kindness and love."

Casimir and the old man were sitting by the fireplace. Snow had been falling all day, and a cold wind now whistled in the chimney. Suddenly they heard the howling of wolves near the house. Casimir looked into his servant's eyes. Neither man spoke.

Before long, a loud knock came at the door. Who could it be? No one had come to Casimir's house in years.

Casimir nodded to his servant. The old man stood up slowly and made his way across the room. At the same time, Casimir put a hand over his eyes and looked at the floor. A squeak and a cold breeze told Casimir that the servant had opened the door. Then he heard a man's voice asking for help. "My wife and daughter are traveling with me," the man explained. "We can go no farther in this storm, and my wife is ill with fever. She will have to be carried from the sleigh."

It was the voice of a good man, Casimir thought. In a way,

the voice made him happy. He could now do someone a favor. This was something he had not had the chance to do in many years. But was it safe? Surely, he thought, no harm could come to these strangers. He would look at them with the kindness he felt in his heart. And what else could be done? His eyes were not half so dangerous as the storm and the wolves outside the house.

Casimir raised his head and looked toward the door. The stranger was a big man with a huge black beard. They exchanged glances, shook hands, and went out to the sleigh.

The man's daughter stepped from the sleigh first. Casimir could not help noticing her beauty, even though the light was dim and the girl was wrapped in a big fur robe. Then Casimir and the man made a chair of their arms. They carried the sick woman into the house. She was put to bed in a warm room, and soon she fell asleep.

The next morning, the woman seemed to be a little better. Casimir asked his guests to stay until she was out of danger. It was hard for Casimir to believe that he was really helping a sick person get well. All his life, he had been making healthy people sick. He was now happier than he had been in years. Every two hours, night and day, he had his servant put wood on the fireplaces in every room. Casimir did the cooking himself, so that the man and his daughter could give all their time to the sick woman. The smile on his face did much to cheer up everyone in the house. The days passed quickly for Casimir. Soon a week had gone by, and then two weeks.

Casimir didn't know it at first, but he had another reason for keeping his guests in the house. It was the girl. During the long winter evenings, she sat with Casimir by the fire. It had been years since Casimir had talked to someone his own age. Now he saw the world through her eyes. It was a world of joy, and love, and hope. Night after night, Casimir watched the light from the fireplace shine on her hair. He hated the coming time when she would have to leave.

The woman's health improved a little every day. In a month, the color had come back to her cheeks. She felt well enough to get dressed and walk around the house. Soon she was able to go for rides in a carriage. By this time it was early spring. Her husband took her riding through the beautiful country around Casimir's house. The nearby farmers were shocked to learn where the strangers were staying. But the woman and her husband laughed at the farmers' odd stories. "What do you mean, 'evil eye'?" they asked the farmers. "One would not find in all of Poland a man more gracious, more gentle, or more handsome than our young friend, Casimir."

The farmers didn't change their minds. "Wait till the grass turns green," they warned. "Then you'll see. The grass under his windows will stay as brown as it's been for these last ten years."

But that spring the grass turned green. Nothing was ever said to Casimir about the evil eye. Such a thing seemed impossible, for now Casimir had only love in his heart. He loved everything—the grass, the river, his house, and his guests. Most of all he loved the girl. When her father finally said that the time had come to leave, Casimir asked for the girl's hand in marriage.

This did not come as a surprise to her parents. They had been watching the two young people. In fact, they had stayed on into the spring, waiting for just this to happen. Their daughter had grown deeply in love with the kind man who had done so much for them. They thought that a better husband would never be found.

A few days later, a small wedding was held in the old stone house, and the happy parents left for home.

That summer the grass beneath Casimir's windows stayed a dark, rich green. It would have grown knee high if Casimir had not cut it every week. He had found a new life. The evil eye bothered him no longer, for his heart seemed too full of love to leave room for anger. And just as joyful as Casimir was his old servant, whose life's work had now been done. Casimir was at last a happy man.

Then something happened. Early one morning, Casimir was awakened by the sound of men singing. He had gone to bed late the night before, and had planned to sleep until the sun was high in the sky. He woke up with a headache. The voices made him angry. He looked out his bedroom window and saw a boat being rowed up the Vistula. Men were singing as they pulled the oars. Suddenly a huge log appeared in front of the boat. The men didn't see it until too late. It crashed into the front of the boat. The men were sent flying into the river.

Casimir cried out. The evil eye was still with him! He watched the men swim to the bank. Then he turned sadly away from the window.

His wife was now wide awake. She lay looking at him with wide-open eyes.

Casimir loved his wife dearly. He would rather have seen her leave his house than hurt her in the smallest way. He loved her too much to put her in any danger. There was only one thing to do. He would tell her the truth, and let her make up her own mind. With a heavy heart, he sat down on the edge of her bed and told the whole story of his evil eye.

When Casimir had finished, she kissed both his cheeks and told him she could never leave his side.

"Didn't you notice that my eyes seem strange?" Casimir asked.

"Of course," she replied, smiling at her husband. "But it only makes the rest of you seem more perfect. Why, if you were *all* perfect, you'd have to live up in heaven! And would I like that?"

Now Casimir had nothing to hide. This made him feel, somehow, that he had nothing to fear. Life passed smoothly until the next spring, when his wife told him that she was soon to have a child.

"A child!" cried Casimir. "Oh, no!"

Not that Casimir didn't want a child. Far from it. Nothing would have pleased him more. But he knew that small children can be unpleasant. There are times when the eyes of the most loving parents flash with anger. Could Casimir always look at his child without anger? No, he decided. "I would rather lose my sight," he told himself, "than bring any sorrow to my wife or child."

Casimir knew what he had to do. But he put it off until the very last minute.

A few months later, two cries rang through the large stone house. From one end of the house came the cry of a baby boy, opening his eyes on the light of the world. And from the other end of the house came the cry of a man in pain who had just looked upon light for the last time.

From that day on, life was different for Casimir. But it remained fairly happy. There were, in truth, some good things that came with the loss of his eyes. Now there was *really* nothing to fear. The windows that faced the fields were broken open, and a fresh breeze blew through the old stone house. Casimir's old servant had become very lame. But now new servants could be hired. People feared Casimir no longer. He made friends with many of his neighbors. His house was often filled with loud laughter, and the loudest of all was Casimir's own.

Of course, there were times when Casimir found that he didn't need eyes to cry real tears. These were the times when he passed his hands over the face and body of his growing boy. As the years went by, Casimir cried more and more often. He wanted so much to see his child. At last the day came when Casimir felt a fuzzy beard on his son's chin. Tears ran down Casimir's face. He had his wife lead him to his room. There he stayed for the rest of the day. He didn't even come out to eat supper.

That night Casimir couldn't fall asleep. An idea raced around and around in his mind. He had buried his eyes in the loose earth at one corner of the house. What if he were to dig them up? Would they still be good? Could he use them to see his son for just a few minutes?

Finally Casimir could stay in bed no longer. He threw back the covers and jumped to his feet. He felt his way along the walls to the front door. Then he walked through the wet grass to the corner of the house.

Casimir dropped to his knees. With his bare hands he dug madly into the earth. Ah, here—no, it was a stone! More dirt flew. Then he felt something, smooth, hard, and round against the tips of his fingers. One eye would be enough! He got to his feet and stood wiping the dirt from the evil eye.

They found Casimir the next morning. He lay on the ground by a corner of the big stone house. A doctor was called at once. But it was already too late. A heart attack, the doctor said, had killed Casimir in the middle of the night.

Only the old, old servant knew the whole truth. It was he who had found Casimir's body. It was he who had seen the evil eye lying in the hole, with its pupil against the earth. And it was he who had buried for the last time the evil eye that had killed the kind Casimir.

A little story with lots of meaning:

THE GOLDEN FISH   The farther east one goes into Europe, the stranger the stories seem to become. If you thought "The Evil Eye" was an odd story, try this one from strange old Russia:

Many years ago, a poor fisherman lived on the shore of a great sea. His life was a lonely one. Summer and winter, good weather and bad, he spent each day sitting by himself in a small boat. Sea gulls were his only company. They made poor friends for the fisherman. But they were better company than the wife who waited in the small gray cottage he called his home.

No matter how many fish he caught, his wife was sure to find something wrong. Even if he arrived home with his basket piled high with fish, his wife would refuse to be happy. "What have you turned out to be?" she would ask in a loud voice. "I married a man who said he would soon own many fishing boats. You and your one little boat! Ha!"

So went his life.

One day, soon after the fisherman had rowed out to sea, he felt a strong pull on the end of his line. It was a fish, and a big one. His only worry was that the line might break before the fish was in his hands. The fish was so strong that it almost pulled him out of the boat. Once he tripped and kicked an oar into the sea. But finally, and with a great splash, the fish landed in the bottom of the boat.

The fisherman had never seen anything like this shiny orange fish. It looked like a four-foot goldfish. He sat down and felt its hard body. Yes, a *gold fish* was just what it was— an enormous golden fish!

Now, the fisherman was already so surprised that when the fish began to speak it didn't bother him at all. In fact, it would have surprised him if the fish had *not* said something.

"Good fisherman," said the fish, "please throw me back into the sea. You and your wife deserve more than a golden fish. I can give you all the things you deserve to have."

The fisherman thought for a moment. Did he and his wife really deserve more than this huge golden fish? What *did* they really deserve? And could the fish really make wishes come true? Well, there was one way to find out.

"What I need most right now," said the fisherman, "is a new oar."

In answer there came a little *pop*. A brand new oar lay across the fisherman's knees! In a minute he had thrown the golden fish back into the sea.

The fisherman rowed home to tell the good news to his wife. He found her preparing some cold fish for lunch. Years of worrying had given her face a pinched look, like a plum trying to become a prune.

"You fool!" she cried, after he finished his tale. "We could have been rich! But no, you had to throw the golden fish away."

Now that the fisherman thought about it, he did feel very foolish. The golden fish now seemed no more real than a half-forgotten dream. Maybe there had been no fish at all. The hot sun sometimes did strange things to a person's mind. Still, it was worth trying a wish. He asked his wife what she wanted most.

The woman had never heard anything so silly. "You can go tell your old fish," she shouted, "that I'm sick and tired of fish! Tell him anything. Tell him I want a big steak dinner!"

The fisherman walked back to the edge of the sea. He stood on the beach and called for the fish, wondering if his wife really deserved a big steak dinner. Suddenly, the huge golden head appeared above the water. The fisherman was almost too surprised to speak. It was all he could do to repeat his wife's wish. Then the fish slapped the sea with its tail and disappeared. The fisherman walked home slowly, feeling, somehow, as though the fish had laughed at him.

But when the fisherman arrived at the cottage, a hot steak dinner was waiting on the table!

His wife was too excited to eat. Right away, she wanted to become the richest woman in Russia, with dozens of servants and a hundred-room house. The fisherman went back to the sea and asked for these things. Then he returned to find a magnificent new home, the grandest house in Russia. His wife, dressed like a queen, was giving orders to a small army of attendants. "What's this!" she cried when she saw him. "Get this dirty old fisherman out of my house! Let him live in the horse barn!"

The fisherman was taken to the horse barn—but not for

long. His wife had never been happy with a heaping basket of fish, and now she was not happy being the richest woman in Russia. In less than an hour she had sent for him. "Go and tell your fish," she ordered, "that I want to own the whole world. I want to rule all the birds in the air, the animals on the land, and the fish in the sea."

Again the fisherman went to the water's edge and called for the fish. When the golden head appeared, he repeated what his wife had said. Then he walked back up the beach, eager to see what he would find.

The huge house was no longer there! In its place was his old gray cottage. A little woman with a pinched face stood sadly in the doorway.

"The big house is gone!" she cried. "The fish has not kept its promise!"

Alas, the golden fish *had* kept its promise. The woman was to have had what she deserved. But a person who wants to be God deserves very little.

The fisherman rushed back to the sea and called out over the waters. But this time no golden head appeared. He stayed there a long time. Evening came, and then darkness. The fisherman felt very foolish as he stood on the dark beach and shouted for the golden fish. His own voice sounded very small indeed against the endless roar of the mighty sea.

THE CAREER OF IGOR IVANOV

... in which a very foolish youth makes us laugh when his silly mistakes work out for the best.

Words We Need to Know:

career   [*ka RIR*]—a job or occupation that one makes his life's work
Melvin wanted to make a *career* of the United States Army.

ferryman   [*FARE ee man*]—a man who runs a ferryboat
The *ferryman* had been going back and forth across the river for ten years.

flatboat   [*FLAT boat*]—a large boat with a flat bottom
Many *flatboats* still go up and down the Mississippi River.

lecture   [*LEK cher*]—a speech; a talk that teaches
In assembly a man gave a *lecture* on home safety.

Myths and Folk Tales Around the World is the title of this book. By now we have learned what *myths* are. We have come part of the way *around the world*. But what about the two words in the middle of the title, *folk tales?*

A *folk tale* is just what the words mean. It is a tale made up by and for "just folks," or common people. A folk tale has no author's name printed under its title. No author's name is known. Instead, a folk tale has many unknown authors. It has been passed from person to person for hundreds of years. By now the story has been told and retold thousands of times. It has been changed and changed. The person who first told the tale would probably not know his own story if he were to hear it today.

"The Career of Igor Ivanov," like "The Evil Eye," can be called a folk tale. It is an old Russian story about a foolish youth whose mistakes work out for the best, bringing him riches and happiness. Don't be surprised if strange things happen, for old Russia was a very strange place.

THE CAREER OF IGOR IVANOV   There once lived in Russia a rich farmer who had three sons. The oldest son was as clever as his father was wise. The second son also had a good head on his shoulders. But the youngest son, Igor [*EE gor*], was probably the most foolish young man who had ever lived.

The father believed that there is a place for everyone in this world. He made a place for everyone on his farm. But after he died, things were different. His sons could not agree on anything. Something had to be done.

It was the clever son who decided what they would do. "My brothers," he said, "since I am the oldest of the Ivanovs [*ee va NOFS*], the farm belongs to me. But the animals belong to all three of us. Now, here's the way we shall split them up."

His plan was simple. They would put all the animals in the barnyard. Then they would open the three barnyard gates. When this had been done, the brothers would jump up and down, shout, and whistle. The frightened animals would run out of the barnyard. Each brother was to get the animals that ran through a different gate.

This was done—but the two older bothers saw that the smallest gate went to Igor. This was a narrow gate meant for people. Most of the animals didn't even know it was there. All Igor received was one young bull. He felt very sad when he looked at his brothers' fine animals.

"Look," said Igor, "both of you have many horses, cows, sheep, and pigs. How can I be a farmer with just this one bull?"

"Ah, you are lucky!" replied the middle brother. "Now you don't *have* to be a farmer. You can go out into the world. You can be anything you want to be."

"A grand career is waiting for you, Igor," added the clever brother. "Alas, we two must stay behind on the farm."

That very day, Igor tied a rope to his bull and started down the road in search of his career. Soon it began to get dark. Igor tied his bull to a small tree. Then he found a bed of soft grass for himself. He lay down and began to eat one of the sandwiches his brothers had given him. But the sandwich tumbled to the ground before it was half eaten. Igor had fallen asleep.

The next morning, Igor could not find the bull. But he did find something else. This was a hole in the ground, where the strong animal had pulled the tree out by its roots. In the bottom of the hole was a large leather bag. Igor jumped down and opened the bag. He peeked inside. It was filled with hundreds of gold coins!

Igor had never seen so much gold. Where had it come from? Had it been buried by robbers? What could he do with all this money? He sat down on the bag and ate another sandwich. The money made him think of rich people. And thinking of rich people made him think of the king, who was richest of all. "I know!" Igor said brightly. "I will take this money to the king!"

So Igor lifted the sack of gold to his shoulder and set out for the king's palace. He had no idea where it was. But he knew that one road can lead in only two directions. He had come from one direction, and the king's palace wasn't there. That left but one way to go.

Soon Igor came to a crossroads. He didn't know which way to turn. As he stood scratching his head, an old man on a donkey came down one of the side roads. The old man had his nose buried in a book. His long hair was as white as snow.

"Here is a man of great wisdom," Igor said to himself. Then he said aloud, "Good man, I am not wise in the ways of the world. Tell me, how do I get to the palace of the king?"

The old gentleman looked up from his book. He pulled on his long white beard. "Don't you see all those signs over there?" he asked.

"Yes, I see them," replied Igor, looking at a post that was covered with signs pointing in all directions.

"Then why are you asking *me?*" said the wise man.

"Alas," Igor replied. "I can see the signs very well, but I can read them not at all."

The old man told Igor that it was the duty of the wise to

lead the foolish. "I am going to the king myself," he added. "Just hold on to the tail of my donkey, and you will not get lost."

So Igor followed in the donkey's footsteps. Before long they came to a wide river. "We will have to wait for the ferry to take us across," said the wise man. "But come, only a fool wastes his time. I will teach you the letters. When you know the alphabet, soon you will know how to read."

Igor said he didn't have time to learn how to read. There were things other than books to look at. Never had Igor seen such a wide river. Nor had he seen a ferry like the one that slowly made its way toward them. It was a large flatboat that moved without oars or sails. A ferryman pulled the boat along by a rope that stretched across the river, from bank to bank.

By the time the ferry arrived, more passengers had joined Igor and the wise man. The youth noticed that they gave the ferryman some money as they stepped into the boat. So he opened his leather bag and handed the ferryman a gold coin. The ferryman's eyes opened wide. All the coins he took in during one day were not worth as much as that one piece of gold.

It was hot on the river. Igor decided to go for a swim. He took off his shoes, socks, and shirt. Then he dived into the water. As he swam in circles around the slow ferry, the passengers opened his leather bag. They filled their pockets with Igor's gold. And then, so that Igor would not notice that the bag was lighter, they filled it with the things that had been in their pockets.

The wise man looked up from his book and saw what the people were doing. He shook his head sadly. "A fool and his money are soon parted," he reminded himself.

184

When the boat was again near land, Igor climbed back on board. "It's a hot day," he said to the wise man. "You should go swimming too."

"No," said the man of wisdom, without looking up from his book. "I have never taken the time to learn how to swim."

Just then the ferryman cried out in alarm. The rope had broken! The ferry started to spin around in crazy circles. It floated down the river. Suddenly it struck a rock and split in two. Igor grabbed his bag and jumped into the water. He swam toward the bank with the other passengers. When they were safely on dry land, they looked to see if anyone were missing. Only the wise man was not among them.

Igor felt very sad. He had liked the old man. But the other passengers seemed strangely happy. Igor wondered why they should be so joyful. Most of them said they were traveling to the king to ask for money.

About the middle of the morning, they arrived at the palace. The king was not in a good mood. One by one, the travelers stepped before the king with their long, sad stories. And, one by one, the king refused them money.

The king was surprised when Igor told his tale. Here was someone who had *not* come to ask the government for money. Instead, he had come to give gold to the king.

"My good man," said the king, "there is a law that all money found in this kingdom belongs to me. But you are the first person who has ever obeyed it. How much gold do you have?"

Igor couldn't speak. He stood on one foot, then on the other. Finally he smiled at the king and emptied his bag on the floor before the throne.

Igor had expected the king to smile, not to howl with anger. And howl the king did. At first Igor didn't know

185

what was wrong. Then he looked down, only to see a pile of old pocket knives, bent nails, combs with missing teeth, and other pieces of junk.

"I thought it was gold!" cried Igor.

Suddenly the king's attendants grabbed Igor's arms. He was given a beating and dragged from the palace.

"I am not wise in the ways of the world," Igor said to the attendants. "What should I have said to the king?"

"You ought to have said that it was a mistake, and that you were sorry it was a waste of time," Igor was told.

A waste of time—Igor liked the sound of the words. He said them to himself as he walked along the road away from the palace. Soon he came to a farmer who stood leaning on a hoe. The farmer was tired, for he had just finished planting a field with cabbage seed.

Igor stopped and looked at the field. "A waste of time," he told the farmer. "A waste of time."

The farmer raised his hoe handle and brought it down with a bang on Igor's head. Igor fell in a heap to the road.

"I am not wise in the ways of the world," Igor explained, looking up. "Tell me, what should I have said?"

"You ought to have said, 'May what you plant grow into nice cabbages,' " replied the farmer. "Now, be off with you."

Igor walked on down the road, rubbing the bump on his head. Over and over he said to himself, "May what you plant grow into nice cabbages. May what you plant grow into nice cabbages. . . ." Before long he passed a graveyard where someone was being buried. "May what you plant grow into nice cabbages!" Igor shouted from the road.

Again Igor was beaten, and again he asked what he should have said. This time he went down the road repeating, "The only true happiness is death. The only true happiness is death. . . ." Late in the morning, he came to a town. Bells were ringing. A wedding party was just leaving a church.

"The only true happiness is death," Igor told the bride and groom.

But the groom was not interested in happiness after death. His fists beat against Igor's head until the poor youth fell to the ground. Then the bride told Igor what he ought to have said.

Igor lay in the dirt of the road. He watched the wedding party until they were out of sight. Then two Russian priests in long brown robes came out of the church. They helped Igor to his feet and brushed the dust off his clothes.

This made Igor feel much better. He remembered the bride's last words. "May you live a long, happy life," he told the priests. "And may you have many, many children."

"What!" cried the priests. "A priest cannot marry! Don't you know that?" For a long time they shook their fingers at Igor and gave him a lecture he didn't understand.

Igor was very unhappy. He sat down on the church steps. He thought about his career. So far he had found no career—unless it was to be beaten every time he opened his mouth. Then the bell in the church rang the noon hour. Igor counted: *one, two, three, four, five.* He had run out of numbers, so he counted to five again, and then to two.

Igor liked the sound of the bell. He sat waiting for it to ring again. He waited a long time. Finally the bell rang, but only once. An idea suddenly came to Igor. He would take the bell!

No one saw Igor enter the church. He climbed up in the church tower and stole the bell. But Igor was so foolish, he didn't know he was stealing. The people of the town saw him walking through the streets with the bell under his arm. But he didn't act like a thief; so, no one looked at him a second time.

Igor carried the bell into the woods. He tied it to the top of a small tree. The wind would shake the tree, Igor thought, and the bell would ring. Then he would be happy. He lay down under the tree to wait for the bell.

Soon Igor fell fast asleep. Soon after that a hungry bear came creeping through the woods. The bear's mouth watered as the animal crept toward Igor's throat.

Ding! Dong! Ding! Again the foolish Igor was lucky. The wind had suddenly come up. The noise of the bell frightened the bear and saved Igor's life.

But poor Igor didn't know what was happening. He sat up and saw some big animal running off into the woods. He didn't know enough to run the other way. Instead, he followed it. In a few minutes he heard a loud scream ahead of him. He went forward on tiptoe and peeked through the bushes.

This time Igor's luck surprised even Igor. A huge brown bear was chasing three robbers into the forest. Igor knew the men were robbers because gold fell out of the bags they dropped as they ran. When the bear had disappeared, Igor ran toward the gold. He almost fell into a hole the robbers had been digging. Then he counted the bags: *one, two, three, four, five; one, two, three, four.*

At first Igor didn't know what to do with his lucky find. Then he remembered what had happened in the king's palace. Yes, he would give this gold to the king too. Only this was real gold. The trouble was that there was so much of it. There was more than he could carry. So he took only a few gold coins and buried the rest in the hole left by the robbers. Then he walked back to the town, back up the road, and back to the king's palace.

"Not again!" shouted the king when he had heard Igor's tale. "You fool, don't you know that one joke is enough! If you bring me any more of your 'gold,' I'll have you thrown in prison. Do you hear! Keep anything you find from now on, and keep out of my palace!"

Igor did as he was told. He kept the gold. He carried the bags home, one at at time, and became the richest man in the country. He built three palaces—one for himself, one for me, and one for you.

There's a party now in Igor's palace. Hear the music and laughter? Come and be one of his guests.

On the serious side:

THE FARMER AND THE SNAKE   Yes, old Russia was a very strange place. In Russia, as in many other places, the snake was feared and worshiped. Snakes were believed to have great wisdom and certain magic powers. And no wonder, with snakes like the one in this story:

A rich and happy king once had an odd dream. As he lay sleeping, he dreamed that he saw a dead fox hanging by its tail above his bed.

The next morning, the king called his wise men together. He asked them the meaning of his dream. When he could learn nothing from the wise men, he sent for everybody in the palace. But still he could learn nothing about his dream.

Finally, he ordered that everyone in the kingdom be called before him. Someone, he thought, would certainly be able to explain his strange dream.

A few days later, an old farmer was ordered to appear before the king. To get to the palace, he had to travel through a wild and rocky part of the kingdom. At one place the narrow road passed between two huge mountains of stone.

When the farmer reached this narrow place in the road, he jumped back suddenly, very frightened. An enormous snake lay in his path. The farmer had never seen such an animal. The snake was three times as long as the farmer was tall. It was as big around as a barrel. Its shiny skin was colored gray, green, and gold. A thin red tongue shot in and out between two long white teeth. Its head weaved back and forth dangerously.

"What do you want on this road?" hissed the snake. "Tell me your reason, and I might let you pass."

The farmer told the snake about the king's dream.

"I can tell you the meaning of the dream," said the snake. "But you must promise to give me half of any reward the king gives you."

The farmer agreed, and the snake moved aside to let him pass. "Tell the king," said the snake, "that a dead fox is a sign of too much cheating and lying in the kingdom."

The farmer went on until he came to the palace. He told the king what the snake had said. The king was happy to have the dream explained at last. He gave the farmer many presents. Then the farmer returned to his home. But he took a much longer road than the one that went past the snake. He didn't want to give the snake half his gifts.

Soon the king had another dream. This time he saw a

sword hanging from the ceiling. He wasted no time with his wise men, but sent at once for the old farmer.

The farmer had no choice. Though he now feared the snake more than ever, he had to return to it. Only the snake would know the meaning of the king's new dream. "Last time the king gave me no reward," he told the snake. "So there was no reward for you, either."

The snake seemed pleased with this. It was again willing to explain the king's dream, and the farmer again promised to give it half of any reward. A hanging sword, the snake said, was a sign of a coming war.

The king was grateful for the news. Not that he liked war, but now he had time to prepare. He formed a large army. When his enemies attacked, they were quickly defeated.

The king was the happiest of men—until, one night, he had a third dream. This time it was a sheep that hung above his bed. Right away the old farmer was ordered to the palace.

The order was received with surprise and fear. The farmer had not kept his second promise to the snake. He had been given a magic sword as one of his presents. With the sword he had chased the snake and cut off a piece of its tail.

This time the snake knew the truth. The farmer could not tell another lie. In fact, there was nothing the farmer could tell the snake except that he was sorry. Shaking with fear, he went and asked the snake to forgive him.

The farmer was surprised when the snake agreed to pardon him for cutting off its tail. Once again, the old man promised to give the snake half of what he received from the king. Then he learned that a sheep was a sign of peace and happiness.

This news pleased the king greatly. He gave the farmer more presents than one man could carry. A horse had to be added to the gifts to take them away from the palace. And the farmer, in turn, was so joyous that he was glad to give half his gifts to the snake. Once more he told the snake how sorry he was. He promised to go home and bring the rest of what the snake really owned.

"No," said the snake. "It was not your fault that you cheated, lied, and cut off my tail."

This was strange, the farmer thought. What could the snake mean? As he asked himself this question, he knew, somehow, that he no longer felt any fear. Why, the snake was really a very beautiful creature, now that its tongue and head were still. No, the change was not so much in the snake as in the farmer's own mind.

"The first time you came," the snake went on, "there was cheating and lying in the kingdom. So you cheated me and then lied about it. The second time, when there was war, you came with a sword and cut off my tail. But now, when the land is filled with peace and happiness, you bring your gifts to share with me. No, good farmer, I want none of your presents. Go home now, and peace be with you always."

The snake then crawled off into a hole in the side of the hill. When it had disappeared, the farmer went home, pleased with the wisdom and understanding the snake had given him.

FROM
The Middle East

The Middle East . . . a land of camels and deserts, of wise men and fools, of great riches and terrible hardships . . . and a wonderland of stories.

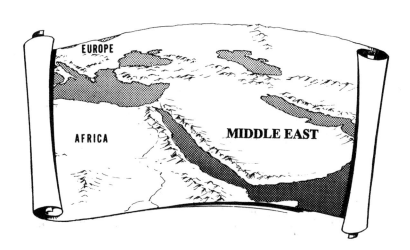

A STORY INSIDE A STORY INSIDE A STORY

. . . in which a beautiful queen tells of an unhappy man who tells a tale of a tail.

Words We Need to Know:

caliph [*KAY lif*]—the political and religious leader of the old Middle East
The *caliph* ruled the Middle East from the magnificent city of Bagdad.

calm [*KAHM*]—quiet; not excited
The dog stopped barking and became quite *calm*.

merchant [*MUR chent*]—a businessman; a person who buys and sells things
A shoe *merchant* opened a new store next to the bank.

unconscious [*un KON shus*]—not conscious; not knowing what is happening; knocked out or asleep
When Henry fainted he was *unconscious* for five minutes.

Once upon a time there lived a king who had a very strange fear. He was sure that there would come a year when no rain would fall. Without rain, plants would not grow. People in the kingdom would have nothing to eat. The king's one thought was to pile up enough food to last a whole year. He had a huge barn built out of stone. Every year he took half the corn grown in the kingdom and put it in the barn. Here, he thought, it would be safe from robbers, rats, and even insects. But one year, when the barn was almost full, a little bird found a small hole up under the edge of the roof. The little bird went into the barn. When it came out, it carried away a grain of corn. Then another little bird came and flew away with another grain of corn. Then another little bird came and flew away with another grain of corn. Then another little bird came and flew away with another grain of corn . . .

Another and another and another. We know, of course, that nothing new will happen in this story. It will not end until the last bird flies away with the last grain of corn. This story is said to be the longest ever told. No one has ever told it all the way through.

But what really *is* the longest story ever told?

No one knows, for sure. But it is probably a tale that is supposed to have taken more than a thousand nights to tell. This story fills sixteen books. It comes from the Middle East. It is called *The Thousand and One Nights*, or, more often, *The Arabian Nights*.

The Arabian Nights is both one story and many stories. It is a very long story in which one character tells another character many short stories. Tales fit inside each other like small boxes inside big boxes. Characters in the short stories tell each other still more tales, giving us stories inside stories inside stories.

A STORY INSIDE A STORY INSIDE A STORY

In the strange wonderland of ancient Arabia, there once lived a very rich king. He sat on a throne made from a

197

single piece of gold. He owned many slaves, camels, and wives. But the king was like many people who have more than is good for them. He became tired of what he owned very quickly.

Especially his wives. No sooner would he marry a new wife than he would start thinking about another. "I have looked at this face too long," he would say. "It pleases me not. Search the kingdom for a pretty new wife for the king!"

Now, in old Arabia, it was not strange for a king to have more than one wife. Most kings kept a small army of wives. But this king wanted only one wife at a time. When he married a new wife, he had the old one put to death. Even in an age when people were not so kind as they are now, this was thought too cruel to be human.

It happened once that this cruel king married a young girl named Scheherazade [*sha hair a ZAH de*]. She had all the beauty and charm of the wives that had gone before. But Scheherazade had something else. She had a mind that was second to none. She never forgot any story she heard, and she had heard every story there was to hear. In her mind she carried every tale and legend of old Arabia. And in her mind she also carried a plan by which she hoped to save her life.

When Scheherazade's day of death arrived, she stayed as bright-eyed and calm as a cat. The cruel king was not pleased. His hangings were always held at midnight. He liked to watch the person suffer through the day and evening. This was his idea of a good time.

A short time before the hour set for her death, Scheherazade sat down quietly before the king's throne. For a few minutes she hummed an old tune and polished her nails. Then, suddenly, she looked up at the king and smiled. "Oh!"

she said. "I almost forgot. There's a story I've been meaning to tell you. This will be my last chance, if you would like to hear it."

The king liked Scheherazade's exciting tales. He nodded his head, and the queen began her story:

I will tell you (said Scheherazade) about a happy caliph who once ruled the great city of Bagdad. Some people said he loved a good joke more than he loved his job. But everyone agreed that he was a kind man who ruled wisely and well.

One sunny morning, the caliph sent for two of his friends. "Let us disguise ourselves and walk through the streets of Bagdad," the caliph said. "We will ask the people how they like the men I have chosen to rule them. Those rulers the people like will be given better jobs in my government. And those the people dislike will find themselves out of work."

The plan pleased the two friends. One thought it was a good joke. The other thought it was a good way to check up on the rulers of Bagdad. So the caliph and his friends dressed themselves as merchants from India. Then they left the palace, to make their way among the people. The caliph was pleased to hear again and again that his rulers were honest and fair men.

About noon, as the caliph and his friends were returning to the palace, they passed over a small bridge. A sad-looking man was leaning on the rail, staring down into the water.

"We are three merchants from India," the caliph said to the man. "Tell us, is Bagdad as great a city as we have heard? Are its rulers good men, or do they fill their pockets with the people's gold?"

The sad-eyed man replied that Bagdad was the greatest

city on earth. Its rulers, he said, were good men who would protect traveling merchants. "All but one!" he went on. "There's a wicked fellow named Ali who rules my part of the city. If I were the caliph, I would take Ali's money, whip him a thousand times, pull off his clothes, tie him backwards on a donkey, and send him riding out of the city!"

"What?" cried the caliph. "Here in Bagdad there is a ruler who deserves such punishment? What has this Ali done to you?"

"I will tell you," replied the sad-eyed man. "But not now. My friends, it is the hour to eat. A good meal is waiting at my home. I should like nothing better than to have you as my guests."

This was odd, the caliph thought. Why should this unhappy man ask three strangers to eat with him? Well, there was one way to find out.

Soon the caliph's party entered the home of the sad citizen of Bagdad. He told them little except his name, which was Abu. They sat down at a table piled high with rich meats and fresh fruit. It seemed as though Abu had expected guests. But the only other person in the house was Abu's old mother. It was she who kept their glasses filled with the finest wine.

During the meal Abu said little. The caliph was as happy as always. But he tried not to act too gay. He felt that it wouldn't be polite to laugh, or to ask Abu again why he hated this ruler. Sooner or later, the caliph thought, Abu would explain everything. But Abu still said nothing. Finally, the caliph could hold his questions no longer.

"Pardon me, Abu," said the caliph. "But we men of India are not so polite as you people of Bagdad. Tell us, why do you ask three strangers to a great meal? And why do you hate Ali, your ruler?"

Abu was silent for a few moments. Then he said, "I will answer both questions at the same time. There is a reason I hate Ali and invite three strangers to my house. And the reason starts with a tale":

I must tell you (said Abu) a little story about a man I know. Just the other day, he was in a part of Bagdad where he had never been before. When the dinner hour came, he went into a small restaurant and asked for beef stew. The stew was terrible. A dog would have walked away from it. The man pushed the plate away from him and started to leave.

"Hey!" called the restaurant owner. "Wait a minute, now. You haven't paid for the beef stew."

"I'll pay for beef stew when I get it," the man said. "What this slop is, I don't know. But no one could call it beef stew."

The restaurant owner rushed outside to find a policeman. While he was gone, the man decided to throw the beef stew into the garbage, right where it belonged. He found a garbage can in the kitchen. But when he lifted the lid, there in front of his eyes was a tail. It was a cat's tail, and with it was the rest of the cat that hadn't been put in the stew!

Soon the owner of the restaurant came back with a policeman. "This man says you ordered beef stew, and then wouldn't pay for it," said the policeman. "Is he telling the truth?"

"It is true that I ordered beef stew," the man replied. "But there is a reason that I didn't pay for it. *And the reason starts with a tail.*"

Now, as soon as the man said *tail*, the restaurant owner turned white. He knew that he was in danger himself. For serving cat meat, he could have been put in jail. A big smile came over his face. "There has been a terrible, terrible mistake," he said. "I remember now—this man *did* pay me. A whole gold coin, it was. And—my word!—I forgot his change." Then he dashed across the room and unlocked the drawer where he kept his money. The finder of the tail left the restaurant with his stomach empty, but with his pockets full. And this (said Abu) ends my tale of a tail.

The caliph and his friends laughed. "You have told a good story," said the caliph. "But how does it explain why you hate Ali? Or why you invited us to this meal?"

"Well, my reason, too, starts with a tale," said Abu. Then he told his guests a very sad story. His father had died several years before. Abu had been left enough gold to last the rest of his life. But a bad friend named Ali had borrowed from Abu until the gold was gone.

Abu had lived for a time by selling the paintings, lamps, and other things in the house. But soon everything had been sold. By this time Ali had become a ruler. Abu went to him and asked for his money back. But no money did he get. Instead, he was whipped until he fell unconscious, and then he was thrown out into the street.

At this point, when all seemed lost, Abu received some good news. His father had known that Abu knew little about keeping money. The old man had divided his fortune into two parts. Half the money was to be kept secret from Abu for a year. So, after Abu had learned his lesson, he was again given enough money to last a lifetime.

"And I learned my lesson well," said Abu. "From that day to this, I have had no real friends. Every day I invite strangers to eat at my house. Then I never speak to them again. If you see me tomorrow, men of India, I shall pretend not to know you."

The caliph looked at his friends across the table. Their host was indeed a strange man. "This is hard to understand," the caliph told Abu. "Is there no one in Bagdad who would make you a good friend?"

Abu stared at the table and shook his head slowly. His unhappy face seemed to show all the sorrow of the world. Then, without warning, he brought his fist down hard on the table. The dishes rattled.

"How I would like to be the caliph for just one day!" Abu cried. "Oh, would I show that Ali a thing or two!"

At this the caliph could not help laughing out loud. He had suddenly remembered what was in his pocket. To protect himself, he carried with him a small bottle of a drug that brought instant sleep. In a few minutes the drug was poured into Abu's wine when he wasn't looking. Soon Abu was unconscious.

Working quickly, the caliph and his friends rolled Abu up in a rug. Then they carried him through the streets to the palace. No one knew that one of the merchants was the caliph, or that the rug had anything inside it.

The next morning, Abu opened his eyes on the foot of a golden bed. He looked about him in wonder. Surely, this was a dream. Curtains made of silver thread covered the walls. From the ceiling hung stars of red gold. Abu shut his eyes tight. He tried to shake the sleep out of his head. Then he looked again. Now an attendant stood at his bedside, holding a silk robe and a pair of silver slippers.

"Your bath is ready, Protector of the People," said the attendant.

Abu pinched his cheeks to see if he were awake. Then he put a finger between his teeth and bit down hard. "Ouch!" he cried. The pain, at least, was very real. He looked again at the servant. "Where am I?" he asked.

"In your bedroom, of course," replied the attendant.

Abu sat up. "Are you sure?"

The attendant had good reason to be sure. For this servant was none other than the caliph himself. He stood looking at the surprised Abu. "Does the caliph feel ill? Maybe a doctor can be——"

"No!" Abu cried. "I am *not* the caliph! Do you hear! Can a man become the caliph in one night? Yesterday I was the sad Abù. So how can I be the happy caliph today?"

Abu scratched his head and looked again at the room. More attendants and slaves now stood against the walls. Abu didn't know what to do. Well, he thought, if he *were* the caliph, he would try giving an order. He would see what happened. "You, there," Abu said, pointing to an important-looking servant. "Go to the house of Ali, one of the rulers of Bagdad. Take his money, whip him a thousand times, and tear the clothes from his body. Then tie him backwards on a donkey and send him out of the city. Tell him the caliph will cut off his head if it is ever seen in Bagdad again!"

Abu held his breath while the servant bowed low and left the room. Now he had given an order. And, what was more important, he had seen it obeyed.

"It is true!" Abu cried. "I *am* the caliph!" His face was happy for the first time in years as a dozen attendants followed him toward his waiting bath. . . .

At this point Scheherazade stopped speaking. The king had become very sleepy. His eyes had grown narrower and narrower as he listened to Scheherazade's story. But his eyes opened wide when Scheherazade stopped. "What!" he asked. "Is this the end?"

"No, not at all," replied Scheherazade. "But it is almost

midnight, the hour set for my death. If I could go on with the story tomorrow . . ."

Scheherazade watched the king closely. She saw him stretch, then look at the clock, at her, and back at the clock. Suddenly she knew that her plan had worked!

"I must hear the end of the story," the king said. "We shall put off your death for twenty-four hours."

And so saying, the king rose from his throne and made his way to bed. Scheherazade's plan had worked for one evening. Little did she know that she would have to keep her story going for a thousand more nights. For only then would the king decide that such a storyteller deserved to live.

From the caliph's palace:

THE CALIPH'S CONTEST Many good stories have come to us from the palace of the happy caliph. In his day Bagdad was the greatest city in the world. Men came to Bagdad from the far ends of the earth. They told the caliph about many strange things. He heard stories of men with tails, of horses the size of dogs, and of sea monsters that could swallow ships. All these things seemed impossible. But men swore that they had seen them with their own eyes. Before long, the caliph came to believe that there was nothing that was really impossible. The world, he decided, was a very strange place.

Once, just for fun, the caliph offered a prize to anyone who could tell him something that was truly impossible. The prize was to be a thousand gold coins. The money was to be given to the person who could make the caliph say, "That is impossible." He set a date for the contest, and had the prize money placed in a glass jar above the palace door.

The contest excited the people of Bagdad. Men, women, and children set themselves to thinking of something that could never really happen. At last the great day came. Thousands of people stood before the palace. A band played as the caliph walked out onto the steps.

A famous clown was the first to try. He rushed forward at once. "Protector of the People," he cried, "news has just come that the moon has fallen to the ground! A hundred of your cities have been destroyed!"

Now, the caliph did not believe for an instant that the moon had crashed into the earth. He felt sure that the clown had made the story up. But still, the story was *possible*. If there was one chance in a million that it could have happened, it was *possible*.

The caliph looked down his nose at the clown. "The moon has fallen, you say?" he asked in a calm voice. "Well, that is possible."

The crowd laughed until the clown left.

Next came a man of great wisdom, the caliph's doctor. The people were surprised to hear a loud noise come from under the doctor's coat. But his face looked so sad that no one laughed. The crowd was silent as he reached under his coat and took out a day-old pig. He held the little pig up to the caliph by one leg.

"Protector of the People," said the doctor, "I have just come from your wives. The truth must be known. Your third wife has just given birth to this pig!"

The caliph looked at the pig with care. Then he nodded. "Yes, that is possible," he said.

The crowd laughed once more, and the doctor, too, left the steps.

A famous fortuneteller was the next person to try. "I

have studied the stars to find what will happen to you, Protector of the People," he told the caliph. "And now, at last, I have found the truth. In the next four days you will grow a long, long tail. In a month your body will be that of a monkey."

"That is possible," agreed the caliph. He could hardly keep from laughing.

"But you will want to live like a monkey, too," went on the fortuneteller. "You will hide in the woods, where you will have seven years, eight months, three weeks, and six days before you die."

The fortuneteller stopped speaking. The people had suddenly become very noisy. Through the crowd was coming a well-known good-for-nothing. His name was Omar, and he had often made the caliph laugh. Now Omar was dressed in rags. His back was bent under the weight of two huge stone jars. He climbed the steps and set the jars at the caliph's feet.

"Protector of the People," Omar began, "you are the best ruler our land has ever had. Everyone knows you have brought peace and happiness to the world."

"That is possible," said the caliph.

"Yes," said Omar, "you have marched at the head of our armies and put your own life in danger. Once you spent all your money to defeat our wicked enemies."

The caliph smiled and nodded, for he knew that this was true.

"My own father, bless his name, told me this," Omar went on. "When you had used all your money, you went out and borrowed money to help save the country."

"That is also possible," agreed the caliph, for Omar was still speaking the truth.

Omar went on in a loud voice. "From my father, Protector of the People, you borrowed these two stone jars filled with gold—twenty thousand gold pieces in all. And you told my father, upon your honor, that you would return the money to his son on this very day!"

"Omar—!" cried the caliph. Suddenly he bent over, holding his sides with laughter. He knew the game was over. He could easily *say* it was possible for the moon to fall, for his child to be a pig, or for him to turn into a monkey. But he could *not* tell Omar that he owed him twenty thousand pieces of gold. He knew Omar would want the money right away. It would be cheaper to pay him the prize.

"You're a sly fox, Omar," the caliph said finally. "You have fooled me. I knew your father. He was a good-for-nothing like yourself. No, I am *not* going to give you twenty thousand gold pieces. I am going to say:

"THAT IS IMPOSSIBLE!"

ABU THE WAG

. . . in which Scheherazade tells how Abu
twice became a happy man.

Words We Need to Know:

imprisoned   [*im PRIZ und*]—having been put in prison, or jail
Most *imprisoned* men do not try to escape.

turban   [*TUR ban*]—a covering for the head made from a strip of cloth
In the Middle East many men wear *turbans* instead of hats.

vizier   [*vi ZEER*]—a high assistant to a caliph
Next to the caliph himself, the grand *vizier* was the most important man in old Bagdad.

wag   [*WAG*]—a funny person; a joker
Susan often laughed at Uncle Charlie, who was a real *wag*.

Was Scheherazade a real person? If not, who invented her? And who made up her stories?

To each of these questions we must give the same answer: no one knows, for sure. We know little about the strange book called *The Arabian Nights*. It comes to us from a time when a city called Bagdad was the most important place in the world. Maybe the answers to our questions lie buried under the sands of the Middle East. Again, no one knows. We cannot give answers; we can only guess.

Probably no "Queen Scheherazade" ever lived. About seven hundred years ago, we now believe, someone wrote down the folk takes and legends of the Middle East. Scheherazade was probably made up as a "teller" of these old stories.

Because Scheherazade was supposed to have told these tales, some people have come to think of her as a real person. Today she is known as "the Queen of Storytellers." Her tales are among the strangest in the world. Some are very short. Others go on, page after page, piling wonder upon wonder. Even the author seems to forget what is happening.

As we have seen, Scheherazade's stories sometimes stop to let the characters tell tales of their own. But the story we are about to read is all Scheherazade's. Here she goes on with the tale of the sad-eyed Abu, the man who woke up one morning to find he was the caliph.

ABU THE WAG   Abu was nobody's fool (said Scheherazade), even if he did let himself be tricked into thinking he was the caliph. After all, what would you have thought? You wake up in the caliph's bed. You are treated like the caliph. You give orders, and you see them obeyed. You know you aren't dreaming. So—you must be the caliph.

The first thing Caliph Abu did was to punish his old enemy, Ali. The second thing was to start for his waiting bath. And the third thing was to decide that it was very nice to be a happy man.

Abu sang loudly as he splashed around in the caliph's bathtub. Twelve attendants stood in a row by the tub. The servants had lined up in the order that they would be needed. Nearest the tub stood the attendant who held the caliph's soap. Next came the royal towel-holder. A bathrobe and a pair of slippers were in the hands of the third. Then came servants holding the caliph's brushes and combs, perfumes, underwear, socks, shoes, shirt, and royal robe. At the end of the line stood a turban-holder and a turban-winder.

That morning the new caliph was late getting to his throne. No sooner had Abu been dried, combed, brushed, and dressed, than he decided to take another bath, so he could be dried, combed, brushed, and dressed all over again. Best of all, Abu liked the turban-winding. For this he moved his head from side to side as the turban-winder ran in smaller and smaller circles around him.

By the time Abu finally reached the throne, the rulers of Bagdad were there waiting for him. Abu was happy to see that Ali was not among them. One by one, the rulers came forward and kissed the ground at the caliph's feet. Then they lined up before the throne, waiting for orders. Abu sat looking at them, wondering what the orders were to be.

But Abu didn't have long to wonder. Suddenly the door opened. Ten guards marched into the throne room. The sound of horns filled the palace. The guards stopped and formed two lines, one on each side of the door. They clicked their heels together and shouted in one voice, "Here comes the grand vizier."

Abu felt a lump in his throat. He knew that the grand

vizier was a very important man. If anyone would notice that Abu were not the caliph, it would surely be the grand vizier.

A big fellow with a smiling, fat face came into the room. "About your business, now," he said to the rulers of Bagdad. He waved his hand, and the rulers disappeared. Then he came toward the throne and bowed down before Abu.

Why, Abu thought, this was the same man he had ordered to punish Ali! He had sent the grand vizier himself!

"Protector of the People," began the grand vizier. He was now on his knees. "You have protected the people again. We found Ali counting his gold. He had far too much money to have come by it honestly. How did you learn he was cheating the people?"

Abu replied that the news had come in a dream. "Last night," he explained, "I dreamed that all my life I had been a sad man named Abu. This Abu had been badly treated by Ali." Then he told the grand vizier to find Abu's house. Abu's old mother was to get four hundred of the gold pieces taken from Ali.

"It shall be done," said the grand vizier, bowing low before the throne. Then horns sounded again, and the grand vizier left the room with his ten guards.

Before the door could be closed, the royal pillow-carriers entered. Their heads were hidden in piles of big pink pillows. These they heaped up before the throne. Soon the pile towered above Abu's head.

Abu started to climb the pile of pink pillows. He found them to be made of the smoothest silk. When he lay down, it was like floating on a cloud. Suddenly ten tray-carriers entered the room. They carried on their heads trays of rich meats, creamy cakes, and fruit so fresh that it still twinkled with dew. Abu wondered if this were breakfast or lunch. But he soon found that the question had no meaning. The meal was to go on all day! He had only to lift his arm, and a choice of the finest food would be at the tips of his fingers. Dancers and singers came and left the room on each other's heels. "Ho! Jolly good!" Abu shouted at the end of each act, or, "Jolly good! Ho!" He wanted to clap, but his hands always seemed to be full of food. "Ho! Jolly good!" Abu cried, and the day raced onward.

Suddenly Abu noticed a single attendant standing at his side. The servant was holding a golden tray. On the tray was a glass of purple wine. Abu knew he had seen this attendant somewhere before. O yes! This was the servant who had first told him he was the caliph.

"Your bedtime wine," said the attendant.

"Bedtime!" cried Abu. "Why, it's hardly afternoon!" Then he watched the attendant pull aside a silver curtain. It was dark outside the window! Abu was surprised. "Time passes fast for a happy man," he sighed.

The food, wine, and pillows had made Abu very sleepy. He would soon have been asleep, even without the drug that the real caliph had put in the wine. The glass was not half empty when it fell from the unconscious Abu's hand.

The real caliph watched the purple wine spread on the pink pillows. Then he started to laugh. He laughed, and laughed, and laughed. The grand vizier entered to find the real protector of the people rolling on the floor. The caliph asked for a handkerchief to mop up the tears in his eyes. Soon the handkerchief was dripping wet, and he had to have another. "Ho! Jolly good!" he would shout, and would again bend over and hold his sides.

Finally the caliph came to his senses. "This Abu is a

214

jolly wag," he said. "I will bring him to the palace and make him my friend. We will call him 'Abu the Wag.' But for now, wrap him in his rug and carry him back home."

The next morning, Abu awakened on a rug in his own house. At first he had no idea where he was. His head felt dizzy. "Ho! Attendants!" he cried. "Ho! Grand Vizier! Ho!"

His cries brought no one except his old mother. "Ho, yourself," she said. "Ho. Ho. Ho."

"Ho!" said Abu. "Jolly good!"

"What's 'jolly good'?" asked his mother.

"Where am I?" asked Abu.

"You're home, now!" she replied. "But where have you been? I didn't see you for a day. Then here you are on the living-room rug."

Abu looked at his mother through narrow eyes. "Who are you?"

"Why, your mother, Abu."

Abu explained that he was *not* Abu—so, of course, his mother could *not* be his mother. He was, he said, the Caliph of Bagdad, and he would now be off to his palace.

But Abu's mother was too quick for him. Before he knew it, she had locked every door in the house. Then she made Abu sit down in a chair. She gave him a long lecture. Slowly, some of his Abu-ness came back to him. Now he didn't know *who* he was. Was it Abu who had dreamed he was the caliph? Or was it the caliph who had dreamed he was Abu? It was his mother who decided the question.

"A strange thing happened yesterday," she said. "While you were gone, the grand vizier came here himself. He gave me four hundred gold pieces."

"Ho!" Abu jumped up. "Jolly good! Ho! You see, I sent

him here—*I*, the Protector of the People. Now, give me those keys!"

Giving Abu the keys was the last thing his mother had in mind. He would surely run to the caliph's palace. He would get them both in trouble. Had her son gone mad, she wondered. But she soon stopped wondering. Abu began to chase her through the house, yelling for the keys. Her loud screams brought the neighbors. They broke in through the windows.

"It's Abu!" cried his mother. "He thinks he's the caliph!"

"Ho! Grand Vizier!" Abu shouted through the broken windows. "Come and get these people! Tie them backwards on donkeys and send them——"

Crash! A neighbor smashed a lamp against Abu's head. He fell to the floor. Once again he was unconscious. Alas, the neighbors thought, the strange, sad Abu was now quite mad. They decided that he should be locked up in a safe place. They would put him in the cellar until he came to his senses.

So Abu was carried to the basement. Before long he awakened for the second time in the same morning. This time his head was not only dizzy. It had a bump on it, too. And this time Abu was not only the caliph. He was an imprisoned caliph, as well.

Abu got up from the dirt floor and went to the window. He looked out between the rusty iron bars. He cried "Ho!" to neighbors in the street. But the people seemed not to hear him. It was as though he were not there. "This is strange," Abu said to himself. "First I was Abu. Then I was the caliph. Now I seem to be nobody at all."

It pleased Abu to be Nobody. Of course, it wasn't like being the happy caliph. But it was better than being the sad Abu. And if he were Nobody, he couldn't get into any more trouble. So Abu was Nobody—until he began to feel hungry. Then a question popped into his mind. Would Nobody have to eat? No, Abu decided. So, after all, he must be Somebody. But, if he *were* Somebody, what Somebody was he? He sat down on the dirt floor to think it over.

About noon Abu smelled something wonderful. Fried camel meat! He hopped up and looked through the bars. His mother was bringing a huge meal on a tray.

"Who are you?" his mother asked. "Are you still the caliph?"

"How *dare* you ask me such a question!" Abu replied.

His mother took a piece of bread from the pile on the tray. She laid it on top of a glass of water. Then she passed the glass through the bars to Abu. "This is your meal," she said. "As long as you are the caliph, you get bread and water. When you decide to be Abu again, you can have the camel meat."

Abu chewed on a piece of the dry bread. He watched his mother walk away with the tray. He tried to keep still, but the smell of the fried camel was too much for him. "Ho!" he cried. "Bring back that meat, old woman. I am Abu, do you hear! Abu! Abu! Abu!"

His mother returned and passed the tray into the cellar. "You might say you're Abu," she said, "but you still talk like the caliph. When you once again speak like my sad Abu, you can come out of the cellar."

Abu sat down on the floor and ate his dinner. When he had finished, he tried to go to sleep. "Maybe I can dream," he said to himself. "If I am really Abu, I can dream I am the caliph. And if I am really the caliph, I can dream I am Abu dreaming he is the caliph."

But sleep was slow in coming. The cold, damp earth made his body stiff and sore. He seemed to have two headaches. One was deep inside his head. The other was right under his hair, where the bump was now the size of a walnut. Very slowly, Abu went into a kind of half-sleep. Then, suddenly, he *knew* he was asleep. He heard the voice of the grand vizier:

"Hello! Is that you? Are you there?"

Abu waited—but nothing happened. He saw no golden bed, no silver slippers, no pile of pink pillows. When he opened his eyes, the cellar was strangely dark. He looked toward the window. Outside the bars was the wide chest of the grand vizier.

"Ho! Grand Vizier!" Abu called. "Look! Down here!"

As Abu went to the window, he saw that the grand vizier was not alone. Beside him stood a smaller man. The other man was wearing the caliph's shoes. His robe was the caliph's. And his turban was the caliph's, too!

"Why!" Abu said aloud. "This is surely the caliph. And that means I must be Abu."

Now, the caliph loved nothing better than a good joke. But he had no wish to play a mean trick on anyone. When news of Abu's trouble had reached him, he had lost no time in coming to help. In a minute Abu was out of the cellar. Soon after that, everything was explained. The caliph gave his new friend a thousand gold pieces. He invited Abu to move to a house next door to the palace.

"I want you to visit me every day," said the caliph. "Friend Abu, you are smiling now. But the lines of sorrow will never leave your face. You remind me of a sad-faced dog that doesn't seem to know its tail is wagging. Yes, we shall call you 'Abu the Wag.'"

218

That very day, Abu the Wag received the caliph's gold. In a week, he had moved next door to the palace. And in a month, he had married the fairest daughter of the grand vizier. He was never to know another day's sadness in his life. For he soon learned that there was something better than being either the sad Abu or the happy caliph. This was being the happy Abu.

The tables turned:

ABU'S RETURN TO LIFE   One day Abu's wife asked for some money to buy silk for a new dress. Abu at once opened his money box. "Ho!" he cried. "The caliph's gold is almost gone!"

Money was something Abu had not worried about for more than a year. He and his wife had lived well, and he had been very kind to his old mother. But now he was nearly out of gold. He knew he would have to ask the caliph for more. This he did not want to do.

"I have it!" Abu said to his wife. "Here's a way we can get a hundred gold pieces, and some silk as well. You go to the caliph. Tell him I have died. He will give you money for a funeral, and silk to wrap the body!"

Now, Abu's wife was almost as much of a wag as Abu himself. She rubbed her eyes to make them red. Then she pulled her hair down over her face. Abu laughed as he watched her walk the few steps to the palace. He could hardly wait for her to return with the money and the silk.

She returned quickly—but, instead of gold and silk, she brought the caliph and the royal doctor. Abu saw them coming. What could he do? He was supposed to be dead. Working quickly, he put some ashes on his face, so the skin would look lifeless and gray. Just before the door opened, he lay down on the floor and folded his hands across his chest.

"There he lies," said Abu's wife. "Alas, his life went out like a candle."

"Dead as a doornail," said the doctor. "Poor fellow. The world will not be the same without him."

"Yes," came the sad voice of the caliph, "when the gods had made our Abu, they threw away the mold."

A teardrop slowly made its way down the caliph's nose, trembled on the tip, and fell to the floor. He told Abu's wife not to worry about the money for the funeral. He said he would send some gold and silk at once. Then he returned to the palace.

Abu had not finished laughing when he thought of going on with the joke. This time things were to be different. Abu would go to the palace himself. He would find the grand vizier. Abu's wife, the grand vizier's daughter, would be the dead person. Now it was Abu's turn to rub his eyes and mess up his hair. On the way to the palace, he began to cry and shout like a madman.

Soon the grand vizier, his doctor, and his ten guards were hurrying with Abu to the house. They entered to find Abu's wife on the floor. Her face was gray with ashes.

"There she lies," said Abu. "Alas, her life went out like a candle."

"Dead as a doornail," remarked the doctor. "This old world will never be the same without her."

"Yes," agreed the grand vizier. "After they made her, they threw away the mold." With tears in his eyes, he promised to do all he could to help Abu. He would start by sending some gold and silk as soon as he returned to the palace.

When the grand vizier had left the house, Abu and his wife howled with joy. "Ho! Jolly good!" Abu cried. He had the next joke all planned. "Now listen, when we get the silk, we will wrap ourselves up like a couple of dead bodies. Then we will go right to the palace to share our laughter."

But there was one thing Abu had forgotten. The grand vizier, to get the gold and silk, would have to go to the caliph. While Abu and his wife were laughing, the grand vizier was entering the caliph's throne room.

"Protector of the People," the grand vizier said. "I bring bad news. The wife of Abu the Wag is dead."

"What!" cried the caliph. "No, you have it wrong. It is Abu who is dead. I have seen his body myself!"

"But Abu lives!" cried the grand vizier. "I have just left him. He was alive and well. But his wife lay on the floor, still as a stone and cold as clay."

Soon Abu saw the caliph and the grand vizier marching toward the house. What had gone wrong? What could Abu and his wife do now?

Abu thought fast. "Ho!" he said. "We will both play dead! Hurry!"

The neighbors had now become interested. Twenty or thirty people followed the caliph and the grand vizier into Abu's house. The room was silent for a time. Then the caliph and the grand vizier told each other many wise things. They spoke sadly of candles, and doornails, and molds. But there was one question they could not answer. Who had died first? Each said that he had seen a different one alive, and the other dead. Finally, the caliph turned to the neighbors.

"I will give a thousand pieces of gold," he said, "to any-one who can tell me who died first."

When Abu heard these words, he leaped to his feet. "Ho!" he cried. "It was I who was the first to die!"

No one had ever seen the caliph laugh louder, harder, or longer. He gave Abu the Wag a thousand gold pieces for answering his question. He gave him another thousand for thinking of a good joke. He gave him a third thousand for being too polite to say he was out of money. And he never let Abu run out of money again.

FROM
The Far East

*M*any of the world's stories come from China, Japan, and the other countries of the Far East. Some of these stories seem strange to us. We find it hard to understand them. They seem to have no point. But other stories of the Far East are liked all over the world. These are the stories about people—and people are the same the world around.

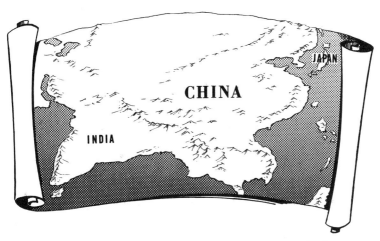

223

CHANG FU-YEN and THE WISE JUDGE

... in which a wise judge and a stone god track down a very clever thief.

Words We Need to Know:

blink   [*BLINK*]—to open and close the eyes quickly
The bright light made Jenny *blink* her eyes.

clue   [*KLOO*]—anything that helps find the answer to a problem
The police found a *clue* that told them who had robbed the store.

courtroom   [*KORT room*]—a court; a room where a judge and jury sit for trials
The judge's high desk in a *courtroom* is often called a "bench."

garlic   [*GAR lik*]—a plant with an onion-like root used to give flavor to meat
Mrs. Berger rubbed the meat with *garlic* before she cooked it.

guilty   [*GIL tee*]—having done some crime
The man was found *guilty* of robbing the store.

shack   [*SHAK*]—a small cabin made of old boards, etc.
The boys built a *shack* in the woods.

soot   [sounds like *foot*]—black powder given off when things burn
Soot will gather on a piece of glass held above a burning candle.

trial   [*TRILE*]—an examination in a court before a judge
The robber was given a fair *trial* in a court of law.

A Chinese folk tale is like a Chinese painting. We see only half the picture. The other half we must make up for ourselves. The reader joins the writer in making up the story.

Chinese stories are often very long tales told in a very few words. What the Chinese can say in a sentence, other people need a paragraph to explain. The story we are about to read could easily fill a book if all the details were filled in.

"Chang Fu-Yen and the Wise Judge" is a kind of early detective story. While reading it, we should remember that the judges of ancient China were nothing like the judges we know today. In old China, a judge was also a policeman, a detective, and a jailer. Here's a story about a judge who solves crimes without clues and makes criminals prove themselves guilty.

CHANG FU-YEN AND THE WISE JUDGE Long, long ago, in the hills of North China, there lived a man named Chang Fu-Yen. Like most Chinese of the time, he was very, very poor. His living came from what little food he could grow in his one small field.

One year Chang planted garlic in his tiny field. He had no other land, so each plant was cared for separately. Not a weed grew in Chang's garlic patch. When the ground was dry, he carried water from a stream over a mile away. All summer long he watched the garlic grow. He knew that good garlic would bring a high price.

When the garlic was almost ready to pull from the ground, Chang began to worry. What if a robber should come in the night? What if his garlic should be stolen?

Chang had worked hard for many months. He wanted to take no chances. He built a little shack in the middle of the field. Every night he sat in the shack and watched for robbers.

But no robbers came. Chang stayed awake for many nights. His eyes became red, and his body thin. At last he decided that there were no robbers in the neighborhood. "My garlic is safe," he thought. "I might as well spend one night sleeping at home."

This Chang did. At last he got a good night's sleep. But the next morning, when he returned to the field, he found that his garlic was gone. Every last plant had been pulled from the earth and carried away.

Chang stood looking at his empty field. His eyes filled with tears. All his work had been for nothing. There was little he could do. He could not hope to find the thief by himself. And he knew of no one who could help him.

Then he remembered. In a nearby city lived a very wise judge, supposed to be the wisest man in China. Chang had never seen this judge. In fact, Chang had never even been to the city. But now he wasted no time. He put on his best clothes and walked down out of the hills to the great city of Peking.

The judge was surprised to see a farmer from the hills standing before him. He looked down from his high bench and asked Chang why he was there.

"Because, your honor, my garlic has been stolen," Chang replied.

"Then why did you not catch the thief?"

"Because, your honor, I was not there when he came."

"Then why did you not bring someone to tell me what the robber looked like?"

"Because, your honor, nobody saw the thief."

"Then why did you not bring some clue, something the thief had left behind?"

"Because, your honor, the thief left nothing behind. I found not even a footprint. There was nothing in the field but my little shack, and it had been there before."

"I see," said the judge. He sat for a while with the tips of his fingers pressed together. Then he spoke. "Chang Fu-Yen, you have told me little. But I think I can help you find the thief."

Chang could not see how. He had told the judge almost nothing. What good was the judge's mind with no facts to think about? How could the judge sit in Peking and find a thief who had disappeared into the hills at night?

"The facts in this case are clear," went on the judge. "Your garlic was stolen. A shack was the only thing in the field at the time. So the shack must have stolen the garlic."

What! A shack steal garlic? Chang could not believe his ears. It seemed impossible. Surely, the wise judge had not said anything so foolish.

But Chang was wrong. The judge *had* said that the shack had stolen the garlic. And what was more, the judge now said that the shack would be given a fair trial. Chang was told to return to his farm and carry the shack to Peking. The trial would be held the next morning.

The news spread fast. As Chang walked home, he found everyone talking about the shack that had stolen the garlic. So strange a trial had never before been heard of. People talked of nothing else.

Early the next morning, Chang carried the shack to Peking. Men, women, and children lined both sides of the road. A crowd of people followed Chang into the city. The courtroom was filled long before the trial began.

Chang entered the courtroom carrying the shack on his back. He was told to put it down in front of the judge's bench. The crowd laughed so hard that the judge had to call for order. When the room finally became quiet, the trial began.

The judge leaned over the bench and looked down at the shack. "Tell me, Shack," he ordered, "did you, or did you not, steal the garlic belonging to Chang Fu-Yen?"

The judge sat as though waiting for an answer. Then, suddenly, the room seemed to burst with laughter. The judge called and called for order. But no one could hear him. His face grew red. It was many minutes before the crowd was calm again.

"I remind everyone in this room," said the judge, "that this is a court of law. Any more of this laughing, and I shall have all of you put in jail. Now, if the shack will not speak, we shall make it speak." He then ordered six guards to beat the shack with clubs. The beating was to go on until the shack answered his question.

Six big men carrying clubs moved toward the shack. Their blows split the old boards. Before long the shack looked like a pile of toothpicks. Nothing so foolish had ever happened in the court of the wise judge. Once more the crowd burst into laughter. They found it impossible to keep still.

"Lock the doors!" cried the judge. "I said no more laughing—and I meant it!" Then he gave orders. Everyone watching the trial was to be put in jail. Everyone was given the same fine—one pound of garlic. No one was to be set free until his fine had been paid.

Soon the families and friends of the people in prison started to bring in the fines. The garlic was put in a large box beside the judge's bench. Each person who brought garlic was asked where he had bought it. The merchant's name was then written on a little tag. The tag was tied to

230

the garlic. In a few days, no more garlic could be had in Peking. Soon the nearby cities had run out of garlic. The judge had it all.

When the last fine had been paid, Chang Fu-Yen was again ordered to court. He could not understand why. He had never understood what beating the shack had to do with finding the thief. Nor had he understood why the judge wanted the fines paid in garlic. Why, he wondered, should the judge want to see him now?

"In this box," the judge told Chang, "is all the garlic in Peking. Your garlic must be here, along with the rest. I want you to look through the box. Look at each bundle of garlic, and set aside those that might be yours."

It took Chang all day to sort through the garlic. There were thousands of bunches. Most of them were old. But some of the bunches were fresh. These, Chang knew, could have come from his field. He set them to one side.

When Chang had finished, the judge came and looked at the tags on the bunches of fresh garlic. "There are only three names here," he told Chang. "All this garlic came from only three merchants."

At last Chang saw what the judge was up to. The shack had been beaten only to make the people laugh. The people had been put in jail only to make their friends and families bring garlic. Yes, Chang thought, the judge was indeed a wise man, a very wise man. He looked up at the judge and cried, "Then one of these three men stole my garlic!"

The judge seemed lost in thought. "Maybe, Chang, maybe," he said. "It might have been one of the merchants. Or it might have been *two*, or all *three* of them. Or it might have been still another man, who later sold your garlic to one, two, or three of these merchants."

Alas, Chang thought, the judge was right. Things were never so simple as they seemed. Oh, to be so wise!

"But never mind," went on the judge. "By tomorrow morning, Chang, we shall know who stole your garlic. For one thing is sure—at least one of these merchants knows who the guilty man is."

The three vegetable merchants were brought to the courthouse. They seemed surprised. Each said that he knew nothing of the stolen garlic. None of them had stolen the garlic himself. Neither had any bought garlic for at least a month.

The judge's eyes passed slowly from one man to another. "Let me tell you something," he said at length. "I am called *wise* by many men. Maybe this is true; maybe not. But wisdom, gentlemen, is not all I have to help me. No, for many years I have had the help of a god, a god of truth. Right now this god is waiting in the cellar of the courthouse. He has never failed to catch a guilty man. Unless you tell me the truth, gentlemen, all three of you will spend the night with this god. Then the truth will be known."

The men still said they knew nothing about the stolen garlic. The judge did as he had promised. He led the three merchants down a dark flight of stairs. Chang followed, carrying a lighted candle like the others. At last they came to a room deep in the cellar. The judge unlocked a heavy door, and the men entered the dark room.

In the center of the stone floor was a great statue of a sitting god. It was carved from a block of white stone. The merchants had laughed at the idea of a statue's doing them any harm. But the smiles left their lips when they saw the statue's eyes. The glassy eyes glowed with a strange red light of their own. They were the eyes of truth, the judge explained. The statue's body was made of stone, but the eyes were those of a god.

"You will see nothing—only the eyes of the statue—until I come back in the morning," the judge said. "It will be dark in here. But remember this, gentlemen. The eyes of truth do not need light to see. They have their own light. So, if you stole Chang's garlic, you had better watch out. Sometime in the night, the god will make a mark on your back. In the morning, we shall all know who is guilty."

The judge took the candles from the three merchants. Then he and Chang went out of the room. The judge locked the door carefully, and the three men were left alone with the gleaming eyes of the god.

The next morning, at dawn, the judge and Chang again walked down the stairs to the cellar room. The door was opened. There stood the three merchants, blinking their eyes into the light.

"Turn around," ordered the judge.

Chang's mouth dropped open. Sure enough, the god *had* left a mark. The back of one of the men was covered with something black!

"This is the man who stole your garlic," the judge told Chang. "See? His back is as black as his wicked heart."

Chang did not know it, but the judge had had the walls of the room rubbed with soot. The thief, of course, had wanted to keep the god from making a mark on his back. He had spent the night with his back pressed tightly against the wall. In trying to save himself, he had marked himself as the guilty man. At once he fell to his knees and told the whole story.

In this way, the wise judge became even more famous. The thief was sent to jail for a long time. Chang Fu-Yen received all the garlic in the judge's big box. He sold it at a high price, became a very rich man, and spent the rest of his days growing roses on his little plot of ground.

Wisdom from old Japan:

A HUSBAND FOR TAMA   We have just read about the wisest man in ancient China. Now let us meet the wisest mouse in ancient Japan. But as we shall see, a wise mouse is not so wise as a wise man.

The most beautiful mouse that ever lived was named Tama. She lived, of course, in Japan, where the mice are so pretty that those of the rest of the world hide themselves in shame. Tama's hair was a soft gray-brown. She had lively, wide-awake little eyes. Her nose was both pointed and pretty. The flutter of her eyelids had to be seen to be believed.

Tama lived with her parents. Their home was the great House of Honda, near the busy city of Yamato. The Honda family was famous from one end of Japan to the other. They owned most of Yamato, and most of the country around. To be invited into the House of Honda was a great honor. Tama knew she was very lucky. Not every little mouse was allowed to live on leftovers from the great House of Honda.

Tama was her parents' only child. One-child families are not often found among mice, but Tama was lovely and loving enough to make any parents happy and proud. She was a very good girl. She always tried to obey her parents, as was the custom in ancient Japan.

When Tama reached the age to be married, her parents

234

began to worry. It was the custom for parents to plan marriages for their children. Tama's father didn't know what to do. Where could he find a husband for so beautiful a mouse?

One day Tama's father took his problem to a very wise mouse. This was an old gray fellow who knew every wall in the House of Honda. "A mouse of Tama's beauty," said the wise one, "must not be married to another mouse. No, she should be the bride of the most wonderful being in heaven or earth. Tama must be married to the sun."

The sun! This idea made Tama's father feel very proud. What other husband could be more warm-hearted, or keep more regular hours?

Without much trouble, Tama's mother and father traveled up in the sky to see the sun. They were greeted in a polite way. The sun listened to their story, and looked for many minutes at a small picture of the beautiful Tama.

"Alas," said the sun finally. "I fear I am not good enough for your lovely daughter. You talk as though I were the most magnificent husband to be found. I fear, my good mice, that you have made a big mistake."

"What do you mean?" asked Tama's mother. "I don't understand."

"Well," went on the sun, "I do what I can to make the earth pleasant and warm. But, to tell the truth, dark clouds often make me feel mighty foolish. A dark cloud that can cut off my sunbeams is surely more wonderful than I."

So Tama's parents went to the largest and darkest cloud they could find. The cloud was not so polite as the sun. "Why do you come to me?" the cloud asked. "The wind is far mightier than I. The wind can push me around in the sky, and can even break me into little pieces."

Tama's parents then went to the wind. It was all they could do to make the wind hold still long enough to hear their story. "I wish I could marry your Tama," the wind replied. "But you shouldn't have come to me. It is true that I can move a cloud. But I cannot move, or even get into, a well-built house. Everyone forgets about me when inside the walls of a good strong house."

Next the two mice went to the largest, strongest house they knew of. This was, of course, the House of Honda. The house lit up in welcome as they drew near. Before long they had told their story for the fourth time.

"The wind was right in saying that my walls are hard to pass through," said the House of Honda. "But the wind was talking about the wind, not about mice. You should know how many mouse holes there are in my walls! I think that the most wonderful husband you could find for Tama would be another mouse."

Tama's parents smiled and bowed down. They thanked the great House of Honda again and again. Now that they were back home, they began to think that another mouse might make a good husband, after all. They hurried off to tell Tama.

Tama had not wasted her freedom. They found her flirting with a handsome young fellow behind a big box of rice in the cellar. He at once asked for Tama as his bride. And her parents, after finding that he came from a good family, gave the marriage their blessing.

Tama and her husband lived a long and happy life. Never for a moment did they think about their children marrying anything but other mice.

THE GREAT BELL
OF CHINA

. . . in which a girl has her fortune told, and
learns what she must do to save her father's
life.

Words We Need to Know:

collapse [*ko LAPS*]—to fall or cave in suddenly
The roof of the house *collapsed* during the storm.

innocent [*IN o sent*]—pure; free from any evil
Many *innocent* children are killed in every war.

liquid [*LIK wid*]—flowing like water; something that can be poured
Steel becomes *liquid* when heated to a high temperature.

mellow [*MEL o*]—soft, rich; pleasing
Betty liked the smooth, *mellow* sound of a saxophone.

mold [*MOLD*]—a hollow form used to give a shape to a liquid as it cools and hardens
Liquid chocolate is poured into *molds* to make Easter bunnies.

studio [*STOO dee o*]—the workroom of an artist
On rainy days the artist painted in his *studio*.

238

Most languages are written across the page, from left to right.

```
R  a  g  w  T  k  l  w  d  m  t  ,  d  l   B
e  n  o  o  h  i  i  a  i  a  o     o  a   u
a  y  o  u  e  n  k  y  f  y     f  w  n  t
d     d  l     d  e  s  f     l  r  n  g  h
   l     d  n        ,  e  w  e  o     u  e
i  a  o     e  o  t     r  r  f  m  t  a
t  n  n  b  x  f  h  b  e  i  t     h  g  C
   g  e  e  t     e  u  n  t  .  r  e  e  h
n  u  ,        t     t  t  e     i        i
o  a     a  t  a  s           W  g  p  g  n
w  g  i     a  l  a  w        i  e  h  a  o
.  e  n     l  e  m  e        n     t  g  e  s
            e  .  e                 e  s  e
```

THE GREAT BELL OF CHINA   Many years ago, there lived in China a very great emperor. Millions of people had to obey his orders. The riches of a great land were his, and his alone.

But the emperor was interested in only one thing. His palace was crowded with works of art. He had more artists in his studios than he had soldiers in his army. In every corner of every room stood a silver statue. Painted screens covered every wall. The pictures on the screens had been painted, it is said, with brushes of a single hair.

Most of all, the emperor loved his bells. To him, a good bell was a work of art. The bell, he thought, was the greatest thing that man had ever made. Bells could be made to look alike, but no two bells ever sounded alike. They could be made in many shapes, in many sizes, and from many metals. The emperor thought of his bells as statues, for they were covered with figures of men and women.

"A bell is the only work of art that can speak," the emperor would often tell his guests. "Paintings and statues can please the eye, but only a bell can please the ear. A bell has a voice, a spirit, and even a *soul* of its own."

One summer day, the emperor called for his best bell maker. This was a man named Fang Tung. Fang Tung had made bells that stood as tall as the emperor himself. He had made bells no larger than the emperor's thumbnail. He had made bells to ring when the emperor was happy, and bells to ring when the emperor was sad. Only Fang Tung could make the great bell the emperor now had in mind.

"I have not many years to live," the emperor told Fang Tung. "I want to leave behind me a bell such as the world has never known. A thousand years from now, when this bell rings, people will stop what they are doing. "Listen!" they will say. "The great bell of a great emperor!"

The bell was to be exactly three times as high as the emperor was tall. Its sides were to show the emperor at three stages in his life. It was to be made of three different metals. Brass, the emperor said, would make its tone loud and clear. Silver would give it a smooth, sweet sound. And gold would make it sound rich and mellow.

Fang Tung listened to the emperor's orders. Then he shook his head sadly. "It cannot be done," he said. "Brass, silver, and gold will never mix. They will not hold together."

"That is your problem," said the emperor. "I will give you a year to learn how to mix the three metals. During the year, you may send for any metal expert in China. But that is when I want the bell—one year from today!"

Fang Tung bowed low before the emperor. Then he left the palace. He knew what would happen if he could not make the great bell. The emperor had only one punishment for failing to carry out an order. This was death. Whether or not the order was possible made no difference.

That evening a sad Fang Tung returned to his family. Gone were his smiles, his laughter, his little jokes. For the first time in years, he did not play with his daughter, Ko-Ning, before supper. Instead, he went straight to his room. He lay down on a mat and stared at the ceiling.

At the supper table, Fang Tung told the whole story to his wife and daughter. "The emperor thinks that brass, gold, and silver will melt together into a new metal," he said. "Alas, I wish it were possible."

"But it *is* possible!" Ko-Ning cried. "You've always said that if you *believe* in yourself, and *try* hard enough, *anything* is possible!"

Fang Tung looked at his daughter's innocent face and eager brown eyes. He smiled sadly. Only Ko-Ning was young enough to have any hope.

The next morning, Fang Tung sent for every metal expert in China. Then he called his workmen and artists together. "It will take a year to make this bell," he told them. "We must do our best the first time. There will be no second chance."

Work on the great bell went forward slowly. First a huge mold was made out of sand and clay. This took many months. But at last the mold was finished. It was ready for the hot, liquid metal that would be poured into it. When the metal had cooled, the mold would be broken open, uncovering a bell of bright new metal.

Or so Fang Tung hoped. Making the mold for the huge bell was a hard job, but it was possible. Making the three metals mix seemed impossible. The experts said that the metals must be heated to a higher temperature than had ever been tried. Maybe this would work; maybe it wouldn't. Fang Tung waited a long time for the experts to think of a better idea. Finally the year was almost gone. He could not wait another day. The time had come to pour the metal.

A special brick furnace had been built, for no one had ever heated so much metal to so high a temperature. The brass, silver, and gold were put into the furnace. A fire was started. The bricks grew red, then white, then brighter than the sun. Just as it seemed that the furnace would burst, Fang Tung gave the order to pour the metal. A door in the side of the furnace was opened. The hot metal flowed out. It filled a clay bowl that was over five feet high. Then huge chains were fastened to the bowl. It was lifted to the top of the mold. The liquid metal was poured from the bowl into the mold. There was just enough.

Two days passed before the metal had cooled. The workmen could hardly wait to open the mold. Fang Tung's life depended on what they found. When Fang Tung gave the word, they quickly attacked the mold with hammers. It fell apart in large pieces.

And so did the bell!

Fang Tung had failed. He picked up a piece of the soft metal and looked at it carefully. It was not one metal at all. In the bright sunlight, he could see that it was made of tiny pieces of brass, silver, and gold. The three metals turned to powder between his fingers. He sent a message to the emperor.

242

Then he went home, to wait for the soldiers he knew would be coming to get him.

But there was something Fang Tung had forgotten. The emperor wanted the bell more than anything in the world—more, even, than Fang Tung's death. If Fang Tung could not make the emperor's bell, who could? So, instead of sending soldiers to Fang Tung's house, the emperor sent a man with a message. Fang Tung was to have another chance—another year to live!

Happiest of all was Ko-Ning. Her own life, she thought, would not have been worth living without her dear father. And to her, a year was a long, long time.

Work was soon started on a second bell. Again a huge mold was made from sand and clay. When the year was almost gone, the three metals were once more heated in the furnace. Fang Tung did everything as it had been done before.

Fang Tung didn't know it at first. But not everything was to be as before. It had made Ko-Ning sad that she could not help her father with the first bell. When work was started on the second bell, Ko-Ning visited an old woman who told fortunes. The girl asked what she could do to help with the bell.

Ko-Ning was told to find a frog with one eye. It would have to be thrown into the liquid metal. Only in this way could the brass, silver, and gold be made to mix. Only in this way could she save her father's life.

Ko-Ning was busy during the months it took to make the second mold. She spent the hours after school looking for a one-eyed frog. She searched everywhere. Most people would have given up, but not Ko-Ning. Finally she found one, on a river bank about a mile from home. It wasn't a large frog. But it had only one eye, and that was what mattered.

Ko-Ning hid the frog under the house. She fed it flies. At last the day came to pour the metal for the second bell. Ko-Ning wrapped the frog in a piece of cloth. She put it in her pocket and went to watch the pouring of the bell.

Ko-Ning had planned to throw the frog into the liquid metal without being seen. But workmen were everywhere. Everyone was looking at the huge bowl. She would have to ask her father first.

Fang Tung smiled when his daughter pulled at his sleeve and asked to throw something into the hot metal. "What is it?" he asked.

"A one-eyed frog," replied Ko-Ning. She held up the small cloth bundle for her father to see. "Just for good luck."

It was a silly thing to do, Fang Tung thought. But it seemed to mean a lot to Ko-Ning. "Go ahead," he told her. "But be careful. Don't get too close. That frog will be dead as soon as it enters the bowl."

Ko-Ning ran toward the bowl. The heat stopped her. She tossed the frog into the glow above the metal. Then she ran back to her father's arms.

Ko-Ning could hardly wait until the metal was cool. At last the time came to break the mold. Would this bell break too, as the first one had? Or would her one-eyed frog do the trick?

The mold broke apart easily. An enormous new bell of golden silver gleamed in the sunlight! The bell seemed too perfect to be the work of human hands.

Only one thing still had to be done. Before the bell was moved to the emperor's palace, the tone had to be tested. Ko-Ning knew that every bell had a sound all its own. Sometimes a beautiful bell would have a bad tone. But no one seemed to worry about *this* bell. Ko-Ning watched as the bell was raised off the ground with strong ropes. Then her father took a heavy hammer in his hands. He got ready to hit the bell on the rim. Beside the great bell, the hammer looked too small to make it ring at all.

The bell did not ring. Instead of a *gong*, there came a *crash*. Cracks like black lightning shot through the bell. For an instant it held its shape. Then, with a great roar, it collapsed into a cloud of dust at Fang Tung's feet.

Ko-Ning was sure that her frog had been too small. The bell, after all, had been a very big one. She did her best to make her father smile. But Fang Tung would not smile. He could not. Even the good news from the emperor failed to cheer him up. Fang Tung was told a third time to make the great bell. This was to be his last chance. The emperor wanted either the bell or Fang Tung's head brought to him in a year's time.

So, for a third time, work was started on a new mold. And once again, Ko-Ning visited the fortuneteller. As before, the visit was kept a secret. But when Ko-Ning came home, her eyes were full of hope. There was a look of deep trust in her eyes now, a promise of something good. Fang Tung knew he could never have finished the mold without Ko-Ning. Her smile kept him going, a day at a time. Sometimes, he even believed for a minute that this third bell would be the one that worked.

Finally the day came when the metal was to be poured. Ko-Ning again went to watch. When the huge clay bowl was full, she again asked to throw something into the liquid metal.

Fang Tung looked at the small cloth bundle in his daughter's hand. "What is it this time?" he asked. "Another frog?"

"You'll see," Ko-Ning replied.

"Go ahead, then," said Fang Tung. "Be careful, now." He

smiled and watched his daughter run toward the bowl. But she didn't stop! She kept on running! Faster and faster she ran—until, with a mighty leap, she dived headlong into the glowing metal.

A shower of white-hot drops tinkled to the ground. Some of the liquid metal spilled over the sides of the bowl. Then all was as before.

Ko-Ning had jumped to her death. Her leap brought tears to the eyes of all who saw it. Fang Tung fainted and fell to the ground. He had to be carried home by two of his workmen.

For a while, the rest of the workmen were too shocked to move. They couldn't understand why Ko-Ning had given her life. Yet Fang Tung was still alive, and *his* life still had to be saved. The emperor's bell had to be finished. The mold stood ready, and the metal had been melted.

Somehow, the metal was poured.

No sign of Ko-Ning was found in the bowl. Her body had become part of the metal—and part of the great bell. When the bell was tested, it was found to be like no other bell ever made.

Fang Tung lay in bed for almost a week. He ate nothing. He said nothing. He knew nothing. Then, in a dream, he heard a voice calling his daughter's name. *Ko-Ning!* it cried, and again, *Ko-Ning!*

Fang Tung sat straight up in bed. He was now wide awake. *Ko-Ning*, it came again. Why, he thought, it sounded like his daughter's voice. No, it was a bell! Fang Tung was sure of it. It was a bell with a sound all its own—the soul of Ko-Ning, crying out for all to hear. It was a sad sound, yet beautiful, too.

Ko-Ning, came the great bell. *Ko-Ning. Ko-Ning. Ko-Ning!*

246

Some will laugh; some will cry:

THE LAZY MAN OF LAOS   In Laos [*LAY os*], a small country south of China, there once lived a man who was very, very lazy. He was so lazy that he never stood up when he could sit down. He never sat down when he could lie down. And when he lay down, it was all he could do to roll over.

Of course, the Lazy Man of Laos never found a wife. No woman would have him. He lived by himself in a one-room shack. Rain dripped through the holes in the roof. Wind blew through the wide cracks in the walls and the floor.

"Work is for fools," the Lazy Man often reminded himself. He kept away from work as though it were a sickness. He called himself a pig farmer. This meant that some thin pigs lived under his house. The pigs were always hungry, and they never seemed to grow at all.

In order to eat, once in a while the Lazy Man had to get a job. He never worked more than a few days at a time. And he never worked for money. He always asked to be paid in food. This saved him a trip to the store.

One fall, the Lazy Man worked for a whole week in a neighbor's rice fields. He was a little ashamed of himself for having worked so many days at a time. But he was proud of the large jar of rice he received at the end of the week. He carried the jar home and put it on the foot of his bed. Then he lay down to think about his good fortune.

"I will keep this rice until late in the winter," the Lazy Man told himself. "Then it will be worth a lot of money. I will sell it, and use the money to buy ten little pigs.

"When the ten pigs have grown large and fat, I will sell them, and use the money to buy a hundred little pigs.

"When these are grown, I will sell them, and use the money to buy a thousand little pigs!"

The Lazy Man was now excited. There seemed to be no end. He could start with his one jar of rice, and become the richest man in Laos!

"When my thousand pigs are fat enough," the Lazy Man went on, "I will sell them, and buy more pigs than my neighbors ever dreamed of owning. Then I will marry. A son will be born to honor his father. When he is old enough to walk, I can send my wife out to look after the pigs. And if she won't work, I'm going to kick her—like this!"

So saying, the Lazy Man raised his right foot into the air. His heel hit the jar of rice. It rolled off the bed and dropped to the floor with a loud crash.

The jar now lay in a hundred pieces on the floor. The rice fell through the wide cracks between the boards. It was eaten at once by the hungry pigs that lived under the shack. The Lazy Man didn't even bother to get up and save a small handful for his supper.

FROM
Africa

*U*ntil a few years ago, Africa was the "dark continent." The rest of the world knew little about it. But today Africa is an exciting place. Important things are happening every day. The world is hearing many African legends and folk tales for the first time. These stories are among the world's best. They show us the "dark continent" in a new light.

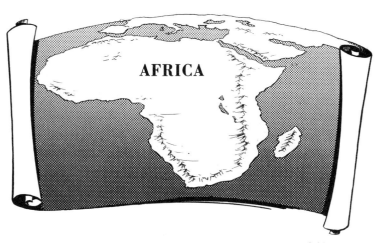

249

THE MAN WHO
OWNED THE MOON

... in which we learn why men are men,
and why monkeys are monkeys.

Words We Need to Know:

cape   [*KAPE*]—a point of land that sticks out into the sea
The southern tip of Africa is called the *Cape* of Good Hope.

crust   [*KRUST*]—a hard covering, like the crust of a pie
The inside of the earth is hot, but the *crust* is cool.

engineer   [*en ji NEER*]—an expert in the planning, building, and use of machines, vehicles, etc.
Engineers are already working on the cars we will see three years from now.

responsibility   [*re SPON si BIL i tee*]—something a person is responsible for, or must care for
A car is a *responsibility* to its owner.

Did you ever hear of a *time machine?*

The idea is simple. A time machine is a big box, about the size of an elevator. You step into it and close the door. Then you push buttons that move you backward or forward in time. When you open the door, you can step out into the world of the future, or into the world of long ago.

The idea of a time machine has always interested people. Who wouldn't like to spend a day in the world of the year 3,000? Or in the world of the ancient Greeks?

The time machine, of course, has never been invented. But people *have* stepped out of one world and into another. About a hundred years ago, an American explorer named Henry M. Stanley traveled through Africa. He found the Africans living much as people did before the beginning of history. Stanley found that it was possible to walk into another world—a world without schools, without science, and without writing.

And what kind of story did Stanley find the Africans telling? Myths, of course. The Africans told myths for the same reasons the ancient Greeks told them. Here is a myth Stanley brought home from Africa. It explains why there are dark spots on the moon, and why men and monkeys are so alike, yet so different.

THE MAN WHO OWNED THE MOON

Did men come from monkeys? Did the grandfathers of the first human beings eat bananas and live in the trees?

Different people have different answers to these questions. Some say *yes;* some say *no.* But the people of old Africa had an answer all their own. They believed that *monkeys* had come from *men!* Here is how they thought it happened.

In the days when monkeys were men, there lived in Africa

a king named Bahanga [*ba HAHNG* a]. He ruled over the ancient country of Bandimba.

One will not find Bandimba on a map. No one had heard of a map in the days of old Bandimba. But King Bahanga knew what land was his. Once a year the king climbed a huge mountain in the center of Bandimba. When he had reached the top, he would turn around slowly and say, "All this is mine!"

King Bahanga lived wisely and ruled well. He had his pick of the best bananas grown in Bandimba. He spent his days in a large log palace. He had the love of his people, and of his many wives. There was only one thing Bahanga wanted that he didn't have. This was a son. His children were all girls.

Finally, after Bahanga had ruled for many years, one of his wives gave birth to a son. Bahanga was very happy. He gave everyone in Bandimba a week's vacation. Then the people, too, were very happy.

Prince Bahang, as the boy was called, grew up quickly. He was always taller and stronger than other boys of his age. His father gave him everything he wanted. The king even allowed him to share the royal power. Prince Bahang ruled over all children his age and younger. When he was five, everyone five and under had to call him "King." When he was sixteen, he was "King Bahang" to half the teen-agers in the country. Before long, the boy ruled over more people than did his father.

But, with all this honor, the prince was still unhappy. The more people he ruled, the more he wanted to rule. The more things he had, the more he wanted to have. When his eyes saw a thing, he would want to own it. And Bahang got everything he wanted. The king loved him too much to say *no*.

Prince Bahang became a very proud youth. He boasted

254

more than he should have. He never made use of the things he owned. But he bragged about them all the time. "I have everything there is to own," Bahang would tell his friends. "My father, the king, cannot say *no*."

Bahang's friends often grew tired of his boasting. One day they had to spend an hour listening to the prince talk about his new canoe. When Bahang had left, they made a plan. "We will tease Bahang," they agreed. "We will tease him about not owning the moon!"

This they did. But the prince wasn't used to being teased. He couldn't take it. Instead of laughing it off, he became angry. He ran to the king.

"My friends say you won't give me the moon," Bahang cried to his father. "But we'll show them, won't we! They are fools, every one of them!"

King Bahanga smiled. "The moon is not mine to give away," he explained.

"What!" cried Bahang. "It hangs in the sky over Bandimba, does it not? I thought everything you could see from the mountain top was yours."

King Bahanga had never thought of it this way. "Why, that's right," he said. "I suppose the moon does belong to me, after all."

"Then I want it," Bahang said quickly. "I want you to give me the moon."

The king laughed. "All right, my son," he said, smiling. "I give you the moon. Take it. From now on, the moon is yours."

Prince Bahang grew angry. First his friends had laughed in his face. Now his father was laughing. "But I want to *own* the moon!" he shouted. "I don't want to just look at it up in the sky! I want to have it here, with me. In my hands!"

The king tried to explain. He told his son that no one had any idea how much the moon weighed. No one knew how high it was fastened to the sky. It would not be possible for the prince to really *own* the moon.

But Bahang was not used to hearing the word *no*. His temper ran wild. "I want the moon!" he shouted. "I want it, do you hear! The moon will be mine, or I shall die!"

These last words were too much for the good King Bahanga. The thought of his son's death made him shake with fear. If Bahang died, who would rule the country when the king grew old? There would be no one to carry on the family name.

"All right," the king said after a time. "I promise you, I shall try to get you the moon. But you must make me a promise in return. You must never speak of your death again."

The prince promised.

The next day King Bahanga called his wise men together. He told them he wanted the moon brought down from the heavens. The wise men wondered if their king had gone mad. No one in Bandimba had ever been higher than the top of the tallest tree.

"The man who gets me the moon will be well rewarded," Bahanga told the wise men. "He will have riches, lands, and much food. He can even stop being a wise man."

The wise men sent for the few engineers in Bandimba. Only an engineer would know how to reach the moon. The wise men and the engineers talked for many days. At last they sent for the king. Bahanga was told that a high wooden tower would have to be built on the mountain. In this way the moon might be reached.

"But is it possible?" asked King Bahanga.

"The moon is up in the sky," the wise men replied. "So, a

tower built up in the sky will reach the moon, if the tower is high enough."

Bahanga thought this over. It seemed to make sense. "Good," he said suddenly. "I shall tell the people about our plan at once. We shall call it the Bahanga Plan. The people of Bandimba will not rest until the moon is reached."

The Bahanga Plan changed many lives. The men of Bandimba were sent into the forests to cut logs for the tower. Boys made the miles of rope that were needed to tie the logs together. Girls did the cooking and looked after small children. And women went out to work in the fields.

In a few weeks, the tower began to rise from the earth. Each of its four legs was bigger around than the king's palace. The legs were farther apart than Prince Bahang could throw a stone. Day after day, logs were pulled up the side of the tower and tied into place.

In two months, the tower was higher than Prince Bahang could shoot an arrow.

In six months, the top of the tower couldn't be seen from the ground. People came from all over Africa to see the tower that disappeared into the sky. "Magnificent!" they said. "O wonder of wonders! All praise be to Bahanga!"

But there were some people who disliked Bahanga's tower. One of these was Aruwimi, the wisest of Bahanga's wise men. "There will be trouble if the moon is moved," Aruwimi warned. "No man should try to reach the moon. It belongs to the gods, and they will be angry."

Aruwimi built a huge canoe. He made it large enough to hold his whole family. "Life in Bandimba has become too dangerous," he told the people. "Everyone should leave the country." But most people laughed at Aruwimi. They couldn't understand his fears. They trusted their king too much to listen to their wise man. Only a few families left Bandimba with Aruwimi.

King Bahanga grew more excited every day. He thought only of reaching the moon. Men who came down from the tower said that they were getting closer and closer. Bahanga could hardly wait. He spent his days watching logs being pulled up the side of the tower. And at night he sat looking at the moon hanging in the sky over Bandimba, like a ripe apple just waiting to be picked.

At last the great day arrived. One evening the chief engineer himself came down to earth. "The tower is finished," he told King Bahanga. He held out his right hand. "With the fingers of this hand, I have touched the moon."

Bahanga hugged the engineer and kissed both his cheeks. The moon had been reached! The moon was his!

The king's hands itched to hold the moon. How proud he would be when he handed it to his son! Bahanga decided to climb the tower himself. *Someone* had to take the moon down from the sky. Why couldn't that person be the king?

Early the next morning, Bahanga started up the ladder that led to the moon. Close on his heels was the prince, with the chief engineer right behind.

Hand over hand they climbed, up, up, up. The people on the ground soon looked like dwarfs, then like dolls, then like dots. By noon the crowd at the foot of the tower had disappeared from sight. It was a clear day. The whole continent of Africa was now spreading out below Bahanga.

Bahanga stopped to look around. Far to the south was the Cape of Good Hope. In the North was a huge desert. On all sides was bright blue water.

"Look," the king told his son. "There it is—Africa! All of it!"

"Then it is all yours," shouted Prince Bahang. "If you can see it, it is yours!"

Bahanga took a deep breath. "Yes," he said with a sigh. "I suppose it is." The idea of owning Africa somehow did not please the king. The responsibility would be too great.

But nothing was too great for Prince Bahang. He had seen Africa. He wanted it. He asked for it.

"Someday, my son," replied his father. "But first, the moon!"

It was a long, hot afternoon. The sun burned down on the bare backs of the three men. But King Bahanga did not stop, even to rest. As the day went on, he climbed faster. When he saw the top of the tower ahead of him, he climbed even faster. The prince, big and strong as he was, could not keep up.

Just as the sun went down, Bahanga reached the top of the tower. He stood alone on the flat wooden platform. A few feet away hung the moon—*his* moon! The king had expected to see it. But at first he could hardly believe his eyes.

The moon was larger than Bahanga had thought. His arms might have reached halfway around it, but no farther. It glowed with a light that seemed to come from the inside.

Bahanga stepped carefully across the platform. He reached out and touched the moon with the tips of his fingers. It was warm, but not hot. It seemed to be made of a sandy kind of stone. He tapped it with the back of his hand. Why, it sounded hollow! He pushed against it hard, and found that it rocked back and forth easily.

Bahanga wanted to loosen the moon from the sky. Could he do it himself? No, he decided. It looked a little too heavy for one man to hold. He would have to wait for his son and the chief engineer.

Soon the prince's head appeared over the edge of the platform. His face looked tired. But his eyes popped open when he saw the moon. He raced across the platform. Then he touched, tapped, and rocked the moon, as his father had done.

Last to arrive was the chief engineer. "Everything is ready," he said. He pointed to a pile of rope on one side of the platform. "We can loosen the moon right now. I had these ropes brought up here to lower it to earth."

Bahanga wanted to unfasten the moon himself. He told the prince and the engineer to stand on different sides of the huge glowing ball. Then he placed his shoulder against the moon. He pushed. The moon only rocked from side to side, so he pushed harder, and still harder. Big drops of sweat stood out on his face. They gleamed like diamonds in the light of the moon. Very slowly, the moon started to roll upward.

Suddenly, there came a loud *crack*. Bahanga's shoulder broke through the crust of the moon. The big ball split open. Fire shot out of a dozen holes. Sparks showered across the night sky. The tower was burning! A huge white flame covered the three men.

Down on earth, the people had cheered when they saw the moon move. "Bahanga has done it!" they had cried. But the cheering had not lasted long.

Bang! The moon burst open. Fireworks lit up the sky. Then the tower caught fire. Burning logs fell to the ground. Flames spread over the forest.

"Run!" the people screamed. "Run for your lives!"

Men, women, and children ran in all directions. As the people ran through the smoke, they became smaller. Hair covered their arms and legs. They tripped over their new tails. They had been changed to monkeys!

The wise man, Aruwimi, watched the monkeys run out of

the burning forest. Some of them he had known as men. Little, lively people had become little, lively monkeys. Big, slow people had been changed to big, slow monkeys. Tears came to Aruwimi's eyes. He knew now what the gods had done. They had changed men who were foolish into foolish animals with tails.

If you don't believe this story, take a good look at the moon some night. Look closely at the dark spots that some people call "the man in the moon." You will see that they look nothing at all like a man's face. They look exactly like what they are—the holes made by King Bahanga, the man who owned the moon.

Also from Africa:

THE LION AND MR. HUNGER Aruwimi, the wise man, often told a story called "The Lion and Mr. Hunger." He wanted to hear what people said when they had heard it. Here is the story.

A rabbit once listened to a lion boast about how strong and brave he was. The rabbit smiled and nodded as the lion talked on and on. But in truth, being neither strong nor brave, the rabbit was not interested. The small animal was bored to death.

Suddenly the rabbit had a bright idea. He waited until the lion stopped for breath.

"Yes, the lion is a mighty beast," spoke up the rabbit. "Next to Mr. Hunger, the lion is mightiest of all."

"Mr. Hunger?" said the lion. "I've never met Mr. Hunger."

261

"Then you surely are a lucky lion," said the rabbit, shaking his head. "If you had met Mr. Hunger, you might not be here today."

The lion laughed. Since he had never really been hungry, he had no idea what the rabbit meant by the words *Mr. Hunger*. "Tell me," he said, "is this Mr. Hunger as large as an elephant?"

"Oh, far larger," replied the rabbit. "Mr. Hunger is so large, he can be in all places at once."

"And is he as strong as a rhinoceros?" asked the lion.

"Mr. Hunger has killed many a rhinoceros," replied the rabbit. "But no rhinoceros has ever killed Mr. Hunger."

The lion refused to be frightened. He roared a mighty roar and shook his head in anger. "Take me to Mr. Hunger," he ordered. "I will show him who is King of Beasts!"

The rabbit shook in his skin. His ears flopped down on his back as he looked up at the lion. In a tiny voice he explained that Mr. Hunger was hard to find. "But I'll find where he lives," the rabbit added. "I'll meet you here in a week, and take you to Mr. Hunger's house."

The lion agreed, and the rabbit bounced off through the bushes. The rabbit had many animals to see, and much to do in the week ahead.

A week later, the rabbit met the lion at the same place. The lion had a wild gleam in his eye. His white teeth looked sharper than ever. "I always go without food before a battle," he told the rabbit. "It makes me a better fighter."

The rabbit jumped onto the lion's head and gave directions to Mr. Hunger's house. Then the lion started off through the forest. "Mr. Hunger lives in a hole in the ground," the rabbit said. "The roof of his house is made of huge logs. The door is

262

a heavy flat stone. I had an elephant open the door, so you could go in and wait for Mr. Hunger."

"Thank you," said the lion. "But won't Mr. Hunger see that the stone has been moved? Won't he know something is wrong?"

"No," replied the rabbit. "After you go in, the elephant will put the stone back where it was."

"My friend, you have thought of everything," said the lion. "I cannot thank you enough."

Soon they came to Mr. Hunger's house. The rabbit jumped down from the lion's head. When the lion had disappeared into the hole, the elephant came to push the stone back in place. Then the rabbit raced away, taking high, happy hops. He could hardly wait to tell all the animals that had helped him build the trap.

The next day, a giraffe passed the trap where the lion was caught. Looking down between the logs, the giraffe saw the lion walking back and forth.

"Yoo hoo, Mr. Hunger," called the giraffe. "Are you at home?"

"No!" the lion roared. "I'm a lion. I'm waiting for Mr. Hunger to come."

"Well," said the giraffe, "tell Mr. Hunger I came to say hello."

Every day, a different animal came to say hello to Mr. Hunger. And every day, the lion replied that he was waiting for Mr. Hunger to come.

Two weeks later, the rabbit learned that the lion was lying down all the time. The mighty voice of the King of Beasts had become very weak. Only then did the rabbit return to the hole.

The rabbit came near the trap silently. He looked down between the logs. The lion lay on the floor without moving.

"Yoo hoo," called the rabbit. "Is anyone at home?"

But there was no answer.

Mr. Hunger had come at last.

Most people who heard Aruwimi's story liked the way the rabbit had tricked the lion. But these people did not understand what the tale was really about. For the point of the story was not that the rabbit had been clever. The point was that the rabbit had tricked an animal who trusted him as a friend.

KINTU AND THE
LAW OF LOVE

... in which we meet the greatest kind of
leader—a man who teaches people to lead
themselves.

Words We Need to Know:

domestic animals [*doe MES tic*]—tame animals; animals that live with man
Dogs, sheep, and horses are *domestic animals.*

foothills [*FOOT hills*]—hills between flat land and mountains
We passed through the *foothills* and into the mountains.

peaceful [*PEECE ful*]—full of peace; quiet
We all pray for a *peaceful* world.

perfect [*PUR fekt*]—as good as possible; with nothing wrong
One hundred is a *perfect* mark on most tests.

266

Not long ago, a woman from England visited the United States for the first time. She went to Washington, D.C. Then she saw New York City. Her last stop was Boston, where she bought a ticket to return to England.

People asked her why she was going home so soon. They reminded her that she had seen only a few cities on the East Coast. After coming all the way across the ocean, why didn't she visit the Middle West? Why didn't she see the Rocky Mountains, the Grand Canyon, and the Pacific Ocean?

At first the woman made excuses. She wanted to be polite to her American friends. Then the truth came out. "I'm traveling alone," the woman said. "And I must stay out of danger. Do you know, the very sight of a bear would scare me half to death!"

We Americans often laugh at the mistakes other peoples make about our country. Yet we make just as many mistakes about foreign lands. What, for instance, do we think of when we hear the word *Africa*? Most of us think of elephants, lions, and huge snakes. But the truth is that many Africans have never seen an elephant or a lion—unless they have visited the government parks, as we go to zoos.

We also make mistakes about the stories told by Africans. Many people don't know that some of the best myths and legends in the world come from Africa. Search the world over, and it would be hard to find a more beautiful legend than the one we are about to read. Its meaning is as old as the history of man, and as fresh as this morning's news.

KINTU AND THE LAW OF LOVE   In the beginning, when the world was first made, everything was perfect. Lying, cheating, and killing were unknown. It was a world without hate, without evil, and without war.

In this wonderful world of long ago, there lived a man

named Kintu. He was one of the first men to walk upon the earth. A holy man was Kintu, gentle, peaceful, and kind. And his heart was that of a little child.

With his wife, Kintu walked through Africa for many years. They were looking for a place to build a house and start a farm. Someday, they knew, they would settle down, raise children, and grow old together. But there was no hurry. Time would wait.

After many years of traveling, Kintu and his wife came to the shores of Lake Uganda. Here was a great valley, hidden from the world by a circle of snow-topped mountains. The soil was rich and black. Brooks bubbled down out of the foothills. Cool breezes blew across the lake.

"Here we will stay," said Kintu to his wife. "Here we have clear air and clean water. Here we have trees for houses and barns. Here the land will be good to us, and we will be good to the land."

Kintu and his wife had brought with them a cow, a sheep, a goat, a pig, a chicken, a sweet potato, and the root of a banana tree. Before long the sweet potato was a potato patch, and the banana root was a banana tree. The animals also grew in number. The one chicken became two, the two became four, and the four became eight.

Children were born to Kintu and his wife, and then grandchildren. These people started farms on the land around Lake Uganda. Before many years had passed, houses and barns dotted the green fields on both sides of Kintu's farm.

The valley was peaceful, and the people were happy. They spent their days working in the fields and woods. Often they looked at the circle of high mountains around them. The world outside the valley seemed strange and frightening. The people were glad to stay in the beautiful land which the good Kintu had found.

268

For many years, Kintu ruled the land of Uganda with wisdom and kindness. In truth, he had little ruling to do. His only law was the Law of Love. "My children," Kintu would tell his people, "if men really love one another, no other laws are needed."

And for a long time, no other laws *were* needed. The people of Uganda did not lie, steal, or kill. They were all children of Kintu. They were all brothers. If a farmer's barn burned down, his neighbors quickly built him a new one. If a man became too old to work, his sweet potatoes and bananas were gathered for him. If children were left without a home, they were taken in at once by another family.

When Kintu was a very old man, the farms that had been spreading around both sides of the lake finally met on the other side. Suddenly there was no more land in the valley. Young men could no longer start farms next to their fathers'. It was then that the trouble started.

Not all men could have farms of their own. There was not enough land. This meant that men were no longer equal. Some men were bosses. Others were workers. Some had too much of the good things of life. Others did not have enough.

The number of people in the valley grew larger every year. But the food supply stayed the same. Soon there was not enough food to go around. Some people had to go hungry.

When the stomach is empty, evil thoughts enter the mind. So it was with the people of Uganda. They started to steal from one another. In this way they learned they could get things without working. They became lazy. Soon no one wanted to work. Neighbor turned against neighbor. Sons rose up against their fathers. Blood covered the land.

But still Kintu made no laws. "If the people want to kill each other," he said, "they will do so, law or no law. The way to stop this killing is to stop people from wanting to kill."

So Kintu traveled through the land, talking about the Law of Love to all who would hear. But few people listened. The young people laughed at Kintu. They called him an old-fashioned fool.

Late one afternoon, Kintu was resting in front of his home. He sat looking out over the green valley where he had lived his life. Suddenly he heard the sound of marching feet. Soon there came the voices of many men. "Kintu! Kintu! Kintu!" they shouted as they came nearer. And then, from the woods near Kintu's house, came a large group of soldiers. Their shields and spears gleamed in the sunlight.

"Who are you?" Kintu asked, standing up. "What do you want?"

The leader of the men stepped forward. "We are your friends, good Kintu," he said. "We want to bring the Law of Love back to Uganda. We want to kill everyone who doesn't believe in love."

Kintu shook his head sadly. "You are as wicked as your enemies," he said.

"But we fight for a good reason!" cried the leader of the army. "We are on the side of love, Kintu. We fight in your name!"

"No man fights in my name," replied Kintu. Then he raised his voice and spoke to the whole army. "Men of Uganda, go home now. Lay down your spears, and the hate will leave your hearts."

But the soldiers were not allowed to hear more from Kintu. "The enemy is waiting!" shouted the leader. "In the name of Kintu, let us march to battle!"

The soldiers lined up and moved away like sheep. Soon Kintu heard the ugly sound of men at war.

Kintu called his wife. He told her they could stay in the valley no longer. "We will leave this wicked place," he said.

270

"We will stay away until stealing and killing have stopped. When the Law of Love returns to Uganda, Kintu will return with it."

Kintu told his wife to dig up a sweet potato and the root of a banana tree. Then he went to the barnyard, to get a cow, a sheep, a goat, a pig, and a chicken. They would take with them no more than they had brought.

And so, as night fell, the good Kintu and his wife walked slowly toward the mountains. Soon they had passed away, hand in hand, into the sunset, into the Great Unknown.

The next morning the news spread like fire. "Kintu has disappeared! Kintu and his wife cannot be found!"

At first the people were afraid. The armies stopped fighting. Everyone hunted for the missing Kintu. A few days earlier, Kintu had been an old man at whom people had laughed. Now he was quickly becoming a legend.

"Why did we let this happen!" the people cried. "It is our wicked ways that made Kintu leave his home. From now on, we will worship his name. We will live by his Law of Love."

The valley was searched, and searched again. But it became clearer with every passing day that Kintu would not be found. And something else also became clear. If Kintu were not to return, a new ruler would have to be found.

A dozen men wanted to rule in Kintu's place. Each said he would rule in Kintu's name. Each said Kintu had given him the job. And each had an army to prove he was telling the truth.

Again Uganda was at war with itself. In the name of Kintu, barns were burned to the ground. In the name of Kintu, men were killed in battle. In the name of Kintu, children were left to starve.

No one really won the war. The fighting ended only when

the country had worn itself out. By that time, only one of the twelve "rulers" was still alive. He became the king.

But there was little left for the king to rule. The valley was in ruins. Houses and barns had been burned. A few thin animals looked for food in weed-covered fields. The people were left without hope.

It was hard for the people to forget the past. It was even harder for them to face the future. But, little by little, the people began to rebuild the country. Children were born who had no past to forget. To them, the Law of Love seemed as real as the stories of war.

The years passed, and old kings gave way to new. The kings all said they ruled in the name of Kintu. But the Law of Love was forgotten. It was replaced with hundreds of other laws.

After many years, a person named Manda became king. As a prince, Manda had often thought about the great Kintu. Manda liked to climb into the foothills and look out over the valley. Sometimes he would pretend to be Kintu seeing the land of Uganda for the first time, many years before. Always he thought about the Law of Love, and wondered if it would really work.

When Manda became king, he decided to test the Law of Love. Every day he crossed a rule off the law books. In a year, all the laws were gone but one. This was the Law of Love.

A great change came over the country. People worked with a new spirit, and smiled with a new joy. Soon Manda's Uganda was as happy a land as Kintu's had been.

Like Kintu, King Manda had little ruling to do. He made it his habit to go often to the foothills. Only when he was far from the palace could he forget he was the great King Manda.

Manda's servants worried about his being alone in the foothills. They loved their master. They warned him about wild animals and falling rocks. But Manda refused to take anyone with him. His attendants did well to get him to carry a spear to protect himself.

But the servants still worried. Unknown to Manda, a servant followed him everywhere he went. The servant stayed far behind, hiding behind a bush or tree whenever the king turned around. The servants didn't like playing this trick on their beloved king. But to let Manda be alone would have been to forget the Law of Love.

One sunny morning, Manda awakened early and started across the fields toward the foothills. He used his spear as a walking stick. He waved to people working in the fields. The sun was warm, and Manda felt good.

Just as the sun became really hot, King Manda entered the forest that covered the foothills. Suddenly he stopped in surprise. His jaw dropped open. Ahead of him, he saw a circle of animals. A sheep, a pig, and other domestic animals sat quietly beside beasts of the forest. In the center of the circle were an old man and an old woman. A long white beard reached almost to the man's waist. He was talking to the animals. Manda was too far away to understand the words. But he could tell that the voice was deep and kind.

Could this old man be Kintu? Suddenly Manda was sure of it. This *was* Kintu!

Manda rushed forward. A lion moved aside to let him pass through the circle of animals. He dropped to his knees in front of the old man.

"My name is Manda," he cried. "I rule Uganda in the name of the good Kintu."

The old man reached out and took Manda's hand. "Rise,"

he said softly. "Do not kneel before me. Are you alone?"

"Yes," Manda replied, standing up. "I am alone."

"I am Kintu," said the old man. "I have heard that the Law of Love again rules Uganda. If this is true, I shall return."

Manda was too happy to speak.

"Do the people of Uganda still tell lies to each other?" Kintu asked.

"No," Manda told him. "It has been years since anyone told a lie."

"Do the people still kill each other?"

"Oh no! It has not happened in my lifetime."

"Then I shall return," Kintu said. "Long have I——"

Suddenly Kintu looked into the woods behind Manda. Then he looked Manda in the eye. "I thought you said you came alone," he said.

Manda looked surprised. "Why, I *am* alone," he told Kintu.

But Kintu still stared at him, and into the woods behind.

"I do not lie!" Manda cried. All at once he turned around, to see what Kintu was looking at.

One of Manda's servants was now standing up behind a low bush. He had been seen by Kintu, and he had come out of hiding. Manda didn't understand why the servant was there. He didn't try to understand. He knew only that Kintu thought he had told a lie. It was the servant's fault. Without thinking, Manda raised his arm and threw the spear.

The instant the spear left Manda's hand he knew what he had done. Both men stood like statues as the spear flew over the ground between them. Then, suddenly, Manda rushed forward.

But it was too late. The point of the spear had found the man's heart.

King Manda dropped to the ground beside his dying servant. He reached down and lifted the man's head. Soon it was over. The servant died with love in his eyes, and with a smile on his lips.

For a long time, Manda looked down at the servant who had loved him. Tears ran down the king's cheeks as he thought about what he had done. He had killed a man who had followed him because of love. He had killed him with a spear carried as an act of love. Now it was all Manda could do to turn around and face the great Kintu.

King Manda stood up slowly. He turned around—and stood still for a moment. Then he shut his eyes tight. When he opened them again, he knew the terrible truth.

Everything had disappeared—Kintu, his wife, the animals, everything! And Manda knew why. Now there was nothing to do but walk back down the hillside, to tell the people what had happened.

To this day, it is said, the great Kintu lives in the mountains. Somewhere in the Great Unknown, Kintu is waiting for evil to leave the hearts of men. There he will wait, the story goes, until we all learn to live by his one law—the Law of Love.

Don't miss the point:

GOSO, THE TEACHER   Much has happened since Kintu walked off into the mountains. Some people have gone on lying, cheating, and killing. But there have always been good people in the world, too. One of these, certainly, was a kind man named Goso. He earned his living by teaching children to read. His classes were held not in a schoolroom, but in the cool shade of a coconut tree.

Every afternoon, when his students had gone, Goso would sit down under the coconut tree. Then he would open a big book of his own and read until dark.

One evening, as Goso sat studying, along came Tanga, the monkey. Tanga climbed the tree to steal a coconut. He picked the largest, hardest, ripest coconut he could find. But, just as he was starting down the trunk, the coconut slipped. Down it fell. It hit Goso on the head.

The next morning, when the students arrived for their lessons, they found their teacher dead. There was a huge bump on his head, and a coconut lay at his right side.

"Someone will pay for this!" the students cried, for they had loved their master dearly. Who had killed Goso? The students talked the matter over. Finally they decided that Koosie, the south wind, had loosened the coconut that killed Goso.

So the students went to Koosie. "How could I have killed Goso?" the south wind asked. "I am not powerful enough to have killed your teacher. If I were so powerful, would I be stopped by someone like Baza, the mud wall?"

Next the students went to Baza, the mud wall. "How could I have killed Goso?" the mud wall asked. "If I were so powerful, would Panga, the rat, make holes in me?"

Next the students went to Panga, the rat. "How could I have killed Goso?" the rat asked. "If rats were so powerful, would Paka, the cat, eat them?"

Next the students went to Paka, the cat. "How could I have killed Goso?" the cat asked. "If I were so powerful, would Kamba, the rope, tie me?"

Next the students went to Kamba, the rope. "How could I have killed Goso?" the rope asked. "If I were so powerful, would Keeso, the knife, cut me?"

276

Next the students went to Keeso, the knife. "How could I have killed Goso?" the knife asked. "If I were so powerful, would Moto, the fire, burn me?"

Next the students went to Moto, the fire. "How could I have killed Goso?" the fire asked. "If I were so powerful, would Magee, the water, put me out?"

Next the students went to Magee, the water. "How could I have killed Goso?" the water asked. "If I were so powerful, would Eenzee, the fly, drink me?"

Next the students went to Eenzee, the fly. "How could I have killed Goso?" the fly asked. "If flies were so powerful, would Tanga, the monkey, eat them?"

Next the students went to Tanga, the monkey. Now, Tanga was very surprised when the students said he had killed their teacher. He thought they had come straight to him. He could think of no excuse. All he could say was, "Yes, I did it. But how did you find out?"

"It was easy," the students replied. "You eat flies, like Eenzee; that drinks Magee, the water; that puts out Moto, the fire; that burns Keeso, the knife; that cuts Kamba, the rope; that ties Paka, the cat; that eats rats, like Panga; that make holes in Baza, the mud wall; that stops Koosie, the south wind; that loosened the coconut that killed our teacher. Tanga, you should never have done it!"

Tanga, the guilty monkey, was too surprised to speak. The students had *not* come straight to him. They had no proof at all. But he had already told them he had killed their teacher. Now he had not a word to say for himself. He was arrested at once and given a fair trial. Soon he had paid with his life for the killing of Goso, the teacher.

FROM
The Americas

We Americans are lucky when it comes to old stories. We have two distinct kinds of tales. First, of course, we have the myths and legends of the Indians. Then, too, we have the legends and folk tales of the pioneer. The stories in this section are of both kinds. They are the stories of one of the world's youngest nations—our nation, America.

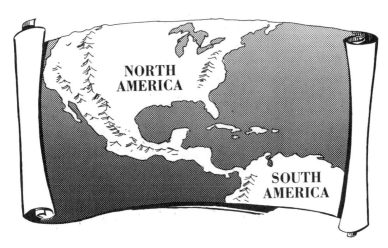

THE DAUGHTER
OF THE STARS

. . . in which a young Indian pays a visit to
the stars.

Words We Need to Know:

lean   [*LEEN*]—thin, having muscles instead of fat
       Bob was brown and *lean* when he returned from camp.
prairie [*PRAIR ee*]—a very large, flat piece of ground covered
       with grass
       Buffalo once lived on the *prairie*.
soar   [*SOR*]—to float through the air
       The eagle *soared* across the sky.
stump [*STUMP*]—the lower part of a tree after the top falls
       or is cut off
       Many ugly *stumps* were left after the storm blew down
       the trees.
wallow [*WAHL o*]—a place where animals roll or lie on the
       ground
       The pigs had a *wallow* in the shade north of the barn.

282

The pages of this book have carried us to many far-away places. We have visited the underworld, the sun, and the moon. We have been to the far ends of the earth. By this time, we have traveled almost all the way around the world. Now we are nearing the end of the road. We have at last come home.

We will start with the tales of the first Americans. The Indians were great storytellers. Like other peoples, they made up myths to explain things they couldn't understand. They believed that thunder was made by a Thunderbird flapping its huge wings. Lightning flashed from the tips of arrows shot by people who lived on the stars. Over all things ruled the Great Spirit, or Father Sky, and his wife, Mother Earth. These stories were being told long before Columbus discovered the New World.

Remember, these stories were written by, for, and about *real* Indians. We will meet neither "story-book Indians" nor "television Indians." The Indians in these tales never heard of books or television. But this didn't stop their lively minds. Hang on, now, for an Indian's trip to the stars!

THE DAUGHTER OF THE STARS

White Eagle was a young Indian brave. This was not his real name. We will learn the reason for this name later on.

Almost every day, White Eagle went to hunt on the prairie. With his bow and arrow, he would walk from his home in the woods out onto the grasslands. He liked to be alone. He liked to be the tallest thing for miles and miles around. He liked to be able to see as far as an eagle could fly.

One day, as he hunted by himself on the prairie, White Eagle came upon a strange sight. The grass in a circle, about ten steps across, had been beaten down. At first he thought the circle was the start of a buffalo wallow. But no tracks

283

led to it except his own. What, then, could have beaten down the grass?

White Eagle decided to find out. He moved off a few steps, and sat down to wait.

The day passed slowly. But White Eagle did not give up. He could wait for hours, like an animal. If he had to, he would wait all night. He knew there would be a full moon.

Just as the sun was setting, the evening star came out. At first it looked like a dot low in the sky. Then it began to grow larger. It became brighter than any star White Eagle had ever seen. Suddenly it seemed to shake itself loose from the heavens. It soared across the sky like a very large shooting star.

As White Eagle watched, the star changed direction and came speeding toward the earth. It seemed to be heading right for the prairie, right for the strange circle near White Eagle!

"Can it be?" White Eagle asked himself. "Is it this star that has beaten down the grass?"

White Eagle was frightened. He lay flat on the ground and tried to pull the high grass over him. There was a strange light in the sky now, but he dared not look. He closed his eyes tight and pushed his face against the ground. The soil smelled cool and damp. He felt his heart beating against the earth and knew, suddenly, how much he loved it. He had no idea what would happen if the star landed in the grassy circle. But he had the feeling that he would not remain alive.

A strange sort of music started to come through the air. It came from no one place, but seemed to fill the whole sky. It sounded something like the wind blowing across the prairie. But it was not the wind, White Eagle was sure of that. It was *music*.

Though he didn't know why, the music pleased White Eagle. He began to feel less afraid. He raised his head and

284

looked around. It was almost as light as day. He looked up in the sky, toward the star.

But it was *not* a star! It was a huge basket, shining brightly and coming closer every minute. It swung back and forth, as though hanging by a rope he couldn't see.

Soon the basket was very near the earth. White Eagle could tell there was something inside it. Then he saw what it was. He could hardly believe his eyes. The basket was full of lovely maidens!

Moving very slowly now, the basket neared the ground. It landed softly on the prairie, and twelve smiling maidens jumped out onto the grass. White Eagle had never seen creatures so beautiful. They had long, golden hair. They smiled with their eyes as well as their lips. Their white gowns seemed to be made of moonbeams.

The maidens joined hands and danced around the basket. White Eagle could stay hidden no longer. He jumped up and ran toward the happy group.

Suddenly he saw her, not three steps away. He stopped in his tracks. The youngest-looking of the maidens was the most beautiful creature he had ever seen. Without thinking, he jumped forward, toward the maiden.

But she was too quick for him. With the others, she leaped back into the basket. Into the sky the maidens sailed, taking the light and the music with them. White Eagle was left alone.

"Alas," White Eagle said to himself. "I shall see them no more."

It took a few minutes for his eyes to get used to the moonlight. Then he started the long walk home. It was to be many hours before he would fall asleep and dream of the heavenly maidens.

The next morning White Eagle was up early. He wanted

to tell everyone in the village about the creatures from the stars. But people laughed at him instead of listening. Even his own family would not believe the story. "You spend too much time alone," his father said. "You dream up these wild tales. The hot sun does strange things to your head."

The chief of the village was old and wise. White Eagle had never talked to him alone. But now he had to. He had to ask the chief before he could marry a girl from outside the village. And White Eagle wanted very much to marry the youngest star maiden—if he could catch her.

"Yes," said the chief, when he had heard White Eagle's story. "You can marry your girl from the stars. But you will never be happy."

"Never be happy!" repeated White Eagle. "Why not?" He felt that he could never be happy *without* his star maiden.

"The people of the stars belong on the stars," replied the chief. "And the people of the earth belong on the earth. This is the way the Great Spirit wants it."

But White Eagle was already making plans to catch the star maiden. After he left the chief, he found a hollow stump in the woods. He put the stump on his shoulder and started across the prairie.

The stump was heavy. It took all day for White Eagle to carry it to the magic circle. The sun was almost down when he got there. He lost no time in climbing inside the stump, to wait for the maidens. The hollow space was just large enough to hold his lean body.

He did not need to wait long. Soon he heard the strange music. Then the heavenly light started to shine through the mouse holes in the stump. He twisted himself around to look through one of the holes.

The basket had already landed! The twelve star maidens

were now dancing around it. He looked for the youngest one, the prettiest. Yes, she was there!

This time White Eagle knew he had to stay hidden. He watched the star maidens. Their dance grew slower and slower, until it was almost a walk. Then they started to sing. White Eagle had never heard such lovely songs. They were singing the songs of the stars.

"Look!" one of the maidens cried suddenly. "That stump —has it always been there?"

The others stood still, looking at the stump without speaking.

"Come, sisters," said the maiden. "It's time to return to the stars. I don't like that stump. How did it get there? No trees grow here on the prairie."

But the others wanted to find out about the stump. They left their suspicious sister in the basket and came toward White Eagle. First they walked in a large circle around him. Then they moved closer. Soon their faces were not a step away from White Eagle's.

"See, the stump is full of mouse holes," said the youngest maiden. "Let's try to push it over. I want to see the mice come running out."

The others agreed. Soon White Eagle felt the stump rocking back and forth—once, twice, three times. Then *crash*, it fell over. It split open. White Eagle found himself lying on the ground, looking up into the faces of eleven surprised star maidens.

No one moved for a moment. Then White Eagle jumped to his feet.

"To the basket!" the maidens screamed. "Run! Run for your lives!"

The star maidens raced across the prairie grass. They

dived headlong over the side of the basket. White Eagle ran after them. He took a flying leap toward the youngest. He caught her by the arm just as she jumped. She landed half in and half out of the basket.

The basket started to rise. White Eagle's fingers were locked around the hand of the star maiden. He would not let go. Either she would be pulled back to earth, or he would be lifted to the stars. To White Eagle, it mattered not which happened. The important thing was that he and his star maiden stay together.

Suddenly the maiden tumbled out of the basket. She fell into White Eagle's arms. For an instant they held tight to each other, like two people caught between heaven and earth. She looked sad, but not frightened, as she waved good-by to her sisters. Then she looked up into White Eagle's eyes.

"I am a daughter of the stars," she said. "I do not belong here on earth."

"But will you stay?" asked White Eagle eagerly. "The minute I saw you, I knew you were meant to be my bride."

The daughter of the stars and White Eagle sat down together on the prairie grass. They watched the setting of the evening star. Then they talked for a long, long time. At last the star maiden said she would marry White Eagle. Hand in hand, they walked through the moonlight to the Indian village.

For a time, White Eagle was the happiest of hunters. The seasons passed quickly. Summer sped by, then fall, then winter. In the spring, a child was born to the star maiden. It was a boy. From the day of his birth, the baby had the strong, lean body of his father and the smiling eyes of his mother. He was the pride of his parents.

The star maiden loved White Eagle dearly. But she

288

couldn't forget that she was a daughter of the stars. As time passed, she thought more and more of her home in the heavens. She said nothing about this to White Eagle. Telling him would not change things, she thought. It would only bring sadness to the man she loved. But every day, while her husband hunted on the prairie, she worked on a basket. Soon it was large enough to hold herself and her son. When it was finished, she hid it in the woods. She would wait until the boy was old enough to walk.

Late one afternoon, White Eagle was returning from the prairie. As he neared the forest, he turned to look behind him. The huge red sun was just going down. It seemed to rest on the far edge of the earth.

Suddenly something came between White Eagle and the sun. It was a woman. She carried something big on her back. And there was something moving in the tall grass behind her—the head and shoulders of a small boy!

At once White Eagle knew what was happening. He raced across the prairie.

But it was too late. The star maiden had already reached the magic circle. As he ran, White Eagle could see her seated in the basket. The child was in her arms. All at once he heard the music. The basket began to glow. It rose slowly from the earth and seemed to swing back and forth a moment. Then it soared into the sky, just as White Eagle fell to the ground in the middle of the magic circle.

For many moons, White Eagle was the saddest of men. He spoke to no one, and he ate almost nothing. He spent his days seated in the magic circle. Most of all, he wished for his son. His wife, after all, was a daughter of the stars. But his boy was an Indian. He belonged on earth.

Unknown to White Eagle, his son felt the same way.

In his new home on the stars, the boy spoke more and more about his father. He could not forget the earth. Finally the star king, his grandfather, decided to send the boy and his mother back to the prairie. They were not to stay. But White Eagle was to be given the chance to return with them.

White Eagle did decide to return with them. A few days later, he climbed into the basket for a trip to the stars with his son and wife. He felt a sinking feeling in his stomach as he soared into the sky. Soon he could see all of North America. Then he saw the big blue oceans on both sides. From high in the heavens, the earth looked round. It was hard to believe his eyes.

White Eagle found that the kingdom of the stars was much like the earth. But it was *not* the earth. Once the star maiden had wished for the sight of her home. Now it was White Eagle who was homesick. As beautiful as the star kingdom was, it could never take the place of his prairie. Finally he could spend not another day in the land of the star people. He took his son by the hand and went to the star king. They were Indians, White Eagle told the star king. They would give anything if only they could return to the prairie.

The star king gave his permission. But they were not allowed to return to earth as men. The star king didn't want people on earth to hear about life in the heavens. He told the two human beings that he would change them into any creatures they wished to become. They could return to earth as anything but men.

That same evening, as the sun was going down, two white eagles appeared in the sky above the prairie. They winged their way in lazy circles over the land they loved. Some people say that they can still be seen at sunset, soaring high against the golden clouds.

A cold story that warms the heart:

THE BLUE MAN OF THE NORTH   Most stories, like "The Daughter of the Stars," are supposed to have happened only once. But here is a story that could have happened over and over again. It might even be happening now!

One evening long ago, an old man was sitting alone on the bank of a frozen stream. The old man's fire was almost out. His thin fingers shook over the low flames. His face was blue with cold. It had been a long, lonely winter for the old man. His only company had been the wind and the falling snow.

As he sat watching his fire go out, the old man heard footsteps coming near him. He looked up from the fire. Walking toward him along the bank of the stream was a cheerful, strong-looking youth with a bunch of flowers in his hand. The young stranger's eyes shone with life, and a smile was on his lips.

"Ah, my son," said the old man, "I see by your flowers that spring has come to the South. I am called the Blue Man of the North, and I have been waiting all winter."

"Waiting?" asked the young man. He did not understand.

"Yes, waiting," replied the Blue Man, looking off into the purple hills. "But never mind that. Sit down. Tell me your adventures, for you must have traveled through many strange lands. We will tell each other stories. In this way, we will pass the cold hours until morning."

The young man agreed, for the sun was already gone from the western sky. He sat down on a stone and watched the Blue Man take out a strange old pipe. A snowbird's head was carved on the bowl, and the stem was more than a foot long. The old man filled the pipe with tobacco and lighted it with a coal from the fire. When this was done, he began to speak.

"I am an old, old man," he said slowly. "And I am not what I used to be. Just a few months ago, I could blow my breath, and the brooks would stop bubbling and stand still. I could make water turn as hard as stone."

"That is strange," replied the youthful stranger. "For *my* breath does just the opposite. When I breathe, the ice in the brooks changes to water, and flowers bloom along the banks."

"In the past," the Blue Man went on, "leaves fell from the trees when I frowned. When I shook my head of white hair, snow covered the ground. Animals hid from me, and birds flew to far-off lands when they saw me coming."

"Again, we seem to be opposites!" said the youth. "Instead of frowning, I smile. And when I do, the trees turn green. A shake of my head brings warm rain to the land. Animals come out of the holes where they have spent the winter. And the birds! Why, their music fills the trees wherever I go."

The two men went on talking until the first light of the sun. A warm breeze came with the dawn, for this was to be the first day of spring.

The old man was silent now. But the air was filled with the sounds of spring. Robins and bluebirds cried for the young man to look at them. The ice in the stream cracked and melted, uncovering the water that had been waiting all winter.

When the sun rose, the youth stood up and stretched. Then he looked down at his friend. He stepped back in surprise. In the light of day, the Blue Man seemed too old to be alive. His face looked dried up, like an apple that has been kept all winter. Indeed, his whole body seemed to have become smaller.

Suddenly the young traveler knew who the Blue Man was. His friend of the night was none other than the Spirit of Winter.

As the day became warmer, the old Spirit of Winter became smaller, and smaller, and smaller. Before the sun was high in the sky, the Blue Man of the North had disappeared. Nothing remained in his place but a small white flower with a pink edge, which was soon picked and placed behind the ear of the smiling Spirit of Spring.

THE SHEEP OF
SAN CRISTOBAL

. . . in which a person learns what she can receive by giving things away.

WORDS WE NEED TO KNOW

coyote [*ky* O *tee*] a wolflike animal of north America
        A coyote killed and ate the little lamb.

ewe [YOO] a female sheep
        The *ewe* tried to protect her little lamb.

inherit [*in* HEH *rit*] to receive money or property when a relative dies
        Someday Carl will *inherit* his parents' farm.

mesa [MAY *suh*] a flat-topped hill with steep, rocky sides
        The sides of a *mesa* often go straight down.

padre [PAH *dray*] Spanish for *father* or *priest*
        The old *padre* walked to his church early every morning.

penance [PEN *ance*] punishment accepted to make up for some evil act
        The padre thought I should do some kind of *penance* for my sin.

San [*san*] A Spanish title meaning *Saint* (*St.*)
        Columbus named the whole island *San Juan Bautista de Puerto Rico*, or "St. John The Baptist of the Rich Port."

shrine [SHRINE] a place (or object) made for the worship of a saint or other holy person
        In Boston we visited the *shrine* of St. Anthony.

STORY INTRODUCTION

This section of the book is called "From The Americas." Its first story, "The Daughter of the Stars," is about Indians. This is just as it should be. The Indians, after all, were the first Americans.

But who were the first settlers from Europe? The English people who came to Virginia in 1607? The Pilgrims? The Puritans? Certainly not. Soon after Columbus's voyage in 1492, people from Spain started to come to the New World. First they settled in Puerto Rico, Cuba, and nearby islands. Then they entered South and Central America. Finally they pushed up through Mexico into what is now the United States.

"The Sheep of San Cristóbal" comes from New Mexico. But remember that at the time of the story New Mexico was not a state. It did not even belong to the United States. It was really the northern part of Mexico, and it belonged to the king of Spain.

THE SHEEP OF SAN CRISTÓBAL   "No! No!" screamed Felipa. "Not Carlos. Not my Carlos! It cannot be!"

The young woman stood in the doorway of her little two-room house. Before her, on the dirt floor, lay the body of her husband. He had been killed by Ute Indians. The dust raised by their horses still hung in the air.

In tears, Felipa sank to her knees. She covered her face with her hands. Why hadn't she been home? Why had she picked that hour—that minute even—to go for water? Together, she and Carlos might have... And where was Manuel?

"Manuel!" she cried. Jumping to her feet, she dashed outside to look for her seven-year-old son. Her nearest neighbors were coming on the run, and behind them, the village priest. Surprisingly, no one had seen the quick Ute raid. They searched the small field next to the house for the boy. Before long everyone guessed the truth. He had been carried off by the Indians. That was the same as death.

The priest held Felipa's sobbing face in his old brown hands. "Come," he said. "Come, Felipa Sandoval. Come to the shrine of Our Lady of Light. And may the Lord have mercy."

Felipa followed the old man to the church. Prayer did not cure the ache in her heart. But it helped her decide to go on living. To go on living, she decided to take over the little farm herself. She decided to plant all the squash and hoe all the beans and pick all the corn. There was no other way that she wanted.

In the days that followed, deep sorrow never left Felipa. She could not forget the Indian raid. But little by little, she learned to take care of the farm. She had always been very religious, and now she spent at least an hour a day on her knees at the shrine. The rest of the time she worked in her field— digging, planting, hoeing, picking. Sometimes she carried a basket of vegetables to the center of Las Colonias to sell. The people of the little town had always liked Felipa, and now they were proud of her. They would buy from her first. Men who cut firewood often dropped off a few pieces by her doorstep. Other people did other little favors. Felipa always thanked them.

There was one man, however, whose favors Felipa did not want. This was Don José Vigil. From his father, Don José had inherited a great many sheep. People said he was the richest man in town, but people also knew that he never gave anything to the poor. It was not Don José's habit to help anyone but himself. Felipa knew the reason for his favors. He was a young man without a wife, and she was a young woman without a husband.

298

At night Don José kept his sheep in a pen beside his house in town. In the daytime he took them to the top of a huge mesa to eat grass. Twice a day, Don José had to pass Felipa's house with his sheep. Felipa would groan when she saw them coming up the dirt road. Leading the way would be Sancho, Don José's big dog. Then would come the sheep, and finally Don José himself. Always he would smile and stop to talk.

Felipa did nothing to lead Don José on. But he would not be stopped. If she would not talk, he would talk for both of them. If she refused a present, he would leave it on the ground. If she hid in the house, he would open the door and walk in. Only if she locked the door would Don José leave her alone. Locking the door was the only way Felipa could think of to avoid Don José and his silly talk of marriage.

Soon Felipa found herself locking the door twice a day. And to her surprise, she sometimes found herself thinking evil thoughts. "If only Don José would fall off the mesa and break his neck!" she would think. Then she would sign and pray to Our Lady for forgiveness.

Before long, however, Don José found a way to get Felipa out of her house. He changed places with Sancho, the big brown dog. Instead of having Sancho lead the sheep, he led them himself. When he got to Felipa's house, he stopped. For a few minutes the sheep stood still on the road. Then, left to themselves, they went into Felipa's field. They began to eat her half-grown bean plants. Felipa had no choice. She came tearing out of the house, shouting and waving her arms at the sheep. Don José stood in the road and laughed.

The same thing happened every morning for a week. What was Don José trying to do? Was he trying to punish her for not liking him? Was he trying to force her to marry him? Without the beans to sell, Felipa would soon have no money. Then what would she do? What *could* she do?

One morning Don José's sheep arrived very early. Felipa woke up to hear them in the field. She looked out the window. They were eating the last of the beans.

Wild with anger, Felipa shot out of the house. First she screamed at the sheep. But what was the use? Her beans had already disappeared. Then she screamed at Don José:

"You are a bad man, Don José Vigil! A bad man! May San Cristóbal throw you off the mesa today! May he break your neck! May you—"

Bursting into tears, Felipa ran back into the house. The door slammed behind her. She didn't watch as Don José shook his head, laughed once, and followed the last of his sheep toward the mesa. The peaceful Sancho was already way ahead.

Three hours later, the body of Don José Vigil was carried past Felipa's house. He had slipped on the narrow path up the side of the mesa. He had fallen and broken his neck.

The news made Felipa feel dead herself. Her anger turned inward. She was sure she had caused Don José's death. All day long she prayed to Nuestra Señora de los Dolores, Our Lady of Sorrows. She could eat nothing. And that night she could not sleep. She kept seeing the eyes of Don José as he fell to his death. They seemed to look right at her, and they made her feel very guilty.

Early the next morning, Felipa hurried to the church. There was only one thing to do. She would have to ask for penance, for some kind of punishment that she thought would make up for her evil words.

"Padre," Felipa cried to the priest. "I am guilty of the death of Don José Vigil." Then she sobbingly told the whole story.

"No," the priest finally said, "you did not cause Don José to die. San Cristóbal would not do such a thing. He would never listen to a wicked prayer made by an angry woman."

300

The old priest looked into Felipa's big brown eyes and went on: "But yes, you *are* guilty. You are guilty of a very wicked prayer. And for that evil act, you must do penance."

"Yes," said Felipa, "I know. Without the penance, I am afraid the rest of my life would be empty."

"Here is what you must do," the priest told her. "You must do penance for Don José, too. You see, he was in some ways an evil man. He never gave to the poor. But no man is all evil. Right now, Don José would want to do good. That is why your penance must be for him also."

Felipa listened as the priest went on. First she was to go to the mesa and gather Don José's sheep together. Then she was to drive them all over New Mexico, to every village. Everywhere she went, she was to search for very poor people in real need. To each of these people she was to give a single sheep. Felipa was to give the sheep away in the name of Don José, with the blessing of San Cristóbal. She was to beg for bread, and eat nothing else. She was to carry only a cup, and use it only for sheep milk.

"If anyone asks you," the priest finished, "say that the sheep are the sheep of San Cristóbal. Have faith, my daughter. San Cristóbal will guide you. Pray often. And at the end, he will give you a sign. You will know that your penance is over, and that you are free of your sin."

Felipa did as she'd been told. First she went to her house to get a cup. Should she change her clothes? No, she decided. She'd keep on what she'd worn to the church, a simple black robe with a hood. Then she headed for the mesa. Her whole body shook as she walked up the path where Don José had fallen.

On the mesa's flat top, she found the sheep in a group. The faithful Sancho had kept them together during the night.

Sancho barked with joy when he saw Felipa coming. He ran

up and pressed his short brown nose against her leg. There on the ground, Felipa saw the bones of three lambs. She knew that coyotes must have taken them during the night.

"You are a good, good dog, Sancho." Felipa scratched the big brown head by her knee. "But you could not do the whole job, could you? Now you have me to help you. And I have you to help me."

Felipa milked one of the sheep. She held the cup of milk out to Sancho. He lapped it up quickly. Then they drove the sheep off the mesa. With Sancho leading, they headed for town. Felipa passed her house, wondering when she'd ever see it again. A few minutes later they came to the house of Don José. Sancho started to drive the sheep into the pen, as he had always done. Felipa ran up and headed the sheep back onto the road. She pulled the gate shut and urged the sheep on by. Sancho stood next to the pen, his head tipped to one side.

Now the sheep were almost to the center of Las Colonias. Felipa looked back at the pen. Sancho was still standing there, watching her.

"Come, Sancho!" Felipa called. "Come! Come!" She clapped her hands together.

For a moment Sancho didn't move. Then all at once he seemed to make up his mind. He rushed toward Felipa, passed her, and took his place far up front.

The sheep moved through Las Colonias and headed out of town. Felipa tried to count them. Because they were moving and close together, it wasn't an easy job. The first time she counted 172. The second time she got 167. Then she noticed that a large black ewe had dropped back to walk at her side. An hour later, the ewe was still there. Felipa looked at her carefully. "I think this sheep wants to be milked," she told herself. "She must be one of the ewes who lost their lambs to the coyotes."

Coming to a grassy spot, Felipa decided it was time to rest.

As the other sheep ate grass, Felipa milked the large black ewe. She drank the first cup of warm milk herself. The second she gave to Sancho. The ewe then wandered off to eat. But as soon as they started down the dusty road again, she came back to Felipa's side.

"You are a good friend, black ewe," Felipa said aloud. "Do you know that I too have lost a child? Can you tell that I share your sadness? Is that why you stay here next to me?"

Before the sun set that day, the black ewe had a name: Negrita. In the evening Felipa milked her again, and again the ewe moved away to eat. But as it got dark, Negrita came back to Felipa and lay down. Felipa lay down too, using Negrita's soft side as a pillow. She knew that Sancho would stay half awake and watch the sheep.

Soon Felipa was sound asleep. Later she dreamed of Don José's face—smiling at her.

Early the next morning the journey continued, with Negrita still at Felipa's side. About noon they got to the first town, San José. Felipa was surprised to find that everyone was waiting for her. The news of her penance had traveled on ahead. Many people offered her bread, more than she could have eaten in a week. She asked and asked, but she could find no one poor enough to be given a sheep.

The same thing happened in the next village, except that there Felipa gave away her first sheep. Everywhere she went, she found that people had heard of her. On the third day her shoes wore out, and at first the dry desert sand hurt her feet. But she kept going. She traveled down the Rio Grande valley, where she found many poor people. Once she discovered a wrinkled old Indian woman who was starving in a mud hut. "In the name of Don José, and with the blessing of San Cristóbal, I give you this large sheep," She knew without asking that the woman was a Ute.

The days turned into weeks, and the weeks turned into

months. Felipa walked through Santa Cruz, up to Chimayo, over to Nambé, and down to Pogoáqua. Nearly every day, she gave away a sheep. The number of sheep grew smaller and smaller. She went past Cuymunque and Tesúque, then over the hills to Santa Fe. Finally there were only a few sheep left. There was no need for Sancho to lead them. He now walked on one side of Felipa, with Negrita on the other.

In Albuquerque, Felipa gave away her next to last sheep. Only Negrita was left. The next town, Felipa knew was La Bajada, and for the first time she didn't want to go on. She prayed that there would be no one in La Bajada poor enough for a sheep. But she knew that if she found the right person, even Negrita would have to go.

Negrita did have to go. Felipa offered her to a thin old man who lay on a mat in the shade of a tree. He was almost too weak to stand up.

"Goodbye, Negrita," Felipa said. "You have been a good friend." As the old man took hold of Negrita, Felipa got down on her knees. She buried her face in Negrita's soft neck. Suddenly she felt tears come to her eyes. She stood up quickly and turned to leave. But all at once, there was Negrita at her side again. The old man had not been strong enough to hold her.

"No, Negrita!" Felipa said. Now the tears were on her cheeks. "You must stay here!" She found a piece of rope and tied Negrita to the tree. But when she again started to leave, a strange thing happened. Sancho stayed behind. He growled at the old man. Then he growled at Negrita. Suddenly he started to bark. He ran at Negrita, sinking his sharp teeth into one of her back legs. The rope broke, and in an instant both animals were back at Felipa's side.

Ashamed of her feelings, Felipa walked on in silence. She could not force herself to take Negrita back to the old man again. But how long, really, could she keep Negrita? The next village was Socorro, which at the time was the last town in lower New Mexico. Surely, someone there would be poor enough to deserve the last of San Cristóbal's sheep.

Felipa entered Socorro with a heavy heart. As usual, the people already knew she was on her way. They offered her bread and answered her questions. No, they said, there was really no one poor enough to get a sheep. Felipa didn't feel quite sure. She then looked into every house. She held her breath at every doorway, but she found no one that deserved to get Negrita.

Beyond the town, on the edge of the desert, was one last house. It was a hut, really, made of mud block, poles, and animal skins. Felipa, with Negrita and Sancho by her side, approached it slowly. A tall man now stood at the doorway. His face was the color of the sun-baked desert sand. His wide-brimmed hat was filled with holes. His clothes were rags.

"In the name of Don José, and with the blessing of San Cristóbal—" Felipa began.

"Ah!" cut in the man. "So you are Felipa Sandoval!"

Felipa nodded. She watched the man smile at her suddenly.

"No," he began, shaking his head slowly. "You will not give your last sheep to me. I am getting old, but I can still work. I am not as poor as I look."

Felipa's heart rose—then fell again as the man went on:

"You should give your sheep to the child in my hut. He seems to be really in need. Only yesterday I traded a piece of cheap jewelry for him. I got him from some Navajo Indians, who told me they got him from the Utes."

Felipa went into the hut. There in the shadows, dressed in Indian clothing, stood her son Manuel.

Feeling her head swimming, Felipa fell to her knees. Was it

true? Had Manuel been kept alive by the Utes? Had he not been carried off and killed?

The boy ran toward her arms, and Felipa knew it was true.

This was her son. She had not held him close to her in a little more than a year.

Waiting outside the hut, Sancho barked twice. Felipa pulled the boy toward the door. Negrita came up and rubbed her leg as Felipa stood blinking in the bright sunlight. Where was the man? She walked around the hut. Had he simply vanished?

Felipa hurried back to the center of Socorro. She asked about the tall stranger. She described him clearly. But the people in town had never seen such a man. The hut, they said, had been built years before for goats. No one had ever lived in it. Now even the goats had given it up.

Suddenly Felipa stopped listening. She knew in her heart who the man had been. She knew that San Cristóbal himself had delivered her little boy to her. And she knew too, as the cloud of her guilt left her, that her penance was over.

For many years, people in New Mexico talked about Felipa Sandoval. They remembered her long walk with the sheep to Socorro. And they remembered even better her journey back home. No one ever forgot the woman with the smiling eyes, the little boy, the brown dog, and the black ewe.

Back in Las Colonias, Felipa found only happiness. Her neighbors had cared for her field, and beans were ready to be picked. And of course everyone in the village, especially the padre, wondered greatly at her story.

(Adapted from *The Native Tales of New Mexico* by Frank G. Applegate. Copyright 1932 by J. B. Lippincott Company. Copyright © renewed 1960 by Frank G. Applegate. Reprinted by permission of J. B. Lippincott Company.)

A PUERTO RICAN ROMANCE

LOVE STORY—NUMERO UNO On the island of Puerto Rico, about eight miles from the city of Ponce, lies a peaceful pond in a small valley. By day it keeps the secrets of birds, fish, and frogs. By night it shares the secrets of the moon—the same moon that two young lovers saw mirrored on its surface nearly 500 years ago. Some people say that the time to visit the pool is at nightfall. Then—if you're lucky!—you can still see the shadows of the two young people sitting side by side on the bank.

Today their names have been long forgotten. We call them simply "the Boriqueno girl" and "the Spanish soldier." No one knows exactly what they looked like. No one knows the language they used to whisper in each other's ears. But perhaps true love needs no language. And true love it certainly was!

We know just enough to piece the story together. The girl must have been born about 1492, the year of Columbus's first voyage. At that time Puerto Rico was called *Borinquen*, its Indian name. The girl's father was a Boriqueno chief. Like most Boriquenos, he had at first welcomed the Spanish soldiers who followed Columbus. He had thought of the Spanish as gods from the heavens, and he had called the sails of their boats *wings*. But now he had changed his mind. His love for the Spanish had turned to hate. And for his daughter to be seen with a Spanish soldier? That was just too much!

"I am a chief," we can imagine him telling her. "And you are a chief's daughter. You will marry a young Boriqueno chief, not a Spanish soldier. The Spanish make fun of our gods. They break up families. They make slaves of our people."

"*They*? Who is *they*? Not my—"

"Your soldier is Spanish, is he not?"

"Yes, but—"

"The Spanish are devils, I say! With my own eyes, I have seen them kill our people. What about the Boriquenos they catch and send away to their mines and farms? You think they feed their slaves? No. It is cheaper to let them starve, and then catch new ones."

"But why can't—"

"No, no, no! You will not marry your Spanish soldier. You will not talk to your Spanish soldier. You will not even *see* your Spanish soldier!"

But see each other they did. The girl knew the perfect meeting place. It was next to a beautiful pond where she often went to swim. On one side of the pond, deep under water, was a hole that led up into a hillside cave. At the smallest noise in the bushes around the pond, she'd just slip into the water. Soon she'd be safely in the cave. where she could stay for hours.

The Boriqueno chief thought he knew what was going on. He often sent a spy to the pool. But no one could catch the two lovers together. The spy would find only the Spanish soldier, dressed in armor and carrying a sword and spear.

The meetings went on. Today we can only guess what they talked about. But she must have told him some beliefs of the Boriqueno people:

How, years before, the land had been cold and dark. Then the sun and moon had first appeared. They had come from a hole in the roof of a cave. After that, men had come from another cave. Big men had come out through a big opening, little men through another smaller opening. At first there were only men. Women lived in the trees, and were very slippery. Finally some tall men with strong hands managed to pull the women down from the branches.

How, when people died, they turned into ghosts. By day, it was hard for the living to see these ghosts. But at night, the ghosts took over the earth. Their shadows were seen everywhere. In the dark, you often couldn't tell the ghosts from living people. To tell them apart, you had to feel them. The ghosts had no navels. That was the only difference.

How, in ages past, Boriquen and the other islands had been the tops of high mountains. There were no oceans, and all people lived on a plain far below. A man named Giaia learned that his son was planning to kill him. So instead, Giaia killed his son. He and his wife placed their son's bones in a dried gourd (a plant like a pumpkin). Much later, they opened the gourd to look at the bones. Some fish jumped out! Giaia and his wife ate the fish. They thought they had a magic supply of food forever. They hid the gourd up under the roof of their house. But four brothers who lived nearby heard about it. One day when Giaia and his wife were absent, they entered the house. They found the magic gourd. Passing it around, they dropped it. It cracked—and water started to pour out! It kept on coming! The brothers fled from the house in ankle-deep water. Before long the water was knee deep. Everyone who could run was heading toward higher land. The water rose until only the tops of the mountains were left.

We can only suppose that the Spanish soldier liked stories such as these. For the romance went on—until one terrible day. One morning a spy sent by the Boriqueno chief came rushing back with big news.

"The Spanish soldier is dead!" the spy cried. "He lies in the bottom of the pool. The metal clothes hold the body down."

The chief and the spy rushed toward the pool. What had happened? In ten minutes they were standing on the bank in shocked silence.

There, lying on the bottom of the pool, was the body of the Spanish soldier. And next to it, holding it in locked arms, was the body of the Boriqueno girl. Her glossy hair swirled like lazy smoke over his shining armor.

Today no one knows how the Spanish soldier died. He may have slipped in. He may have been murdered. But the case of the girl is clear. Swimming down from her cave, she had seen the body. She had chosen death at his side over life without him.

Their love lives on, some people say. That is why you can still see their dim shadows on the bank of the pool, with joined hands and meeting lips. . . .

HOW POCAHONTAS
SAVED MY LIFE

. . . in which we learn the little-known
story of a well-known tale.

Words We Need to Know:

grindstone   [*GRIND stone*]—a large round stone used for sharpening knives, axes, etc.
            Jimmy turns the *grindstone* while his father sharpens the ax.

savage   [*SAV ij*]—a wild and ignorant person
            Captain John Smith thought of the Indians as *savages*.

vein   [*VANE*]—a blood vessel, or tube, that carries blood to the heart
            Sometimes the *veins* can be seen under the skin on the back of your hand.

whopper   [*HWOP er*]—a tall tale; an enormous lie
            The fisherman told a *whopper* about a big one that got away.

Myths. Legends. Folk tales. Which kind of story do we Americans most like to tell?

Not myths, certainly. Today people believe in one God, not in a whole family of gods and goddesses. Also, we have science to help us understand the world around us. We don't need myths to explain the things we see.

Folk tales are told in all parts of America. Almost every town has its haunted-house story. But most of these tales are not known by everyone in the country. Few people in Massachusetts have heard the folk tales of the Mississippi Valley. And few people in Louisiana know the folk tales of New England.

It is, however, legends that we most like to tell. We Americans love our heroes. When we run out of true stories about them, we start making up false ones. Everyone has heard at least one story about Davy Crockett. He really lived, even if most of the stories about him are legends. Most of us have heard of Johnny Appleseed, the strange little man who planted apple trees from Pennsylvania to Illinois. He really lived, too. So did Casey Jones, the railroad man who died in a crash, giving his own life so that others might be saved.

Most legends are made up after the people they are told about have died. But sometimes people start legends about themselves. Such a person was Captain John Smith. He was too good a storyteller to let the truth spoil a good tale.

HOW POCAHONTAS SAVED MY LIFE Almost everyone knows the story of the Indian princess, Pocahontas [*po ka HON tis*]. We have all heard how she saved Captain John Smith. Yet almost no one knows the "story" of this story. Few people have read the tale as Smith wrote it. And there is not one person alive today who can prove that the tale is true—or that it is not true.

Here is a chance to become an expert. First we will read

313

the tale as Smith told it in 1624. Then we will learn something about Captain John Smith. Finally we can try to decide on the truth of the story. Is Smith telling what really happened? Or is he telling the biggest "whopper" of all time?

✦ ✦ ✦

The year 1607 should always be remembered. This was the year we settled Jamestown, Virginia, the first successful English town in the New World. There was trouble from the beginning. Three times I had to use guns to make the people stay. Small groups were always trying to steal our boat. They wanted to escape the life they had chosen. But my orders were to stay or die. So we stayed—and many died.

Life was not easy. The weather was damp. We did not have the right food. Sometimes we did not have *any* food. Many people grew sick and died.

But the biggest danger was the Indians. A few of them were friendly, and we used these as guides. But most of the savages stayed in the woods, out of sight, waiting. How well I know!

One day in the fall of 1607, I decided to do some hunting. I took one of the Indian guides and went into the woods. All of a sudden, from out of nowhere, two or three hundred Indians came at me at once. I shot some of them right away. Then I took a garter off my leg. I used it to tie my guide's arm to mine. I held him in front of me as a shield. This made the Indians stop firing arrows. I had been hit in the leg, and had many arrows in my clothes. But I was not badly hurt.

When the Indians had seen what my gun could do, they kept out of sight behind rocks and trees. I tried to escape. I untied my guide, but he ran away. Without him I was lost. Soon I was wandering in a wet swamp. Before long the mud and water came up to my knees. I stopped. It was beginning to get cold. I could see the eyes of Indians behind bushes all around me. I waited, hoping they would go away. But they didn't. Finally, when I was near death with cold, I just threw away my gun.

For some reason, the Indians had decided to let me live —for a while, at least. They led me to a campfire and rubbed my legs and arms until I was warm. Then I asked to see their chief. I was taken to him at once. I had no toys or beads with me, so I gave the chief my round compass. The savages looked at the little needle which always pointed north. They couldn't figure it out. They poked at the needle with their fingers. But they couldn't touch it because of the glass. This made them even more excited. They had never seen glass before. They seemed interested when I told them the size of the earth, and of the great oceans and strange lands that covered it.

In about an hour, however, I was tied to a tree. The Indians stood in a half circle in front of me. They got ready to shoot. But suddenly the chief held up the compass. He shouted something. The Indians laid down their bows and arrows. Then they led me away through the woods. Two big fellows held my arms, and on each side of me were six guards. They never took the arrows from the bows they held in front of them.

Soon we arrived at their town. Here were thirty or forty houses made of mats. The women and children came out and stood looking at me as though I were a white monster. The men marched in a large circle. They kept this up a long time. Then, one by one, they stepped inside the circle. They started to dance in all kinds of strange ways, singing, yelling, and howling.

All the Indians were by now painted red. On their heads they wore the skins of white birds with wings spread. Hanging from their heads were pieces of copper, white shells, and feathers. Some wore the rattles from the tail of a strange snake that lives in the New World. When the savages had finished dancing, I was taken to a long house made of mats. Here I was left with thirty or forty tall fellows to guard me. I was brought more deer meat and bread than twenty men could have eaten. Were they trying to fatten me up before they killed me? It looked that way. But I went on living.

Two days later, I was led to the home of a sick boy. The chief asked me to make the boy well again. Now I knew they thought I might be a maker of magic. I saw a chance to escape. We had a drug at Jamestown, I told the chief, that would make the boy well. If he would let me go, I would travel to Jamestown and return with the drug.

But the chief would not agree. Instead, he wanted my help in attacking Jamestown. We would all go to Jamestown together, conquer it, and get the drug. The Indians had waited until winter to start the war, he said. Now I could give them help. If I would do this, I could have my freedom, much land, and the friendship of the Indians.

But to this *I* would not agree. I frightened him with stories of guns that could kill a hundred Indians at a time. I made up tales of other Indians who would help us if we were attacked.

Finally we agreed on a plan. I wrote a letter to Jamestown, asking for the drug and some other things. But no one wanted to take the letter. My stories had frightened the

316

Indians too much. They were also afraid of the letter itself. They thought that the paper could speak.

Not long after this, a fire was made in the center of the house where I was being kept a prisoner. Mats were spread on each side of the fire. The guards made me sit down on one of the mats. Then they went out, leaving me alone for the first time. Before long a great ugly savage came dancing in, painted black with coal and oil. Many snakes and animal skins hung down around his face. The tails were tied into a kind of crown on the top of his head. Around the crown was a circle of white feathers. The Indian was a terrible sight, all painted black, with the skins and snakes hanging down and a rattle in his hand. He began to sing while he made a circle of meal around the fire. Then three more of the devils came in. These were painted half red and half black, with huge white circles around their eyes. As they joined their leader in the dance around the fire, three more came in. But this was to be all.

After a long dance, all seven of the creatures sat down next to me. They shook their rattles and sang what sounded like a prayer. The veins in their foreheads grew large. Sweat poured from their oiled bodies. Then, still singing, they rose to their feet and took out grains of corn and little sticks. They placed these, one by one, on the mat near the circle of meal. This kept on until night. None of us had anything to eat or drink. I felt every minute that I would be killed the next. But when evening came, baskets of food again appeared, and we feasted happily. This went on for three days.

On the third day, they told me the meaning of it. They wanted to see if I would bring them harm. The circle of meal was supposed to stand for their country. The sticks stood for my country, and the corn for the great sea between. What they found out from all this, I never knew. But I learned that they thought the world was shaped like a saucer. They lived in the center.

Once they showed me a bag of gunpowder. It had come from some Englishman they had killed. They were saving it until the next spring, to plant it as they did corn.

I was taken to the town where lived Powhatan [*pow a TAN*], their king. Here they led me into another long house. A loud cry went up when I came in. Two rows of men were sitting along each side, with two rows of women behind them. All were painted red, and all wore white feathers on their heads.

Powhatan himself sat on a low throne before the fire. He wore a great robe of animal skins, with their tails left hanging. His wife was also there. So was his daughter, Pocahontas, who was about thirteen years old. Pocahontas was not her real name. It is the Indian word for *playful*. I learned later that her real name was Matowaka. The savages didn't want me to know her real name. They thought I might hurt her with my white-man's magic.

Powhatan's queen brought me a bowl of water. I washed my hands, and dried them on a mop of feathers. All this time Powhatan was talking with his chiefs. The Indians then feasted. But I could eat nothing. I could only sit and wonder what Powhatan was saying. At the end of the meal, two great stones were brought into the long house. They were laid at Powhatan's feet. Suddenly I was grabbed by as many Indians as could lay their hands on me. I was dragged forward. My head was laid on the stones, so it might be beaten with clubs.

Many, many times Pocahontas asked her father to spare

318

my life. But old Powhatan sat with a face of stone. Pocahontas finally saw that words alone would not save me. She
took my head in her arms and laid her own upon it to save
me from death.

My life was saved. I should have been happy, but my
heart was sad. I still thought I would be put to death. This
fear had been with me for over six weeks.

But Powhatan, not long after, said we were friends. He
told me he would trade my life for two large guns and a
grindstone. He was also ready to give me land and to honor
me as his son.

Why Powhatan changed his mind about me, I have never
known. But soon I left for home. Twelve Indians went
with me, to carry the guns and the grindstone back to
Powhatan. The next day I stood once again in the fort at
Jamestown. I had been among the Indians for six or seven
weeks.

At first the Indians didn't want to take the guns back to
Powhatan. They would take the grindstone, they said. But
the guns were too heavy. I wanted to keep my word to
Powhatan, so I decided to show them what the big guns
could do. I took one of the guns outside and aimed it at
a tree that was covered with ice. The gun went off with a
great roar. Ice came falling down. The savages ran off into
the woods, half dead with fear. But at last they calmed down
and agreed to take the guns, as well as other presents we
gave them for their wives and children.

(Adapted from Smith's *Generall Historie of
Virginia, New England, and the Summer Isles*,
1624)

✦   ✦   ✦

Is the story of Pocahontas true?

No, say some people. We have no proof that it happened. All we have is the word of a man who liked to stretch the truth. Smith wrote the story of his adventure twice. The first time was in 1608, right after it took place. The second time was in 1624, long after he had returned to England. In 1608, of course, people knew how long he had been among the Indians. It had been about three weeks. But by 1624 these three weeks had been stretched to "six or seven." In the 1608 story, he says that it took eight men to guard him. But by 1624 this number had grown to "thirty or forty." And, most important, the early story does not describe his rescue by Pocahontas. This is strange. Smith was not a man who kept quiet about his adventures. Why should he have waited so long before telling the Pocahontas tale to the world?

For those who don't believe the story, the answer is simple: Smith made the whole thing up. A lot had happened between 1608 and 1624. Pocahontas had grown up, married an Englishman, and traveled to England. She had been introduced to the Queen of England, and her name had become famous. In 1617 she had died. This meant that Smith could join her name to his in any story he liked. No one could prove he was not telling the truth.

Other people, however, think the tale is true. After all, they say, when a person *says* a story is true, we should believe him until someone proves differently. Smith's life was already full of adventures. Why should he have dreamed up another? And if he didn't describe his rescue by Pocahontas in the 1608 story, so what? There are many things he left out of the short 1608 story. Maybe other things seemed more important at the time. Maybe he didn't want to say that a young girl had saved his life. Maybe it wasn't until Pocahontas had become famous that Smith thought people would be interested in her part in his adventure.

Who is to decide? Probably no one will ever be able to say *true* or *false*. But there is one thing on which we can all agree. The story is famous not because it is either true or false, but simply because it is a very good tale.

Another tall tale:

DAVY CROCKETT KILLS A BEAR   Captain John Smith was not the only American who started legends about himself during his own lifetime. Davy Crockett, too, had a lot to say about himself. Here is the way Davy Crockett describes a bear hunt in the woods of Tennessee. His English is not the best, but it is excellent for a man who had gone to school fewer than a hundred days. Notice that this adventure, too, took place long before it was written down. And here again, we have only the author's word that the tale is true.

✦   ✦   ✦

About the biggest bear I ever killed was one I stuck with a butcher knife. At first I didn't know just *how* big that bear was. It was dark by the time I got to the place where my dogs had him up a tree. All I could see was a kind of black lump up where the branches started. But I had seen his tracks, and I knowed he was a screamer.

I could see the lump, but not plain enough to shoot at, as there was no moonlight. I had fallen in a creek and was shaking with cold. I knowed I couldn't aim my gun. So I set in to hunting for some dry wood to make me a fire. But I could find none. What I did find was that the ground was full of great open cracks. The earthquake of 1812 had left these cracks in places all over West Tennessee.

The only thing was to shoot by guess. I pointed my gun as near the lump as I could, and fired away. But the bear only clomb up higher and got out on a limb. Now I could see him a little better. I loaded up my gun and fired. But this time he didn't move at all. I started to load my gun for the third shot, but the first thing I knowed the bear must have slipped. He was down on the ground, fighting with the dogs.

They were fighting all around me. I had a big butcher knife in my belt, to cut up the bear with after he was dead. I took it out. The night was miserable black. Now and then I could see a white dog I had. But the rest of the dogs, and the bear, were dark. I couldn't see them at all. By and by the bear got down in one of those cracks in the ground, about four feet deep. I could tell the biting end of him by where his teeth snapped at my dogs.

I had laid down my gun in the dark. Now I began to hunt for it. I felt around and got hold of a pole, so I thought I would punch the bear with that. I did so, and when I would punch him, the dogs would jump on him, and he would bite them terrible. He didn't seem to mind my punching as much as he minded the dogs. I wondered how long he would stand still. Could I get down in the crack and maybe get my knife into him?

I got my dogs down in front of the bear to keep his head busy. Then I got down in the crack behind him. I crept up till I could feel his fur in the dark. I felt my way along his back till I came to the place where I knowed I would have to stick him. Then I made a big jump with my long knife. Got him right through the heart. He just sank right down easy, and I got out of there in a hurry.

322

I suffered very much that night with cold. Everything I had on was wet and frozen. I knowed I would freeze if I didn't warm myself some way. So I yelled a while, and jumped up and down, and threw myself around all sorts of ways. But this wouldn't do, for my blood was now getting cold. I had the chills coming on all over me. I was so tired I could hardly stay awake. But I thought I would do the best I could to save my life. Then, if I died, nobody would be to blame.

So I felt around till I found me a tree that I knowed wouldn't have a branch on it for thirty or forty feet. I clomb way up to the first branch, locked my arms around the tree, and slid down to the bottom. This made the insides of my legs and arms feel mighty warm and good. I kept on doing this till daylight. How many times I clomb my tree and slid down I don't know. But I reckon at least a hundred.

In the morning I cut up the bear and found me enough dry wood to make a fire. This was about the biggest bear I ever killed. It was all I could do to carry the meat home. It was about thirty miles, but I reached home the second day. This made fifty-eight bears I had killed during that fall and winter.

In the spring I went out to get me a few more bears, and in about a month I killed forty-seven. This made one hundred and five bears I had killed in less than a year.

(Adapted from Crockett's *Narrative of the Life of David Crockett of West Tennessee*, 1834)

ABRAHAM LINCOLN
and ANNE RUTLEDGE

. . . in which we read of the greatest joy, and the greatest sadness, in a great man's life.

Words We Need to Know:

awkward — [*AWK ward*]—not graceful or smooth in movement; clumsy
The *awkward* boy knocked a glass off the table.

innkeeper — [*IN kee per*]—a person who runs an inn, or a small hotel
Adam's father bought a small hotel and became an *innkeeper*.

fiancé — [*fee ahn SAY*]—a man engaged to be married
Miss Miller's *fiancé* is now in the army.

fiancée — [*fee ahn SAY*]—a woman engaged to be married
Anne Rutledge was probably never the *fiancée* of Abraham Lincoln.

quilt — [*KWILT*]—a thick bed covering
On cold nights Sol slept under a *quilt*.

sympathy — [*SIM pa thee*]—a feeling of sadness for another person's sorrow or trouble
We should have *sympathy* for people who are sick.

The greatest legends are told about the greatest people. As soon as someone dies, tall tales about the person are born. We cannot really call these stories "lies." There is almost always some truth in them. And, more often than not, the persons who start these stories believe they are telling the truth.

Abraham Lincoln is often called one of the greatest people of all time. It is not strange that he should be the hero of one of the greatest legends of all time. This is the story of his romance with Anne Rutledge.

Lincoln died well over a hundred years ago. Today we know that there is little truth in the Anne Rutledge story. But this does not really matter. Most Americans *want* the story to be true. They are lucky, for there is just enough truth in it to keep it alive forever.

The legend of Lincoln and Anne Rutledge has been told by many authors. We will read the story as told by William H. Herndon, Lincoln's law partner and friend for many years. Remember that Herndon wrote this story more than fifty years after it was supposed to have happened. The legend had grown as the facts had been forgotten.

ABRAHAM LINCOLN AND ANNE RUTLEDGE

I knew Abraham Lincoln. He was my law partner for over twenty years. The last five of these years I ran the office alone. Mr. Lincoln had more important business. He was President of the United States.

Mr. Lincoln was my good friend. I have always been proud that there was never any real trouble between us. I loved the man, and I worship his name to this day.

A bullet ended Mr. Lincoln's life in 1865. This was over twenty years ago. By now much has been written about him. Some books about Lincoln are full of small mistakes. Others give the reader legends, not facts.

It is now time for the truth to be told. Before long the

327

last man who ever shook Lincoln's hand will have gone from the earth.

I will try to tell the truth about Abraham Lincoln. People who love him will have little to fear. The whole truth will never harm such a great man. His life will stand the test of truth, or any other test. Someday his fame will reach the highest place in American history.

Here is the story of the great romance of Abraham Lincoln's life. Our hero falls in love for the first time. I know that many people will not agree with me about his love for Anne Rutledge. Most books about Lincoln leave out this part of his life, or give it only a few lines. Some authors even say that the love story is a legend.

But these authors are wrong. I knew Miss Rutledge myself. Our fathers were good friends. More than twenty people have told me that the love story is true. These people know what they are talking about. They saw it happen under their very eyes. I now repeat what I have said before—that the romance with Anne Rutledge was the happiest, and the saddest, chapter in Mr. Lincoln's life.

Abraham Lincoln was about twenty-five years old when he took a shine to Anne Rutledge. Her father, James Rutledge, owned a small hotel in New Salem, Illinois. In 1833 Mr. Lincoln came to live at this inn. Lincoln was working long hours every day. He was studying law in the evenings. It is hard to see how he found the time to look twice at Anne.

But Anne Rutledge was not the kind of girl one sees every day. She had beautiful blond hair, blue eyes, and very light skin. She was on the thin side, and short, about five feet, two inches. Her cheerful ways and quick smile made her the most popular young lady in the village. Her mind was as fast as a whip. She had, I believe, spent some time away at school. Her education was at least as good as Lincoln's.

It was not a case of "love at first sight." For one thing, the young Mr. Lincoln was too shy to tell her how he felt. She was probably the only really nice girl he had met up to that time. Her hands were soft, her heart was kind, and her head was full of good common sense. She was a real *young lady*.

But there was another reason that the romance was slow in starting. This reason was more important. Miss Rutledge was engaged to someone else, a young merchant named John McNamar. He had come to New Salem from New York State. In less than five years he had made a small fortune. It seemed only right for the town's most popular girl to be the fiancée of its most important young man. Lincoln probably thought so, too. He and McNamar had come to New Salem at about the same time—and McNamar had done far better.

Though Anne was engaged to McNamar, no wedding date was ever set. There was something he wanted to do before he married. "When I left New York," he told Anne, "I also left my parents, and my brothers and sisters. They are still poor and in need. When I came out West, I had a plan. I was going to make a fortune, and then go back to help my family. I am now going to return to New York. If I can, I will bring my family back to Illinois with me."

A few days later, Anne watched her fiancé leave for the East. Then a long wait began. A week went by without news from McNamar. Anne waited eagerly for a letter. The week grew into a month. She began to worry. Why didn't she hear from him? Something must have happened. But what?

Anne's friends told her to give up hope. They said that McNamar would never be heard from again. He had turned out to be no good. Maybe he was running away from some crime. Or he might have left Anne to go off and marry another woman.

The people Anne called her friends told her these terrible things. Friends can do strange things to each other. In meaning to help, they can actually do harm. When a person's so-called friends think that he or she has made a mistake, how little sympathy they seem to have! But Anne Rutledge was not a person to give up easily. She still thought she would hear from McNamar. She had faith. She waited.

At last a letter came. It explained everything. In passing through Ohio, McNamar had become sick with a fever. For almost a month he had been too ill to leave his room. But now he was well again. He was on his way to New York.

More weeks passed. Anne finally received another letter. McNamar had reached his old home. His father's health was very poor. The return trip would be delayed.

More time went by. At last McNamar's father died. But still McNamar did not return. He wrote that he would have to stay in New York a while longer. Other letters followed. Each was less of a love letter than the one before. The language grew more polite and proper. It was as if he were writing to a stranger.

Anne began to lose faith. Had McNamar's love grown cold? Often she asked herself this question. She had not given up hope before, but now her heart grew sick.

At this point, into our story steps Abraham Lincoln, tall, awkward, and shy. He had learned that McNamar no longer wrote to Anne. It seemed that the engagement had been broken by McNamar himself. This meant that Anne was free. Now it was Lincoln's turn.

330

Anne didn't know what to make of the way Lincoln now acted. Was she still engaged to McNamar? She didn't really know. Lincoln's smiles and little jokes surprised her. But she didn't know if they pleased her. She could not yet tell. The McNamar question would have to be settled first.

Lincoln's new happiness surprised everyone in New Salem. He had never been what one would call a happy man. But now he was full of life and joy. "He seemed to see the bright side of every picture," one of Anne's brothers wrote me many years later. The people of New Salem were on Lincoln's side. They wanted Anne to forget McNamar.

McNamar, too, was surprised when he later heard of the change in Lincoln. As he told me after Lincoln's death, "Mr. Lincoln was not paying attention to any of the young ladies when I left for my home in New York. There was no trouble between us. It was just the opposite. I had every reason to believe him my very good friend."

Little by little, Anne turned to Lincoln. He began to take her everywhere she went. He would call for her when she was ready to return home. In the evenings Anne often went to "quilting bees." She and her friends would make quilts and talk, talk, talk. Anne was very quick at sewing. Her fast fingers could make the needle fly. She was invited to every quilting bee in town.

One time, while Anne sat sewing at a friend's house, Lincoln stood waiting outside. Men were supposed to keep away from quilting bees. The parties were for women only, and men were out of place. But Lincoln could not stay away from Anne. He went into the house quietly. Then he sat down by Anne's side as she worked on the quilt.

He whispered into her ear the old, old words of people in love. Her heart beat fast. It nearly burst with joy. Her fingers became awkward with the needle. She was so excited that she made her stitches uneven and crooked. Her friends looked at each other and nodded.

The owner of this quilt kept it until a few years ago. She would show her visitors the uneven stitches Anne Rutledge had made as Lincoln sat by her side.

Anne had a clear, ringing voice. She often sang for Lincoln when they were alone. He liked to hear her sing. In fact, he liked everything about her. Soon he saw that he was falling in love. And love was new to him. He thought that falling deeply in love would be like falling into a well with no bottom. As he found himself coming near the edge of the well, he tried to stop. He needed time to think it over.

But it was too late. Soon he fell in—in love with Anne. He asked her to be his bride.

At first Anne would not say *yes* or *no*. She could not. It was as though her heart and mind were at war. Her heart said *yes*, marry Lincoln, do what you really want to do. But her mind said *no*, do what you promised, wait for Mc-Namar. For days the battle went on. Lincoln kept asking for an answer. Anne knew she would have to tell him something. But she couldn't make up her mind. The fight inside her started to take her strength. She began to grow weak.

When Anne's answer finally came, it was neither *yes* nor *no*. She said she would marry Lincoln—but she must be given time to write McNamar. As soon as news came from McNamar that the old engagement was broken, she would tell the world that she was going to marry Abraham Lincoln.

So Anne wrote a sweet letter to McNamar. The slow mails carried it to New York. But no answer came. Days passed, and then weeks. To Lincoln, the weeks of waiting must have seemed like years.

Finally, Anne gave up hope of a reply. She looked at Lincoln and smiled. Her eyes told him what at first her lips would not say. He had won. She was ready to become Mrs. Abraham Lincoln.

Now that they were engaged, Lincoln told Anne what she must have already known. He was very poor. He was still a student. She must give him time to finish his law studies. Then, said Lincoln, nothing would be able to keep them apart.

To this Anne agreed. She told herself that her troubles were over. "As soon as he finishes studying," she said to her brother, "we are to be married."

But the thought of another love kept coming back to Anne. She couldn't forget McNamar. She couldn't help wondering if she had done the right thing. She had said *yes* to Lincoln, but McNamar's name and face kept popping into her mind. Her heart and her head were still at war.

Her health began to fail. The color left her cheeks and her eyes grew dim. Late in the summer of 1835, she took to her bed. A fever was burning inside her body.

Lincoln often came to see Anne during the early days of her illness. His long, kind face would be lined with sorrow as he entered her room. Then he would stand looking down at her white face against the whiter pillow. Once, sick as she was, she sang for him. The song was one he had always liked. It was a hymn that began, *Proud man, give up your selfish ways.* It was to be the last song she ever sang.

Day by day, Anne grew thinner and weaker. At last her doctor said that she must be left alone. Her room was to be kept quiet. No visitors were to enter.

But Anne kept asking for Lincoln. She would not take no

for an answer. Finally, she demanded to see him. There was nothing else the family could do. Lincoln was sent for.

When Lincoln arrived at Anne's bedside, the door was closed behind him. They were left alone. What happened at this last meeting was known only to him and the dying girl. We can only guess what was said, and what was left unsaid. But we know that Lincoln was very unhappy when he left the house. His friends worried about his going out of his mind.

A few days later, Anne fell asleep for the last time. She died on August 25, 1835. It was the saddest hour of Lincoln's life. In speaking of her death and her grave, he once said, "My heart lies buried there."

Anne's death made Lincoln very sad. He seemed to lose interest in everything. He spent his days walking by himself. Sometimes he would go off into the woods. His friends feared that he might try to take his own life. Lincoln must have had this same fear. He said later that he had never dared to carry a pocket knife.

Lincoln's friends started to watch him carefully. They tried to cheer him up, but his sadness only grew worse. Finally they sent him to the house of one of his good friends. This was Bowlin Green, a kind man who lived a mile south of town. Here, hidden in the hills, Lincoln stayed for a few weeks. Under the care of the good Bowlin Green, he slowly became more like himself again. Then he went back to New Salem, back to his law books, and back to his life.

The saddest chapter in Lincoln's life had ended. But it would never really be over.

(Adapted from William H. Herndon's *Abraham Lincoln*, 1888)

The best-known American legend:

GEORGE WASHINGTON AND THE CHERRY
TREE   Every American knows what George Washington did with his little hatchet. The tale has been told for
more than 150 years. It has been put into many schoolbooks.
Millions of children have read the story and learned that
they should always tell the truth.

In a way, this is strange. For the story itself is probably
not true. As our last reading of this book, let us see how the
famous legend was born.

A few years after the first President's death, a book called
The Life of George Washington appeared. It was bought in
large numbers. The author of this book was a man named
Mason Weems.

"Parson" Weems, as he was called, was a book-peddler,
preacher, and writer. He told his readers that he had been
the minister of Washington's church. He filled his book with
stories that could only have come from someone who had
known Washington well. But in truth, Weems had never
been the minister of Washington's church. He had probably met Washington a few times, but the two men were
never friends. Weems knew almost nothing about his hero's
early years. But this didn't stop him from writing many
pages about Washington's youth. Where there were no facts
to fill the pages, Weems made up stories. And wonderful
stories they were!

Weems was careful to give some "proof" for the story of
the cherry tree. He said it had come from an old woman, a
good friend of the Washington family. But he failed to say

who this woman was. And no one has ever known why she never told her interesting story to anyone else.

Here, then, is Weems's story of the cherry tree. Notice that nothing is said about cutting it down.

✦ ✦ ✦

When George was about six years old, he was made the owner of a little hatchet. He liked the hatchet very much, and was always going about chopping everything that came in his way.

One day, in his father's garden, he tried the hatchet on a beautiful young cherry tree. He forgot for a moment that the tree was his father's favorite. Pieces of bark fell off, and the hatchet cut deeply into the wood.

The next morning, his father saw what had happened. He came into the house at once. With much anger he asked who had killed his cherry tree. He said that he would not have traded the tree for a hundred dollars. But nobody could tell him anything.

Soon George and his hatchet appeared. "George," said his father, "do you know who killed that little cherry tree yonder in the garden?"

It was a tough question. George looked at his shoes for a moment. But he quickly knew what he had to say. He looked up at his father with the sweet face of youth. His eyes were bright with the charm of all-conquering truth as he bravely cried out:

"I cannot tell a lie, Pa. You know I cannot tell a lie. I cut it with my little hatchet."

"Run to my arms, you dearest boy," cried his father in great joy. "Run to my arms. Glad am I, George, that you killed my tree. For you have paid me for it a thousand times over. Such an act of honesty is worth more than a thousand trees, though loaded with fruit of the purest gold."

(Adapted from Weems' *Life of George Washington*, 1806)

✦   ✦   ✦

So ends the story. But the "story" of the story goes on. About the time Weems wrote this tale, his own son is supposed to have cut down one of his favorite rosebushes. Like the young Washington, the child told the sad truth. This act of honesty, however, failed to save the boy from receiving a good hard spanking.

HOW WELL DID
YOU READ?

OLD, OLD, STORIES

DIRECTIONS: *Choose the ending that best completes each sentence.*

1. Greece is a country in a) Asia b) Europe c) South America.
2. The ancient Greeks were a) publishers of the first myths b) ancestors of the modern Greeks c) gods and goddesses.
3. The Greeks thought that the sun was a) an angry god b) larger than the earth c) a ball of fire.
4. The Greeks believed that the earth was a) a flat square b) smaller than the sun c) shaped like a saucer.
5. Most myths were made up a) to explain things the Greeks couldn't understand b) to tell to children c) to make the Greeks famous.
6. Most Greek myths are about a) 1,000 years old b) 2,000 years old c) 3,000 years old.
7. Greek myths were first told aloud instead of read because a) the Greeks had no printing presses b) the myths had not been translated into other languages c) the plots could not be written down.
8. Zeus was a) the goddess of wisdom b) the king of the gods c) the god of the sea.
9. The gods and goddesses a) lived peacefully on Mount Olympus b) could all throw lightning from the sky c) quarreled the way human beings do.
10. Myths are still read because they a) are good stories b) explain the world to us c) have Greek characters.

QUESTIONS FOR THOUGHT AND DISCUSSION:

1. Why is it better to have many cities joined together in states and countries than to have each city a separate country? Think about transportation, language, travel, defense, and money.
2. How might the Greeks have explained why we have spring, summer, fall, and winter? Try making up gods or a myth of your own to explain the seasons.

341

THE MYTH OF PHAETON

DIRECTIONS: *Read each sentence carefully before deciding whether it is true or false.*

1. Phaeton's friends laughed at him when he said that his father was Helios, god of the sun.
2. The palace of Helios was on the eastern edge of the earth.
3. Helios's attendants were all men.
4. Helios could look down from the chariot without growing dizzy, but Phaeton could not.
5. Helios was right when he told Phaeton that it is foolish to be too brave.
6. Phaeton was shocked and frightened when he first saw the fiery horses.
7. Helios told Phaeton never to use the whip on the horses.
8. Zeus ended Phaeton's ride because he thought the boy might burn up everything.
9. The horses became quiet when they no longer felt Phaeton pulling the reins.
10. The myth of Phaeton explained to the Greeks why no trees grow on the tops of high mountains.

QUESTIONS FOR THOUGHT AND DISCUSSION:

1. How does this myth show that "he who is too brave is foolish"?
2. How might the myth have ended if Zeus hadn't been there to throw a bolt of lightning? Can you make up another ending?

342

CERES AND PERSEPHONE

DIRECTIONS: *One of the following words belongs in each sentence below. Place the words in the proper sentences:*

VENUS, SUMMER, MOON, SPED, EARTHQUAKE, ECHO, GRAPES, POMEGRANATE, WINTER, HARVEST, PLUTO, QUIVER, ORANGE, FLOWERS, CUPID.

1. The Greeks believed that long ago it had been _____ all year long.
2. Ceres was the goddess of the _____.
3. One day Persephone went to pick _____ and never returned.
4. An _____ answered Ceres from across the lake.
5. Persephone's friends and Ceres _____ to the place where the girl had last been seen.
6. Cupid carried a bow and _____ of arrows.
7. Cupid's beautiful mother was the goddess _____.
8. The king of the dead had come to earth because of an _____.
9. Ceres learned that her daughter was married to _____.
10. Persephone had sucked the juice from six _____ seeds.

QUESTIONS FOR THOUGHT AND DISCUSSION:

1. The myth of Ceres and Persephone explained to the Greeks why we have summer and winter. Today we really know why we have seasons. What makes the seasons change?
2. The Greek god who has stayed with us the longest is Pluto. By what name is he known today? How has he changed in three thousand years?
3. The Greeks knew that there is a mixture of good and bad in most people. How is this shown in the character of Ceres?

PROMETHEUS AND PANDORA

DIRECTIONS: *Match the sentence beginnings in Column A with the sentence endings in Column B.*

A	B
1. Ceres	a. opened the little box.
2. Zeus	b. once saw that humans had enough to eat.
3. Epimetheus	c. was given stubbornness.
4. The mouse	d. was the blacksmith of the gods.
5. The fox	e. saw nothing on earth to interest him.
6. The mule	f. was given timidity.
7. Man	g. carried a flaming torch to earth.
8. Prometheus	h. was the only creature without a difference.
9. Vulcan	i. was not busy when Zeus gave him a job.
10. Pandora	j. was given slyness.

QUESTIONS FOR THOUGHT AND DISCUSSION:

1. Today, of course, we no longer believe that Prometheus brought fire to earth. We like the story because it tells of someone who was brave enough to do what he thought was right, even though he knew that he would be punished. Do you know any other stories like this?
2. Zeus thought that fire was too dangerous for man to have. Would you have agreed? What does man have today that is even more dangerous?
3. Sometimes the story of Pandora is told another way. Instead of the little box being full of troubles, it holds good things, like health, beauty, and happiness. When Pandora opens the box, all these good things fly out and are forever lost. Only hope is left. Which story do you think is better? Why?

BAUCIS AND PHILEMON

DIRECTIONS: *Number the sentences in Group I in the order in which the events happen in the story. The first two have been done for you. Then go on to Group II.*

GROUP I

a. __2__ Zeus asked Hermes about the temples on earth.

b. _____ Vehicles pulled by horses forced the two gods off the paving stones.

c. _____ Hermes learned that the earth people had fooled him.

d. __1__ Zeus sent his messenger Hermes down to earth.

e. _____ Two gods in disguise passed through the gate of clouds.

GROUP II

a. _____ A pitcher seemed to fill itself with wine.

b. _____ A kind man asked Zeus and Hermes to spend the night.

c. _____ The old people's cottage was turned into a magnificent temple.

d. _____ Baucis and Philemon shared their food with the travelers.

e. _____ The town was covered by a peaceful lake.

QUESTIONS FOR THOUGHT AND DISCUSSION:

1. In the first part of the story, we learn that Zeus is worried about man. What are the two main reasons for this worry?
2. "Men have become selfish," Zeus says in the story. "They do favors only for money." Do you think that Zeus would say this today? What true stories do you know about people who have done favors and *not* wanted money?
3. Many old stories have a moral, or lesson, back of them. They teach the reader to think certain things, or to behave in certain ways. Does "Baucis and Philemon" teach the reader anything? If so, what?

KING MIDAS AND
THE GOLDEN TOUCH

DIRECTIONS: *Use one word from the story to fill each of the following blanks. You may use a word more than once. See how many words you can remember without looking at the list below.*

1. a rich king named _____
2. a crown of solid _____
3. a darling daughter named

   _____
4. for the goddess of the _____
5. a dark vault full of _____
6. lighted by a single _____
7. a box of gold _____
8. a pail of gold _____
9. "What a happy man you

   _____"
10. the god of _____

11. Bacchus gave Midas one

    _____
12. the gift of the golden _____
13. a robe of golden _____
14. an embroidered _____
15. a cup of steaming _____
16. Iris became a golden _____
17. a bath in a _____
18. a pail of _____
19. a dress that was _____
20. one small and tender _____

Words: ARE, CLOTH, COFFEE, COINS, DUST, GOLD, HANDKERCHIEF, HAPPINESS, HEART, IRIS, MIDAS, RAINBOW, RIVER, STATUE, SUNBEAM, TOUCH, WATER, WET, WISH.

QUESTIONS FOR THOUGHT AND DISCUSSION:

1. On his second visit, Bacchus tells Midas that the king is now "wise" instead of "smart." What is the difference between being *smart* and being *wise*, as the words are used in this story?
2. People who find it easy to make money are often said to have the "golden touch." Is this always bad? Is everyone with the "golden touch" a King Midas? Explain.
3. Many people can guess some of the things that happen in this story before they take place. What events did you think were going to happen? What made you think so?
4. There is no daughter in the ancient Greek myth. Most people don't know that she was added only about a hundred years ago by an American author named Nathaniel Hawthorne. Why does adding the daughter make the old story better?

ULYSSES AND CIRCE

DIRECTIONS: *The following sentences are all false. Make them true by changing one word in each sentence. (Do not change the word was.) The first one is done for you.*

1. The city of Troy was built on a plain. (Change *plain* to *hill*.)
2. The Greeks dreamed of conquering Italy.
3. The Trojan War lasted nine years.
4. The Greek soldiers traveled home by land.
5. Food and other things were thrown overboard to please Zeus.
6. Ulysses was King of Greece.
7. The Lotus-Eaters ate meat.
8. The soldiers used their paddles to row to Circe's island.
9. All the men went to explore the island.
10. Ulysses told jokes to those who stayed behind.
11. Ulysses waited for days on the beach.
12. The soldiers heard Circe screaming inside the palace.
13. Circe was a beautiful mermaid.
14. The men were changed into goats.
15. Only the feet of the men were not changed.
16. Ulysses met a young goddess near the palace.
17. The beautiful Circe wore a green gown.
18. A magic coat protected Ulysses from Circe's tricks.
19. Circe was forced into a corner by Ulysses' wand.
20. Ulysses and his soldiers stayed with Circe a month.

QUESTIONS FOR THOUGHT AND DISCUSSION:

1. Ulysses is remembered because he was so clever. How does he show this in the legend we have read?
2. What part of a man stayed the same when Circe changed him into a pig? Why was this so terrible? What do you think Circe did with her pigs?

ULYSSES AND THE CYCLOPS

DIRECTIONS: *Here are twenty "scrambled sentences." Put the words in each sentence in the right order. The first one has been done for you.*

1. country was Ithaca in Greece a.   (Ithaca was a country in Greece.)
2. King of Troy was Ithaca and of conqueror Ulysses.
3. The water drink couldn't sea Greeks.
4. green to blue from water The changed.
5. on Soon island an they landed.
6. the Cyclopes wanted to meet Ulysses.
7. about the Everyone knew Cyclopes.
8. sheep herded monsters The.
9. a big was Behind a big rock cave.
10. The watched the monster the cave Greeks enter.
11. the jug of Greeks The wine a Cyclops gave.
12. the Cyclops Ulysses to lied.
13. The the blinded Greeks Cyclops.
14. sheep over the Cyclops tripped The blind.
15. The hearing after No-man shrugged about Cyclopes.
16. fleece grabbed the fingers Ulysses' sheep's.
17. to A sheep Ulysses carried freedom.
18. Cyclops the Ulysses shouted at.
19. raged at monster The blind Ulysses.
20. The rock a Ulysses monster at threw.

QUESTIONS FOR THOUGHT AND DISCUSSION:

1. How does this legend show that Ulysses was a clever man? Explain this sentence: *Ulysses saved the wine, and the wine saved Ulysses.*
2. Does anything in the story show that Ulysses thought of the Cyclops as a being with feelings and rights of his own? In what ways is the giant human? In what ways is he like an animal?

348

CUPID AND PSYCHE

DIRECTIONS: *Choose the ending that best completes each sentence.*

1. Psyche was unhappy because a) she had no boy friends b) her sisters disliked her c) she was so beautiful.
2. Venus decided to punish Psyche because of the girl's a) love for Cupid b) exquisite beauty c) silly pride.
3. Venus told Cupid to make Psyche fall in love with a) a kind, good man b) a mean, wicked man c) Cupid himself.
4. Cupid found Psyche a) in her four-poster b) thinking about her dream-man c) in her father's garden.
5. As Psyche stood on the hill, she a) turned into Venus b) was lifted off her feet by the wind c) heard the sound of a brook.
6. When Psyche opened her eyes, she saw a) a blue palace b) Cupid, the god of love c) a table set for a single person.
7. Psyche was most suspicious during the a) day b) evening c) night.
8. When she lighted the candle, Psyche expected to see a) Cupid, the god of love b) an ugly monster c) her dream-man.
9. Cupid was awakened by a) a drop of hot wax b) the gleam of gold-tipped arrows c) the light of the candle.
10. Cupid left Psyche because of her a) pride b) suspicion c) sadness.

QUESTIONS FOR THOUGHT AND DISCUSSION:

1. "Love and suspicion cannot live in the same house," Cupid says at the end of the story. What does this mean? Is it true?
2. Psyche's life would be easier today. People no longer believe in Venus. But do very beautiful girls still have problems other girls don't have? What are some of them?
3. The word *psyche* today means *soul, mind,* or *inner person.* Why is this a good name for the character in the story?

THE HAMMER OF THOR

DIRECTIONS: *Number the sentences in Group I in the order in which the events happen in the story. Then go on to Group II.*

GROUP I

a. _____ Two ravens landed on Woden's wide shoulders.

b. _____ Thor was remodeled to look like Freya.

c. _____ Loki was thrown into the air by the Thunderer.

d. _____ Thor searched everywhere for his sledge.

e. _____ Freya fell to her knees and asked to stay in Asgard.

GROUP II

a. _____ Thor's hand trembled against the lips of the Frost Giant.

b. _____ The hammer of Thor was thrown at the Frost Giant.

c. _____ Thor and Loki saw dwarfs making things out of metal.

d. _____ Thor told Loki never to laugh at him again.

e. _____ A leg of beef disappeared under Thor's veil.

QUESTIONS FOR THOUGHT AND DISCUSSION:

1. There are no human characters in the myth of Thor and his hammer. This is an important difference between the myths of Northern Europe and those of Greece and Rome. Think of at least two other differences.

2. After Thor had almost killed Loki, why did Loki take Thor's side in the argument with Woden? Why did Loki offer to go with Thor as a maid?

3. In what ways is Freya like the Venus we met in the Greek and Roman myths? In what ways is she different? Do the differences tell us anything about the peoples who invented the two goddesses?

4. Not long ago a boxer from Northern Europe boasted of his right fist as "the hammer of Thor." Why did he say this?

SIR GAWAIN AND THE GREEN KNIGHT

DIRECTIONS: *Read each sentence carefully before deciding whether it is true or false.*

1. A strange knight in green armor rode into King Arthur's palace on New Year's Eve.
2. The knight carried a green shield and rode a green horse.
3. The stranger's helmet was the only thing that was not green.
4. The Green Knight offered his battle-ax to the knight who would strike him one blow.
5. Sir Gawain chopped off the Green Knight's head in a fit of anger.
6. The Green Knight put his head back on his shoulders before he got on his horse.
7. Gawain's horse galloped through the North Country to the Green Castle.
8. Gawain was offered a horse on which to escape.
9. Gawain's life was spared because he was smarter and more clever than the Green Knight.
10. Two years pass from the beginning of the story to the end.

QUESTIONS FOR THOUGHT AND DISCUSSION:

1. In what ways were the knights of the Middle Ages like the gods of ancient Greek times? Why did the Green Knight have almost to *be* a god in order to test Gawain's honor?
2. How does this legend show that a knight was supposed to be polite to women, honest, and brave?
3. Who remembers the Greek myth about Phaeton? In that story Helios tells Phaeton that it is foolish to be too brave. Do you think the knights of the Middle Ages believed this? Why, or why not?

THE PIED PIPER OF HAMELIN

DIRECTIONS: *Here are twenty "scrambled sentences." Put the words in each sentence in the right order. The first one has been done for you.*

1. mayor not hear The dogs the did.   (The mayor did not hear the dogs.)
2. The house was a rat mayor's hotel.
3. Germany is in Hamelin.
4. The jacket like a stranger's patchwork quilt looked.
5. clothing was His pied.
6. stranger a not The peddler was.
7. Mice were the rats in the compartment above.
8. He had three shiny feet about a pipe long.
9. The marched rats the before mice.
10. The marched three mice times around.
11. The faster rats than marched the mice.
12. The crowd the mayor when out a came made noise.
13. The Kuppelberg River Weser Hill flows near.
14. For the different tune every Piper had a creature.
15. The rats told the trained Piper that been the mayor had.
16. The streets followed the rats through the Piper of Hamelin.
17. Fifty was paid but offered was thousand fifty only.
18. The mayor the Piper laughed at.
19. The laughing hill marched into the children Piper the.
20. A sad saw joyful boy a sight.

QUESTIONS FOR THOUGHT AND DISCUSSION:

1. The Pied Piper smiles only twice in the story. What are these two times? What do you suppose he is thinking when he smiles?
2. Why is the lame boy the saddest person in town? How is his sorrow different from that of the children's parents?
3. What lesson did the Pied Piper teach the world?

THE EVIL EYE

DIRECTIONS: *The following sentences are all false. Make them true by changing one word in each sentence. (Do not change the word was.)*

1. The Vistula is a river that runs through Hungary.
2. Green fields lay on two sides of Casimir's great stone house.
3. A bearded man arrived in a carriage and asked for help.
4. Casimir knew his glance might bring ruin to the lives of his four guests.
5. During the long evenings, the girl talked to herself by the fireplace.
6. The girl's parents wanted her to forget Casimir.
7. Casimir was awakened one morning by men fighting on the river.
8. Casimir found that he didn't need eyes to see.
9. Casimir was most unhappy when he punished his son.
10. The old servant saw the eye lying in the hole with the pupil turned up.

QUESTIONS FOR THOUGHT AND DISCUSSION:

1. Why could this story never really have happened? Suppose for a moment that the evil eye could be true—is there anything else that could not have happened?
2. In what ways did Casimir show that he had a kind heart?
3. Why did Casimir try to keep the guests in his house? Can you think of three reasons?
4. "That summer the grass beneath Casimir's windows stayed a dark, rich green." This sentence has two meanings. One of these has nothing to do with grass or windows. What are the two meanings? Find the sentence in the story if you have to.
5. Why didn't the evil eye kill the old servant when he found it in the hole?
6. The last two stories have had very unhappy endings. Many folk tales end unhappily. Why should sad stories last longer than the happy ones people sometimes say they like better?

THE CAREER OF IGOR IVANOV

DIRECTIONS: *In all stories, certain characters do certain things in certain places. Match the characters in Column A with the actions in Column B, and then with the places in Column C. Here is the answer to the first one:* Igor's father made a place for Igor on his farm.

A	B	C
1. Igor's father	a. hit Igor on the head	k. near a cabbage field.
2. Igor's brothers	b. took a gold coin from Igor	l. in the king's palace.
3. The wise man	c. made a place for Igor	m. on his flatboat.
4. The ferryman	d. chased the robbers	n. in their barnyard.
5. Igor	e. discovered Igor couldn't read	o. in front of a church.
6. A farmer	f. cheated Igor out of his animals	p. on his farm.
7. Two priests	g. gave Igor a long lecture	q. in his own palace.
8. Some robbers	h. were burying gold	r. at a crossroads.
9. A bear	i. ended his career	s. in a hole.
10. Igor	j. emptied his bag onto the floor	t. into the woods.

QUESTIONS FOR THOUGHT AND DISCUSSION:

1. Just how foolish is Igor? Can he read or count? Can he tell time? How do we know?
2. How does the story show that all wisdom is not found in books?
3. Why is Igor able to steal the bell? Why might a smarter person have been caught?
4. Why does the king let Igor keep the nine sacks of gold? What might a smarter person than Igor have done?
5. The following sayings are taken from the story. What do they mean? Do you agree with them? Why, or why not?

> *One road can lead in only two directions.*
> *It is the duty of the wise to lead the foolish.*
> *Only a fool wastes his time.*
> *A fool and his money are soon parted.*

A STORY INSIDE A STORY
INSIDE A STORY

DIRECTIONS: *Choose the ending that best completes each sentence.*

1. This story is really   a) one story   b) two stories   c) three stories.
2. The story which is told straight through from beginning to end is   a) the story of Scheherazade and the king   b) the story of Abu and the caliph   c) the story of the man in the restaurant.
3. Scheherazade tells the king a story   a) to cheer him up   b) to save her own life   c) to teach the king that he should be as happy as the caliph in her tale.
4. The caliph and his friends disguise themselves as merchants from India to   a) play a trick on Abu   b) fool the people   c) find out about the rulers of Bagdad.
5. Abu asks the merchants to his home because   a) he asks strangers to be his guests every day   b) he knows one of the merchants is the caliph   c) he is angry with Ali.
6. Abu seems to live   a) alone   b) with his mother   c) with his wife.
7. The caliph carries a drug   a) to protect himself   b) to play jokes on people   c) because he is ill.
8. In the whole story, we hear of Abu being unconscious   a) once   b) twice   c) three times.
9. Abu thinks he really is the caliph when   a) he wakes up in the caliph's bed   b) an attendant tells him so   c) he sees an order obeyed.
10. At the end of the story, Scheherazade is sure that   a) her death is put off for one day   b) she must talk for a thousand more nights   c) she will die in twenty-four hours.

QUESTIONS FOR THOUGHT AND DISCUSSION:

1. Which character do you think of first when you see each of the following words? Why? *Calm, cruel, wise, greedy, sad, happy, dishonest, beautiful, smart.*
2. Can you tell what happens in each of the stories without telling the other two? Try it.
3. Does Abu's tale of a tail have much to do with the rest of the story? Why does Abu tell it?

355

ABU THE WAG

1. Scheherazade thinks Abu is a fool because he lets himself be tricked into believing he is the caliph.
2. At the beginning of this part of the story, Abu thinks he is the caliph.
3. The caliph's turban is the last piece of clothing he puts on in the morning.
4. Abu leaves the palace to punish his old enemy, Ali.
5. Abu's mother never believes for a moment that her son is the caliph.
6. Abu decides he is Somebody because it would be impossible for Nobody to be imprisoned.
7. Abu discovers that a person can have two headaches at the same time.
8. Abu knows that he is Abu when he sees the real caliph with the grand vizier.
9. The caliph decides on the name *Abu the Wag* at the end of the story.
10. At the end of the story, Abu knows that one can be happy only when playing the part of someone else.

QUESTIONS FOR THOUGHT AND DISCUSSION:

1. Early in the story, Abu says, "Time passes fast for a happy man." What does this mean? What has happened to Abu to make him say this?
2. What are some bad things that might have happened if Abu had been the caliph for a week, or a month? Why is it hard to be happy by pretending you are someone else?
3. Suppose you could be someone else for a day. Whom would you choose to be? Why? Try to describe that day from morning till night.

CHANG FU-YEN AND THE WISE JUDGE

DIRECTIONS: *Fill the blank spaces in the sentences below. Choose your answers from among these words:* SPIDERS, BEANS, CROWD, ROBBER, BRAVEST, GARLIC, SOOT, CANDLE, BOX, SHACK, GUILTY, PAIL, MURDERER, TWO, THREE.

1. Chang Fu-Yen planted _____ in his small field.
2. The _____ left no clue behind him.
3. A _____ was put on trial in the courtroom.
4. The _____ was put into jail for laughing.
5. The judge collected a big _____ of garlic.
6. _____ vegetable merchants were called to the courthouse.
7. A god, the judge said, would mark the _____ man.
8. The three men blinked when they saw the _____ in the judge's hand.
9. The back of one of the men was covered with _____.
10. _____ of the men were not guilty.

QUESTIONS FOR THOUGHT AND DISCUSSION:

1. While reading detective stories, most people like to guess what will happen next. Did you know why the judge was collecting garlic before Chang himself guessed the reason? At what point in the story did you see what the judge was doing? Look back if you have to. Did you guess the end of the story? At what point?
2. In the beginning of the story, the judge says that he has no clues. But this is not true for long. What are the clues in this detective story? How are they found?
3. This is a strange story, but does anything really *impossible* happen? Explain your answer.
4. Does the guilty man think the judge's story about the god might be true? How do we know?

THE GREAT BELL OF CHINA

DIRECTIONS: *Match the sentence begininngs in Column A with the sentence endings in Column B.*

A	B
1. The emperor was	a. rich and mellow.
2. The emperor kept artists	b. rich and cruel.
3. The emperor told Fang Tung	c. died an instant death.
4. Gold was used to make the bell	d. to use brass, silver, and gold.
5. Ko-Ning was both	e. lived on in the great bell.
6. Ko-Ning was told	f. when the third bell was made.
7. The second bell collapsed	g. busy in his studios.
8. Ko-Ning jumped to her death	h. innocent and hopeful.
9. The body of Ko-Ning	i. to find a one-eyed frog.
10. The soul of Ko-Ning	j. when hit with a hammer.

QUESTIONS FOR THOUGHT AND DISCUSSION:

1. What did the fortuneteller tell Ko-Ning on her second visit? Why should Ko-Ning have been so happy and hopeful when she returned home?
2. Of whom did the emperor want people to think when they heard the bell? Is this what happened? Why, or why not?
3. Why did Ko-Ning show her father a little cloth bundle before she jumped to her death? Did she carry another frog?
4. In ancient China children were supposed to honor their parents. How is this shown in the story we have just read? What was good about this custom?

THE MAN WHO OWNED THE MOON

DIRECTIONS: *Number the sentences in Group I in the order in which the events happen in the story. Then go on to Group II.*

GROUP I

a. _____ The chief engineer told Bahanga that the tower was finished.

b. _____ The king told Prince Bahang that he could have the moon.

c. _____ Prince Bahang's friends teased him about not owning the moon.

d. _____ Logs were tied together to make a high tower.

e. _____ Bahanga saw the Cape of Good Hope.

GROUP II

a. _____ Sparks from the moon set fire to the tower.

b. _____ Bahanga's shoulder went through the crust of the moon.

c. _____ Aruwimi knew why some men had been changed to monkeys.

d. _____ Men who had watched the moving of the moon were changed to monkeys.

e. _____ The king thought about the responsibility of owning all Africa.

QUESTIONS FOR THOUGHT AND DISCUSSION:

1. This myth explained two things to the people of old Africa. What two things? How did it explain them?

2. Would Bahanga have tried to reach the moon if it had not been for the prince? (Yes or no?) What do we know about Bahanga that tells us so?

359

KINTU AND THE LAW OF LOVE

DIRECTIONS: *The following sentences are all false. You can make them true by changing one word in each sentence. (Do not change the word was.)*

1. Kintu was one of the first men to walk upon the waters.
2. For many years Kintu wandered through Asia.
3. Kintu and his wife looked for a place to start a school.
4. They finally settled down near Lake Victoria.
5. They brought with them a cow, a sheep, a goat, a pig, and a turkey.
6. They planted the root of a coconut tree.
7. After many years, there was not enough water in the valley for the people's needs.
8. Some people in the valley had to go out.
9. Trouble started, but still Kintu made no plans.
10. Kintu talked about the Law of Wisdom throughout the land.
11. The young people clapped when Kintu spoke.
12. A group of students marched to see Kintu.
13. "No man fights in my army," Kintu told them.
14. Kintu and his wife walked off into the Great River.
15. The land of Uganda was ruined by a storm.
16. King Manda liked to climb into the foothills and pretend he was God.
17. Manda's wife worried about his being alone.
18. Both domestic and wild animals sat in a circle around Manda.
19. Manda killed a servant who had hated him.
20. Somewhere, the great Kintu is still waiting for evil to leave the hearts of animals.

QUESTIONS FOR THOUGHT AND DISCUSSION:

1. This story is like many others we should know. Explain how "Kintu and the Law of Love" is like one of the following: the myth of Pandora and the troubles; the story of Adam and Eve; the story of Noah and the ark.
2. "No man fights in my name," Kintu says. What does he mean? Would most people today agree with him?

THE DAUGHTER OF THE STARS

DIRECTIONS: *The following paragraph is a summary of the story. Some of the most important words have been left out. The paragraph would mean little to anyone who has not read "The Daughter of the Stars." Fill the blank spaces with words that are used in the story. You may use a word more than once. See how many words you can remember before looking at the list below.*

A young Indian named (1)_____ (2)_____ often hunted on the (3)_____. Once he found a circle in which the (4) _____ had been beaten down. At first he thought it was a buffalo (5)_____. He waited. Toward evening a (6)_____ seemed to soar across the sky. The Indian saw that it was a big (7)_____ holding twelve lovely (8)_____. It landed on the earth. The next day the Indian hid his lean body in a hollow (9)_____. When the (10)_____ came, they pushed it over. The Indian caught the one he liked best. She said she was a (11)_____ of the (12)_____. But she agreed to live on (13)_____ and marry the Indian. After she had a child, she built a (14)_____ to return to the (15)_____. Her father, the (16)_____ (17) _____, allowed her (18)_____ to come later. But the Indian grew homesick. He and his son were changed into white (19)_____. Then they returned to the grass-covered (20)_____.

Words: BASKET, DAUGHTER, EAGLE, EAGLES, EARTH, GRASS, HUSBAND, KING, MAIDENS, PRAIRIE, STAR, STARS, STUMP, WALLOW, WHITE.

QUESTIONS FOR THOUGHT AND DISCUSSION:

1. White Eagle fell in love with the star maiden the first time he saw her. How does this story show the danger of "love at first sight"?
2. Why didn't the star maiden tell White Eagle that she wanted to return to the stars, since she was planning to leave him anyway?
3. White Eagle chose to be turned into the bird of the same name. If you had to make the same choice, what animal would you choose to be? Why?

THE SHEEP OF SAN CRISTOBAL

DIRECTIONS: *Here are twenty "scrambled sentences." Put the words in each sentence in the right order. The first one has been done.*

1. Indians had been killed husband by Felipa's. (Felipa's husband had been killed by Indians.)
2. Lady Felipa of the shrine prayed at Light of Our.
3. Don Felipa to marry wanted José.
4. his father's sheep José Don inherited had.
5. the sheep mesa went to the morning Every.
6. in Felipa's field Don José's ate sheep.
7. death for Felipa asked Don José's.
8. old Felipa her story to the told Young padre.
9. penance to Felipa was do.
10. poor sheep people had to give to Felipa.
11. sheep killed had three Coyotes.
12. to milk the dog offered Felipa.
13. ewe beside A large Felipa walked.
14. Felipa gave people Then bread.
15. And sheep giving started people Felipa.
16. is in The city of New Albuquerque Mexico.
17. a single Finally sheep Felipa had.
18. a man Felipa told about A boy.
19. the toward ran The mother boy.
20. the man thought Felipa knew who she had been.

QUESTIONS FOR THOUGHT AND DISCUSSION:

1. Unlike most of the selections in this book, "The Sheep of San Cristóbal" could be a true story. What is your opinion?
2. The story contains several *morals* (lessons or meanings). In your opinion, what is the main moral?
3. If you can, find out about the Ute Indians of the old Southwest. How did they differ from the Navajos and Pueblos?

HOW POCAHONTAS SAVED MY LIFE

DIRECTIONS: *Choose the ending that best completes each sentence.*

1. The first English settlement in the New World was at a) Plymouth, Massachusetts b) Jamestown, Virginia c) Boston, Massachusetts.
2. Captain John Smith was surprised by over two hundred Indians as he was a) fishing b) hunting c) paddling a canoe.
3. Smith gave the Indian chief his a) gun b) compass c) belt.
4. Smith says that he was guarded by a) two or three savages b) eight or ten savages c) thirty or forty savages.
5. The Indians were saving their gunpowder to a) make some more like it b) attack Jamestown c) plant as they did corn.
6. Pocahontas was about a) thirteen years old b) eighteen years old c) twenty-three years old.
7. Captain Smith was not told Pocahontas's real name because a) it was too hard to pronounce b) she was always called by her nickname c) the Indians feared his magic tricks.
8. Powhatan planned to kill Smith by a) beating him with clubs b) shooting him with arrows c) opening his veins.
9. Powhatan offered to trade Smith's life for a) a drug to save a boy's life b) a grindstone and two guns c) two grindstones and a gun.
10. The story of Pocahontas was told a) right after it happened b) about sixteen years after it happened c) about thirty-two years after it happened.

QUESTIONS FOR THOUGHT AND DISCUSSION:

1. What kind of a man was Captain John Smith? What have we learned about him that might make us believe he was telling the truth? What have we learned that might show he was stretching the truth, or telling a lie?
2. How does Smith seem to feel about the Indians? What interests him about them? What are some important things he seems not to notice?
3. Think of three mistakes the Indians made about things that were new to them. Why was each mistake made?

ABRAHAM LINCOLN AND ANNE RUTLEDGE

DIRECTIONS: *Read each sentence carefully before deciding whether it is true or false. Answer according to the story.*

1. William H. Herndon was the law partner of Abraham Lincoln.
2. Herndon says that the story of Anne Rutledge is a legend.
3. Lincoln was about thirty-five years old when he met the innkeeper's daughter.
4. At first Lincoln was too shy to tell Anne how he felt about her.
5. Anne's first fiancé went back to New York when he heard of his father's death.
6. Anne's friends had little sympathy for her feelings.
7. Anne thought Lincoln was awkward and shy, but she liked his clear, ringing voice.
8. Anne became ill after she had promised to marry Lincoln.
9. Lincoln was at Anne's bedside when she died.
10. Lincoln's friends had little sympathy for his feelings.

QUESTIONS FOR THOUGHT AND DISCUSSION:

1. Does Herndon say that he saw Anne Rutledge and Lincoln during their romance? If not, how did he learn so much about it? What "proof" does he give that the story is true? Does this proof seem to be enough?
2. Herndon collected the "facts" for this story after Lincoln's death. This was about thirty years after the death of Anne Rutledge. Many of Herndon's facts came from Anne's relatives. Would they have told him the same things thirty years earlier? Why, or why not?
3. Many Americans would believe this story even if it were proven false. Why should people *want* to believe such a sad story?

BRINGING OUR STORIES TOGETHER

The pages of this book have carried us through thousands of years and thousands of miles. So far we have thought about only one story at a time. Now comes the time to bring our stories together. Reading means little if we fail to think about what we read.

See how many of the following questions you can answer. First take a few minutes to glance back at the table of contents. Look at the title of each story and try to review it quickly in your mind. You may want to place a bookmark in the table of contents to find it easily while you are answering the questions.

1. What is a myth? A legend? A folk tale? Can you give an example of each? Can you give another example from a different part of the world?

2. Think quickly of a story you liked very much. Would you call it a myth, legend, or folk tale? What kept you interested in the story as you read it. Was it adventure? An interesting character or plot? Explain.

3. What facts about the world were explained at one time by myths? How did the different myths explain these things? Give examples. How are the same things explained today?

4. Describe the life the Greeks made up for their gods. In what ways was this life similar to that of the Greeks themselves? In what ways was it different?

5. Why did the Greeks, and later other peoples, stop making up myths? Did this mean there were to be no more tales about the gods? What modern stories are very similar to myths? Explain your answer.

6. The names of some of the gods and goddesses are still with us today. What things in the modern world are called by these names, or by names very like them (as *cereal*, for example, is like *Ceres*, the goddess of the harvest)? Don't forget the days of the week and the planets.

7. Many heroes have paraded through the pages of this book. Which hero did you find most interesting? Was it the hero himself or his adventures that interested you? Suppose your hero had been born into the modern world. What sort of a person might he have become? What might be his occupation?

8. Folk tales seem to pass from one part of the world to another more easily than do myths. Why might this be true? Did any of the folk tales in this book remind you of stories you already knew? Explain.

9. Many stories in this book, especially the folk tales, have a *moral*, or lesson that they teach the reader. Usually this moral can be put into a single sentence, often a well-known saying. The moral of "The Myth of Phaeton" might be said to be "Look before you leap." What morals can you think of for any of the other stories?

10. Are human beings always the same, or do they change as we go from country to country and from time to time? In what ways were the ancient Greeks, for instance, similar to the people of today? In what ways were they different? How might these differences be explained? Are people *themselves* different, or are they different because they were born into different "worlds"?

11. The geography of the ancient Greeks was very different from ours. What was the Greeks' picture of the earth and the heavens? What other world-pictures have we read about? In what stories?

12. The past 3,000 years have seen the rise and fall of many different forms of government. Explain which stories from the book can be used to show the following: a) the joining together of families under one ruler to form small kingdoms; b) the age of small kingdoms; c) the age of large kingdoms and powerful kings; d) the end of the age of kings; and e) the growing importance of the common people.

13. What stories, or parts of stories, made you laugh? What characters or actions did you laugh at? Can you think why?

14. Which kind of story—myth, legend, or folk tale—do we Americans most enjoy? Can you give an example of such a story

that was started by its hero during his own lifetime? Give the title of another that was made up after the hero's death.

15. People have always liked stories about clever characters. We have read several such tales. It shouldn't be hard to think of a few characters from this book who are famous because of their cleverness. Starting with clever characters, make a list of all the characters you can match with each of the following:

a) cleverness   f) honesty   k) kindness and modesty
b) bravery   g) laziness   l) boastfulness and false pride
c) foolishness   h) greediness   m) love of parent for child
d) wisdom   i) loyalty   n) love of child for parent
e) selfishness   j) cruelty   o) love between man and
                                                      woman

PRONUNCIATION GUIDE

Apollo [*a POL o*] — Greek (and Roman) god of music and poetry

Asgard [*AHS gard*] — Home of the Norse gods

Bacchus [*BAK us*] — Roman god of wine and happy times

Baucis [*BAW sis*] — Aged woman who was rewarded for being kind to Zeus and Hermes in disguise

Camelot [*KAM a lot*] — Palace and court of King Arthur in England

Casimir [*KAS i mer*] — Polish owner and victim of "The Evil Eye"

Ceres [*SEE reez*] — Roman goddess of the harvest

Chaos [*KAY os*] — Confused, disordered space supposed by the Greeks to have existed before the world was made

Circe [*SUR see*] — Enchantress who changed Ulysses' men into pigs

Coventry [*KUV en tree*] — City in England, home of Lady Godiva

Cupid [*KEW pid*] — Son of the Roman goddess of beauty, Venus

Cyclopes [*sy KLO peez*] — More than one *Cyclops*

Cyclops [*SY klops*] — One-eyed monster who trapped Ulysses in a cave

Daedalus [*DED a lus*] — Greek inventor, father of Icarus

Echo [*EK o*] — Greek maiden who died for love of Narcissus

Epimetheus [*ep i MEE thee us*] — Brother of Prometheus and husband of Pandora

Eurydice [*yew RID i see*] — Beloved wife of the Greek musician Orpheus

Freya [*FRAY a*] — Norse goddess of love and healing

Godiva [*go DY va*] — English woman said to have protested high taxes by riding naked through the streets

Hamelin [*HAM a lin*]	—German city supposed to have been cleared of rats by the Pied Piper
Helios [*HEE li os*]	—Greek god of the sun
Hercules [*HUR kew leez*]	—Greek hero famous for his strength
Hermes [*HUR meez*]	—Messenger of the Greek gods
Icarus [*IK a rus*]	—Son of Daedalus, flew too near the sun
Igor Ivanov [*EE gor ee va NOF*]	—Foolish character in Russian folk tale
Ithaca [*ITH a ka*]	—Greek island ruled by Ulysses
Laos [*LAY os*]	—Small country south of China
Leofric [*LEE o frik*]	—Husband of Lady Godiva
Loki [*LO kee*]	—Norse god with wicked ways
Midas [*MY dus*]	—Ancient king granted "The Golden Touch"
Narcissus [*nar SIS us*]	—Greek youth who fell in love with his own reflection
Orpheus [*OR fee us*]	—Greek singer and musician
Pandora [*pan DOR a*]	—Wife of Epimetheus, opened the forbidden box
Penelope [*pe NEL o pee*]	—Wife of Ulysses
Persephone [*per SEF o nee*]	—Daughter of Ceres and wife of Pluto
Phaeton [*FAY a ton*]	—Human son of the Greek god Helios
Philemon [*fi LEE mon*]	—Husband of Baucis
Pluto [*PLOO toe*]	—Greek god or ruler of the dead and lower world
Prometheus [*pro MEE thee us*]	—Bringer of fire to men on earth
Psyche [*SY kee*]	—Roman princess loved by Cupid
Pygmalion [*pig MAY li on*]	—Greek artist who fell in love with a statue
Ra [*RAH*]	—Egyptian god of the sun
Scheherazade [*sha hair a ZAH de*]	—Storyteller of the *Arabian Nights' Entertainments*
Thor [*THOR*]	—Norse god of thunder
Ulysses [*yew LIS eez*]	—Brave ruler of the Greek island of Ithaca
Valhalla [*val HAL a*]	—Norse "Hall of Heroes" for dead soldiers

Venus [*VEE nus*]   —Roman goddess of love and beauty
Vistula [*VIS choo la*]   —River in Poland
Vulcan [*VUL kan*]   —Blacksmith of the Roman gods
Woden [*WO den*]   —Ruler of the Norse gods
Zeus [*ZOOCE*]   —Ruler of the Greek gods